prentice-hall
scientific foundations of nursing practice series

Dorothy E. Johnson, Editor

Behavior and Illness
Ruth Wu

Behavior Modification: A Significant Method in Nursing Practice
Michael D. LeBow

scientific foundations of nursing practice series

Behavior and Illness

Ruth Wu

Department of Nursing
California State College
Los Angeles

prentice-hall, inc.
englewood cliffs, n.j.

Library of Congress Cataloging in Publication Data

Wu, Ruth
    Behavior and illness.

    (Prentice-Hall scientific foundations of nursing
practice series)

    Includes bibliographies.
    1. Nurses and nursing. 2. Sick—Psychology.
I. Title. [DNLM: 1. Attitude to Health—Nursing
texts. 2. Sick Role—Nursing texts. WM 100 W956b 1972]
RT86.W8   610.73   72–6124
ISBN 0–13–074146–9
ISBN 0–13–074138–8 (pbk.)

Cover photographs by Englewood Hospital, Englewood,
N.J.; Harold M. Lambert from Frederic Lewis, Inc.;
and Elizabeth Wilcox.

10 9 8 7 6 5 4

Printed in the United States of America

PRENTICE-HALL INTERNATIONAL, INC., London
PRENTICE-HALL OF AUSTRALIA, PTY., LTD., Sydney
PRENTICE-HALL OF CANADA, LTD., Toronto
PRENTICE-HALL OF INDIA PRIVATE LIMITED, New Delhi
PRENTICE-HALL OF JAPAN, INC., Tokyo

Contents

Foreword

The growth of nursing as a profession and a scientific discipline has been rapid in recent years. New orientations and emphases in nursing education are readily apparent. New organizational patterns to facilitate professional practice are being sought and found. Nursing practice becomes increasingly significant and sophisticated as knowledge is developed along many fronts and is brought to the service of patients. In the face of these changes, and because the knowledge potentially available for practice no longer can be contained within the boundaries of the comprehensive course textbook approach in education, this new approach to the subject matter underlying nursing practice is offered.

The SCIENTIFIC FOUNDATIONS OF NURSING PRACTICE SERIES consists of a number of relatively brief monographs, each dealing with a specific and circumscribed topic. Each monograph is designed to order and integrate pertinent knowledge drawn from widely dispersed sources. Collectively, the series will attempt in time to cover all essential areas, thus providing the fullest scope possible. Such an approach appears to have a number of advantages. The treatment of single topics in separate books permits great flexibility in use in educational programs that vary markedly in the structure and level of courses offered and in the content encompassed or emphasized. It allows the examination of each topic in greater depth than is possible when many issues or concepts must be considered in a comprehensive text, and it encourages consideration of new and emerging foci of interest and development. It avoids the sometimes disjointed nature of publications with multiple authors while simultaneously offering presentation of diverse topics by those especially well qualified to do so. And, finally, it may encourage the development of specialized interest and competence by the advanced practitioner.

The major emphasis in this series is on selected nursing problems. The first concern is for problems that patients are likely to experience in any setting in which nursing is practiced, even though the patients will differ along such dimensions as age; sex; medical diagnosis; and degree, severity, and chronicity of the illness. To the degree made possible by existing knowledge, these problems are described and explained, and the scientific basis for their identification and nursing management is provided. The tentative nature of the basis for prescription in particular will be emphasized, and it is hoped that the presentation will excite in the student or practitioner the skepticism and challenge essential to future contributions to knowledge in the field.

Other volumes in the series cover other aspects of nursing as a field of study and practice. One provides an introduction to the profession and the discipline. Others attempt to synthesize and order knowledge about human behavior in health and illness as a basis for understanding the nature of nursing problems. Still others examine the diagnostic process in nursing, modes of scientific inquiry, and certain treatment methods. Both the underdeveloped nature of nursing knowledge and the steady growth of that knowledge demand that the series remain open-ended, flexible, and subject to early revision.

The scope of nursing practice is broad, and a wide range of knowledge and skills is required among its practitioners. No series of monographs or group of texts can provide adequately for the needs of all students or practitioners in the field. This series is focused upon the needs of baccalaureate and higher degree students but will also serve the needs of many other professional practitioners. The SCIENTIFIC FOUNDATIONS OF NURSING PRACTICE SERIES is an attempt to place in the hands of this group stimulating material of outstanding quality in subject matter and presentation.

Dorothy E. Johnson
Professor of Nursing
University of California
Los Angeles

Preface

The assessment of patient behavior is a necessary tool for the intelligent practice of nursing. This evaluation is needed to confirm the presence of a patient problem and to prescribe an appropriate course of action. It is a necessary step toward achieving the nursing goal of conserving the patient's energy, which will be needed in the recovery process. Thus, if the nurse understands the events to which the patient is responding, and the kinds of behaviors such events tend to evoke in persons with specific demographic variables, she is in a better position to predict with some precision the behaviors that will follow. If she assesses the behavior to be inappropriate or ineffective, she can intervene to alter the conditions so that the resources of the individual are best conserved. An accurate assessment requires knowledge of man and knowledge of the event to which he is responding. For nursing, the event is illness or the threat of illness. The purpose of this volume is to provide an understanding of the nature of illness. It is intended for the student nurse who already has some understanding of man's reactions to the usual day-to-day fluctuations of his environment and consequently is now ready to observe critically man's response to illness or the threat of illness.

The book is divided into two parts. The first half presents a description and analysis of the most common events experienced by sick people: illness, treatment, and hospitalization. Illness is dissected conceptually into its denotable and phenomenalistic aspects. The denotable features can be physically encountered or measured by the observer, whereas the phenomenalistic aspects are known only by the person experiencing the illness. It is necessary for the nurse to understand both aspects. Behavior is known to be directly influenced by the person's perception of the event to which he is responding. The nurse must concern herself with *how* illness is experienced as well as with the measurable manifestations of illness.

Superimposed on the experience of illness for many patients are the events of treatment and hospitalization. Again the knowledge needed to understand the patient's behavior under conditions of hospitalization and treatment is not only the objective data about these events but also how the particular events are experienced or perceived.

Following the above exposition the reader is introduced to the concept of behavioral stability. A basic assumption is that behavioral stability is achievable in illness and, further, that it is dependent upon the kind, amount, and effectiveness of the nursing and medical measures applied. Another premise is that less energy is expended during periods of relative stability vis-àvis periods of relative instability. Thus the goal of nursing care is to help the patient achieve and maintain a state of relative stability. This concept of behavioral stability provides the reader with a theoretical framework from which to assess patient behavior.

The second half of the book presents a discussion of four categories of behavior: health behavior, illness behavior, sick role behavior, and impaired role behavior. This is an attempt to look at behaviors systematically, to examine the determinants, and to offer an explanation(s) for the observed relationships.

The author hopes that those engaged in nursing practice and theory building will view this work as an initial effort to extrapolate and synthesize what appears to be a convergence of concepts and ideas from several fields: sociology, psychology, public health, and medicine. Furthermore, it is hoped that the reader will respond by systematically relating the perceptual processes described herein to the variety of behaviors displayed by persons who are experiencing illness or the threat of illness, in order to test the relevance or utility of the concepts for nursing practice.

There are many individuals to whom the author is indebted. The study was started when the author was a member of the U.C.L.A. School of Nursing Faculty and received its primary impetus from her associations with Dorothy Johnson. Many of the concepts in the text reflect her contributions. I am particularly grateful to Betty Jo Hadley for her valuable suggestions, to Lulu Hassenplug for her encouragement and support, to the "junior" faculty and students who helped write portions of the text, and finally to my husband, Joe, and sons, Randy and Jim, for their patience and understanding during the many weeks and months of writing and rewriting.

Ruth Wu
Department of Nursing
California State College
Los Angeles

one | *Introduction*

Illness is a universal phenomenon that is experienced by people in all societies. It has been with us since the beginning of time. Like birth, death, work, and play, illness is an accepted part of our lives. It is talked about, heard about, and "seen" in all segments of society, and yet its definition and its very nature remain elusive.

There are two basic reasons why a study of the nature and meaning of illness is both logical and necessary for nursing. In the first place, such knowledge provides content for a foundation upon which the care component of nursing may be based. *Care* is "providing comfort and support in times of anxiety, loneliness, and helplessness. It is listening, evaluating and intervening appropriately."* The consequence of care is said to be comfort—another vague, ambiguous, and imprecise term. What do we mean by *comfort*? Comfort is best measured in terms of some calibrated, felt tension level of the human organism. Thus comfort can be said to be experienced when tension level is maintained within an optimal range, neither too high nor too low for the individual. *Tension* is defined as a "state of being stretched or strained," and it manifests itself in the

*From "American Nurses' Association's First Position on Education for Nursing," *American Journal of Nursing*, 65, No. 12 (December, 1965), 106–11.

human organism through changes in behavior (Johnson, 1961, p. 65). It is possible to identify a class of behaviors for any given individual, with few exceptions, as indicative of tension above or below his optimal range. In concert with gross observable behavioral changes there are certain physiological or biochemical changes. For example, Mason and Brady (1964) have demonstrated the existence of a relationship between the amount of urinary 17-OHCS excreted and the degree of environmental disturbances experienced. They showed that during the weekends when the hospital wards were quiet and pleasant, patients excreted less urinary 17-OHCS than during the weekdays when the wards were busy and hustling. Obviously more research is needed on the psychoendocrine systems in order to increase our understanding and control of human behavior.

If the nurse's responsibility is to assist in the regulation of tension, with the goal of comfort, she must have a sound base of knowledge about man and illness. She must recognize that man is not only a biological organism but also a psychological actor, a member of a society, and a bearer of culture. He is a biological organism with vital processes that are characteristic of life or of living matter. He is a psychological actor in that he feels, acts, and engages in such activities as thinking, learning, talking, and perceiving. He is a member of a society in that he not only occupies a status, both ascribed and achieved, but he also enacts one or more roles through interaction with others. He is a bearer of culture in that he carries the beliefs, values, customs, and mores from generation to generation. All of these facets of man must be understood singularly and jointly, for it is their combined effect that guides and determines man's total behavior.

An analysis of man's behavior is incomplete without an analysis of the events to which he is responding. For nursing, the main events are illness or the threat of illness. Nurses must recognize that illness is not only a disease with biological alterations but also a psychosocial phenomenon. Knowledge of bio-psycho-socio-cultural man and of the nature and meaning of illness with all of its ramifications becomes a diagnostic or assessment tool for the eventual control and prediction of behavior. If the nurse has a profound understanding of man and of the events that he is experiencing, she will be in a better position to reduce or minimize those features that create tensions above or below his optimal range. She will be equipped to achieve, within the limits of the disease process, her goal of comfort and support.

The second basic reason for this study is that knowledge of the nature and meaning of illness can also contribute to an understanding of the cure component of nursing. Obviously the care and cure components of nursing are interdependent and interrelated. Cure activities are necessarily intertwined and frequently inseparable from the nurse's care activities. Cure activities include the multitude of medical and surgical treatments prescribed by the physician, plus the instructions for the promotion of health and the prevention of disease and/or its complications. Recognizing the varying conceptions of illness among sociocultural groups can help explain the different coping techniques that are used to deal with health problems. If the nurse is aware of the values, beliefs, and attitudes the individual associates with a given health problem, she is in a better position to help the individual accept the recommended therapeutic plan and/or associated hospitalization. Acceptance of such a plan facilitates recovery.

Superimposed upon the experience of illness, as implied above, are the experiences of treatment and hospitalization. Either of these experiences is capable of displacing illness as the object or event to which the individual is responding at any given point in time. Therefore it is essential that the nurse gain an understanding of the nature and meaning of treatment and hospitalization, as these experiences may produce responses quite different from those produced by the illness per se. The meaning of illness may influence the meaning attributed to the treatment plan, and vice versa. If the patient views his illness as common, familiar, and curable, he may have no qualms about the treatment plan, knowing it to be a necessary means to his goal of recovery. Conversely, if he views his illness as terminal or without a known cure, he may react to the treatment plan with skepticism, doubt, and even fear. Knowledge of these events provides additional content from which a nursing diagnosis can be made and a plan of intervention prescribed. Thus, an understanding of the nature and meaning of illness, treatment, and hospitalization is seen to be both logical and necessary for the education and preparation of nurse practitioners.

In the following chapters an attempt is made to analyze each of the above events both in terms of its objective, denotable features and in terms of its subjective, phenomenalistic features. Assuming that the reader has a basic understanding of bio-psycho-socio man, knowledge of the nature of illness should add to her understanding of the behaviors associated with the event. It should provide clues to the observed incongruency between what is known about the illness and how it appears to the person experiencing it.

REFERENCES

"American Nurses' Association's First Position on Education for Nursing." *American Journal of Nursing*, 65, No. 12 (December, 1965), 106–11.

JOHNSON, DOROTHY "The Significance of Nursing Care," *American Journal of Nursing*, 61, No. 11 (November, 1961), 63–66.

MASON, J. and J. V. BRADY "Sensitivity of Psychoendocrine Systems to Social and Physical Environment," in *Psychobiological Approaches to Social Behavior*, eds. P. H. Leiderman and David Shapiro. California: Stanford University Press, 1964, Chap. 1.

two | *The Nature of Illness*

The search for a more clear and precise definition of illness begins with the dictionary, and it then proceeds to a perusal of the medical, sociological, and public health literature for a more detailed discussion and analysis of the essence of illness. *Webster's Dictionary* (1967) defines illness as an "unhealthy condition of body or mind." Illness is also called a malady, ailment, disease, or infirmity. The dictionary does not provide any clear distinction between these five words. All of the terms could be used to refer to an unhealthy state, an impairment of the normal state, a bodily disorder, or a poor, deteriorated state.

Suchman (1963) suggests that it might be useful to distinguish between the words *disease, sickness,* and *illness.* Disease, he suggests, refers to the medical entity that is defined in terms of biological and physiological functioning; whereas illness refers to a social entity, a status that is defined in terms of social functioning; and sickness refers to the reaction of the individual in terms of his own feelings and to the reactions of others toward his illness. In other words, Suchman distinguishes between a disease process, an illness condition, and a sick role. He also states that two persons may have the same disease but have different degrees of illness (incapacitation) and different degrees and types of sickness (reactions). Further, he says that two people may have the same disease and the same conditions of illness but have different degrees and types of sickness.

This situation is possible only because all these terms are relative concepts subject to social and personal as well as to medical interpretation. For example, an individual who is defined as ill by others may not consider himself to be ill, and therefore he will behave as if he were well. The distinction between a process, a condition, and a role is necessary, but the use of the above terms to make this distinction seems superfluous. Disease, illness, and sickness are terms that are used interchangeably, and learning to distinguish between them appears to have little heuristic value for nursing. For instance, learning to associate the term *sickness* with the sick role, when it is used by the average layman to describe a condition or disease process, seems only to add to an already confusing situation. Therefore, for the purposes of this book and to minimize semantic difficulties, the terms sickness, malady, infirmity, ailment, and disease will be used more or less synonymously with illness.

In summary, whether illness is viewed as a process, a condition, or a role depends upon the perspective from which it is viewed. As suggested by Suchman, from the medical perspective illness is viewed as a process, whereas from the sociological perspective illness is viewed as a status with rights and obligations, and from the psychological perspective illness is viewed as something that elicits a reaction both in the actor and in those with whom he interacts. Each occupation defines illness according to the particular contribution or service it makes to society.

What then shall be nursing's definition of illness? In the light of nursing's defined role, illness is best described as an event or happening that offers content for scientific observation and study, i.e., an experience that evokes a certain class of behaviors. Viewing illness as an abstraction allows us to widen our perspective so as to encompass a variety of experiences, rather than limiting ourselves to a single discrete entity or a thing-in-itself. Thus, the individual may consider illness to be either a disease process, a position in society with certain expectations, or some punishment for wrongdoing. In other words, illness can represent all or none of these qualities. Recognizing that illness is an experience subject to varying interpretations provides the nurse with a broad base from which to assess and to make predictions about patient behavior.

Recognizing that illness is an event that is experienced does not, however, solve the problem of the nature of illness, for we need to know what distinguishes the experience of illness from other experiences. For example, what distinguishes the experience of illness from, say, the experience of unemployment? Rules for conceptual learning state that there are relevant cues that distinguish one class of things or events from another dissimilar class of things or events. In other words, on the basis of some common feature(s) two or more distinguishable events can be classified and set apart from other events. The bases upon which these things can be classed or grouped are legion. The most familiar method is that of using physical similarities such as color, size, and form. On a different plane, common or similar functions may provide a basis for grouping. Thus, there is little physical similarity between an orange and a loaf of bread, but the fact that both are used for similar purposes places them in a class called food.

The problem that confronts us is to identify the basis upon which things or events can be classified as illness. It is possible to use physical similarities as a basis for distinguishing illness from other phenomena. Thus, all persons manifesting physical aberrations such as fever, abnormal cell count, broken bones, and tumors are experiencing illness. Illness can also be distinguished on the basis of some common function. Accordingly, any action of the body to protect itself from harm and injury represents illness. Another basis for distinguishing illness from other phenomena is causation. Thus, all conditions caused by pathologic organisms or by trauma can be classed as illness.

It can be seen from the above that any number of dimensions may be used for distinguishing one class of things from another. The task is to select the one or more dimensions that have the most relevance for the practice of nursing. Shall the distinction be made on the basis of etiology, consequences, or structural changes? Is it possible to identify some sort of rule for combining and/or using the relevant attributes involved in the definition of illness? Identifying and recognizing the phenomenon of illness will be facilitated if the relevant attributes and conceptual rules are known.

DEFINITIONS OF ILLNESS

A review of the literature reveals five different but somewhat overlapping definitions of illness: primitive, medical-physiologic, ecologic, equilibrium, and social. Although these models overlap each other in terms of sharing certain attributes, each is presented separately as a definition of illness in order to emphasize its distinctiveness from the others. An attempt is made to examine each definition in terms of content (i.e., the substance of illness), causation or etiology, diagnosis or mode of recognition, and mode of intervention. Admittedly, the models are crude. A model is not a theory. It is merely a way of looking at or examining something from which certain deductions can be made.

Primitive Model

Ambiguity in the use of the term illness has been common practice throughout the history of man and particularly so in the annals of medicine. As medicine has gained in its search for the cure and prevention of disease, the definition of illness has undergone corresponding changes.

For centuries illness was personified as an autonomous force or "being" that attacked man, dominating him and killing him. Man was viewed as a passive agent in that he had no power to defend himself against the attacker. This autonomous being was thought to settle somewhere in the body, and the job of the witch doctor or medicine man was to find the place where "it" had settled and to drive it out of the body. Magical and ritualistic practices were designed to appease the evil spirits and to drive the illness away (Sequin, 1946).

During the Middle Ages the idea of illness as an autonomous being was displaced by the mystical concept of sin as the cause of everything evil. Illness was viewed as punishment for committing a sin or misdeed. Healing could only be achieved through supplication, confession of sin, and reaffirmation of one's faith in God. The common discomforts such as colds and constipation were accepted as part of one's existence, but the more serious and disabling conditions were attributed to the work of a malevolent demon or of an offended God.

Ignorance combined with fear forced primitive man to resort to superstitions and belief in supernatural beings for the explanation of all phenomena. Illness was no exception. Things that occurred together or sequentially were said to be causally related, when in fact there may have been no relationship. This was the basis for many old wives' tales, folk beliefs, and practices. Since primitive man spent most of his time in the fields, much of his healing practices came from direct observations of the herbs and plants that the animals sought when they were sick. Through many years of trial and error, remedies were developed, and they were then transmitted from one generation to the next. Success with these "home" remedies provided proof of their validity, and failures were ignored or rationalized away. These culturally derived and generally nonscientific beliefs and practices continue to show their influence on the interpretation of illness today.

Further support for the demoniac concept of illness came with the discovery of bacteria. Now the demon was said to be in the form of a germ that attacked and killed. Pure speculation was replaced by "rational" scientific thought. With the invention of the microscope the demon could actually be seen. Comments such as the patient "is fighting the illness" or "is resisting the illness" reflect the influence of the primitive concept of disease on present-day thinking.

The primitive model viewed illness as an autonomous, amorphous being that attacked and killed. In other words, illness was seen as an evil force that struck a defenseless person. The individual was held responsible for the attack, but he had no power or defenses to fight back. Recognition of illness during this period was mostly intuitive, speculative, and empirical. It disrupted life, and primitive man learned to deal with it according to his existing beliefs and understandings about nature. Belief in supernatural beings and spirits was reflected in the mode of intervention that was directed primarily at appeasing the evil spirits and implementing various techniques to drive the illness out of the body.

The Medical-Physiologic Model

Transition from a magical and religious conception of illness to a scientific conception was a gradual process that lasted over many centuries. Hippocrates had no patience with the idea that disease was a punishment sent by the gods. Every disease, (he said) had its own nature and arose from external causes (as opposed to supernatural causes). He attributed the supposedly divine origin of illness to man's inexperience and ignorance.

Discovery of the scientific method with its emphasis on making direct and objective observations, as opposed to speculations, resulted in a concept of illness based upon anatomic changes in the organs, tissues, and cells; i.e., illness was conceived to be an organic phenomenon. The relevant attributes or cues of illness in this model were the presence of aberrations from normal body structure and function. Based upon the correlation of clinical observations with laboratory findings it was possible to identify and to classify such clinical entities as rheumatic heart disease, pulmonary tuberculosis, typhoid fever, and diphtheria.

As medicine continued to match clinical observations with laboratory findings, problems of incongruence became apparent. Certain similar pathological organisms were found capable of producing different anatomic and physiologic changes among individuals, and different organisms produced similar observable manifestations. What happened was that in man's feverish search for bacteria and viruses as the cause of illness other factors tended to escape detection. Medicine soon realized that man was not a passive being attacked by organisms but rather an active being with abilities to resist the aggressor. Individuals varied in their ability to resist and to defend themselves against the attacking organism. Medicine observed that there was a direct relationship between the strength of an aggressor and the severity of illness and an inverse relationship between the strength of the organism's defenses and the degree of illness. In other words, the stronger or more virulent the disease-producing agent, the more serious the illness; the better the body was able to defend itself, the less severe the illness.

The medical-physiologic model viewed illness as some underlying defect or structural aberration that must be identified, prevented, removed, counteracted, neutralized, or corrected. Efforts were directed towards discovering pathognomonic signs that fit into the frame of some medical classificatory scheme. According to this view, illness was biologically determined by such agents as bacteria, viruses, and toxins. It was considered to be morally neutral. The severity of illness was a function of the strength of the aggressor or disease-producing agent as opposed to the body's resistance. Thus the observation of different responses to similar disease-producing agents was attributed to individual idiosyncrasies. The recognition of illness was supplemented with laboratory analysis, and speculation was replaced by scientific procedure in which the emphasis was on the directly observable and measurable manifestations of illness.

Ecologic Model

Dissatisfaction with the limitations of the medical model next resulted in the development of an ecologic model that considered the relationship of man to his total environment as it influences his health. Ecologists stated that the cause of illness or injury is three-pronged: the disease- or injury-producing agent, the resistance or susceptibility of the host, and the environmental situation that brings agent and host together. The agent may be virulent or weak, the host may be susceptible or able to resist the agent, and the environment may be favorable or unfavorable to a "forceful" impact. Illness is not caused by a single discrete, disease-causing or injury-causing agent acting upon an otherwise normal and healthy person; it is caused by many factors both within and outside the organism.

Although at first glance it seems that this model places emphasis on the immediate and specific causation of illness, advocates of this approach are quick to point out the importance of including the net balance of accumulated environmental effects. Long-term effects of the environment can serve to strengthen or weaken the basic constitution of the host; they may also affect the developing potential parasite or other agents that cause illness; and finally, they may gradually create the immediate situation in which the precipitating event may occur.

The ecologic model states that illness is a function of genetic man plus the total effects of his environment (Rogers, 1960). In other words, the occurrence of illness is dependent upon man's heredity or genetically derived characteristics and upon the current and accumulated effects of the environment as they act upon his body and mind. The notion of resistance, predisposition, and immunity take on wider meaning in this model. Environment is of two kinds, according to Rogers: intrinsic and extrinsic. The intrinsic or internal environment includes such factors as age, sex, hereditary characteristics, inherent mentality, and temperament. It is difficult at this point to distinguish between Roger's concept of "genetically derived characteristics" and the intrinsic environment. The external or extrinsic environment is said to include physical properties, such as the climate and topography; biological properties, such as bacteria and viruses; and sociocultural properties, such as values, beliefs, and societal norms.

The ecologic model explicates and reinforces the notion of predisposition as an important determinant of the degree of illness. Knowledge of the causation or agent of illness has no utility, according to the ecologist, without an accompanying analysis of the medium or source of the attack. In other words, the factors that put a phenomenon into motion are secondary to man's inherent disposition to respond in a determined way. Recognition of the role of predisposition helps to explain why certain people react differently to the same stimulus and similarly to different stimuli.

The ecologic model does not really offer a different definition of illness; it is only an extension of the medical model. Thus its relevant attributes are the same as those defined by the medical model. The ecologic model is a further attempt to explain the causation of illness. Its contribution lies chiefly in its recognition of a class of variables not previously well defined plus its attention to the interactional process between the medium and agent. The organism may or may not actively resist the force or aggressor, depending upon the strength and character of its predisposition and the facilitatory or inhibitory effects of the environment. This notion is further developed in the equilibrium model.

Equilibrium Model

The equilibrium model views illness as a disturbance in equilibria. The interactional process between man and his environment, alluded to in the ecologic model, is subject to constant change. This process is constantly being influenced by factors that also may be constantly varying. As long as the process remains in balance, the person is said to be experiencing health/wellness. When the proper balance between man and his environment is upset, according to Menninger (1963), certain processes in the organism develop in a manner prejudicial to its life. This imbalance between the aggressive or self-destructive forces and the constructive or integrative ones represents illness. It reflects a failure of the body's adaptive, self-regulating powers to maintain the balance (constancy of the internal milieu) in the face of stress, physical and emotional, arising from inside and outside of the organism.

This model differs from the medical-physiologic one in that it considers illness to be a dynamic process rather than something static and unchanging that fits into some nosologic classification. It views illness as a reaction of the whole organism, biological and psychological. The dualism between mind and body no longer exists. The equilibrium model also recognizes that factors other than those that initiated the illness process can significantly influence its course and outcome. For example, financial worries could slow down and impede full recovery.

This model adopts the causal explanations offered by the ecologist in terms of the interplay between a class of stressors and the defensive reactions of the body. In other words, illness is a consequence of all factors in a reaction—internal and external stimuli as well as the predisposition of the individual.

The individual is reacting constantly to the stimuli of his environment, adjusting himself to them, and maintaining equilibrium through shifts of some kind and degree. The changes in equilibrium caused by these shifts are usually compensated for so rapidly that an imbalance does not become a problem. Stimuli that do not cause an upset in the balance are described as physiologic. In the event that the stimulus is powerful enough to disrupt the equilibrium, it becomes pathologic. The individual is unable to deal with the stimulus, and the balance is upset beyond immediate righting. An imbalance may also occur from overreactive defenses. The individual's defenses respond in a manner that is out of proportion to the demands of the situation. Unsuccessful attempts to restore the balance appear as signs and symptoms of disease.

The equilibrium model views illness as a failure of the body's self-regulating powers to maintain the constancy of the internal milieu. It represents an imbalance in man's physiologic adaptation to multiple physical and emotional stresses. Recognition of this imbalance is by means of the scientific procedure introduced in the medical model. The relevant attributes are the signs and symptoms of disease that are the manifestations of an imbalance. Intervention is directed towards encouraging, nurturing, reinforcing, and strengthening behaviors that will restore the balance.

Social Model

The sociologist views illness as "an impairment of capacity to perform one's social roles and/or valued tasks relative to his status in society" (Parsons, 1958). It is viewed as a social phenomenon that disrupts regular patterns of living.

Hadley (1964) defines illness as a "status in which there is a disturbance in one or more spheres of an individual's capacity to meet minimum physical, physiological, psychological, and social requirements for appropriate functioning in the given sex category and at the given growth and developmental level." The criteria for measuring "minimum requirements for appropriate functioning" utilize the dimensions of age, sex, and development rather than status. Certain physical, physiological, and psychological behaviors can be expected to appear at different stages of growth and development, and incapacity to perform at the minimally expected level can be viewed as illness. In order to avoid the ambiguity of "optimal" or "normal" capacity, from which "impairment" can be measured, Hadley substitutes the terms "minimal" and "appropriate," suggesting that these behaviors are discernible and that they allow for individual variations beyond a minimal level. She suggests that if an individual cannot meet certain minimum requirements appropriate to his age, sex, and developmental level, he is experiencing an impairment that she defines as illness.

The advantages of Hadley's modifications over the earlier sociological definitions of illness lie in her attempt to be more definitive. Since individuals occupy more than one status and play a variety of roles, and since some occupations and social positions require more physical stamina than others, it seems logical to eliminate this relative criterion from the assessment of illness. There is perhaps greater unanimity associated with the expectations of a given age, sex, and developmental level than with an occupational or family status. Hadley has thus limited herself to these three criteria, which she has identified as relevant to a definition of illness.

The sociological model defines illness in terms of the social position or role an individual is expected to occupy or play. The four models discussed previously explained illness in terms of causality, physical manifestations, and consequences to the individual's stability, whereas the sociological model is focused on the consequences of the impaired condition to society. This definition enables individuals other than the patient and doctor to modify the meaning of illness according to different situations and the changing needs of the social system. Sometimes the requirements of the social system will take precedence over purely medical and humanitarian conditions and will provide a different basis for defining illness; e.g., the demands of the system may not allow certain persons to be called ill, since the economic needs of the community take precedence over the individual's medical condition. Society assigns a status depending upon the needs of the community, and it evaluates capacity in terms of these needs. However, not all conditions defined as illness by certain segments of society are recognized as such by the community. For example, exemption from social role obligations is not always granted to the ill. Generally, the more dim the prognosis the more likely is the individual accorded the status of illness and all the rights and obligations that go along with such a status.

The average layman aligns himself along with the sociologist in his definition of illness. In an interview with 60 well people, ages 20 to 50, Sweetser (1960) found that interference with usual activities appeared to be the most important condition associated in the layman's mind with illness. If the individual had persistent signs and symptoms (commonly associated with illnesses) that failed to limit activity, the individual generally speaking was *not* viewed as ill. This was particularly true in the older age group, as changes in body structure and function were attributed to the aging process.*

Although Bauman (1965) investigated the different attitudes of people toward health and physical fitness, the findings reported

---

*Twaddle (1969) reports a similar finding. Older males in his study defined themselves as "not well" when a change in feeling occurred, e.g., the experience of pain and weakness, incapacity to perform one's normal role, and appearance of certain changes in the body that were viewed as important to survival and longevity (p. 108).

tended to reflect conceptions of illness. Her study included 182 chronically ill patients in an outpatient clinic and 252 medical students, both groups from the East Coast. The clinic patients tended to use their own health status as a referent for defining health. The most frequently mentioned criterion for health by the clinic patient was the ability to do everyday activities in line with usual role obligations, whereas the medical students tended to use the absence of signs and symptoms as a criterion of health. Most definitions given by both groups included more than one criterion. However, reference to a feeling of well-being as a criterion of health was rarely mentioned by either of these groups.

In contrast to the above findings, students enrolled in a nursing school on the West Coast found that among 50 adult medical patients interviewed in a nearby hospital the most frequent response given to questions concerning their definitions of illnesses was "not feeling well."* They also found that healthy nonnursing students enrolled in the local university tended to define illness as a state of feeling; e.g., "feels bad all the time," "tired and run-down," "don't feel well," "irritable and complaining." This is a rather interesting observation, especially since Bauman has noted a relationship between educational background and the criteria given for health. The person with a formal education, she found, was more apt to use absence of signs and symptoms as a criterion of health, whereas the person with no formal education tended to use a subjective referent such as his overall feelings to define health. Since the students did not analyze their data in terms of age, education, social class, religious affiliation, and physical condition, as did Bauman, it is unfair at this point to make any comparisons except to note that by virtue of being college students they might be classified as having a formal education. The apparent inconsistency of responses between the group of medical students and the group of nonmedical and nonnursing students can be attributed to:

1. The focus of the interview, one on the definitions of health and physical fitness and the other on illness.
2. The differences in the subjects' academic majors, the former group majoring in a health-related field and the latter in fields other than health.

The second most common criterion of illness held by both groups, university students and hospitalized adult patients alike, re-

---

*Survey conducted by U.C.L.A. nursing students as a class assignment.

lates to performance: "can't get up and around," "can't do your job and support your family," "have to study in bed and can't get your work done," and so on. These findings support the notion that the layman defines illness along sociological lines, that is, based on his ability or inability to carry out usual daily activities.

Thus the relevant attributes that apparently distinguish illness from other phenomena are three: an interference in performing one's usual daily activities, a feeling of not being well, and the presence of signs and symptoms or changes in body structure and function. The presence of one or more of these attributes is taken as an indication of illness.

In summary, the social model views illness as an incapacitation to perform social roles and tasks. There is no attempt to explain the cause of illness. Recognition is based on a general feeling of not being well plus an inability to perform at the level usually expected. The individual generally seeks confirmation from a medical person. When illness is recognized, the individual is allowed to occupy a special status with certain rights and obligations.

CRITIQUE OF THE MODELS

Except for the ecologic model, all of the models differ in their view of the nature of illness. (See Table 1). The primitive model views illness as an autonomous being that attacks and kills. The medical-physiologic model defines illness along certain static and divisional lines that fit into some nosologic classification (clinical syndromes). The equilibrium model defines illness as a dynamic process that is constantly changing, and the social model defines illness as an incapacitation in performance ability.

The scientific procedure provided impetus for a rational approach to the study of illness. With the exception of the primitive model, the cause of illness was attributed not only to some disease— or some injury-producing agent—but also to the inherent predisposition of the host and to the character of the environment. Medicine moved from an intuitive, speculative, and empirical mode of diagnosis to a scientific, rational approach that used all kinds of observational and measuring techniques.

The form of intervention varies among the models, depending upon whether illness is conceptualized as a demon to be driven out of the body, a physical aberration to be surgically removed or corrected, or a dynamic process in which the forces of aggression are being resisted by the body's defenses. In the last case, intervention is directed toward facilitating and supporting the process, so that a balance is restored. Finally, when illness is viewed as an incapacitation to perform one's usual roles and tasks, intervention is directed toward exempting this person from his usual obligations so that he can get on with the job of getting well and can resume his role obligations.

The problem now is to select the model that is best suited for nursing and best distinguishes illness from other phenomena. Although the medical and equilibrium models view the content of illness differently, they rely on the same manifestations for its recognition. Changes in body structure and subsequent function, changes that comprise a clinical syndrome or exceed the normal constancy of the internal milieu, become the signs and symptoms of illness.

A source of confusion in regard to the equilibrium model is the assumption that the presence of signs and symptoms reflects a failure of the body to adapt to stress. In other words, a state of imbalance implies that the body has either overreacted or underreacted to environmental stimuli. This is not necessarily so. Sometimes the body's defenses react in direct proportion to the strength of the aggressor so that a state of balance exists. This is an example of adaptation. Adaptation is involved every time the individual encounters illness or a similar event. When adaptation exceeds physiological limits, the process is described as maladaptive and is considered pathological. Signs and symptoms are the manifestations of both physiologic and pathologic adaptation. An increase in red blood cells beyond the normal range to compensate for the decrease in the percent of oxygen absorbed due to low atmospheric pressure experienced in high altitudes is an example of physiologic adaptation. It represents a new balance outside of the "normal" range required to cope with the stressful environment. Failure to respond appropriately to the reduced atmospheric pressure resulting in oxygen want is an example of maladaptation (pathologic adaptation).

Another example is the variation of the body's responses to invasion by pathogenic organisms. In an effort to deal with the toxins produced by the organism, the body's temperature-regulating mechanism may respond by producing heat to kill the organism. A new balance is achieved as the fever attempts to rid the body of the organism, an example of physiologic adaptation. Conversely, if the body's temperature-regulating mechanism were defective and did not produce the necessary heat, or produced too much heat, to deal with the organism, without the assistance of drugs the individual would lose the battle. Thus, when the body fails to respond to a level commensurate with the degree of threat, it is an example of maladapta-

TABLE 1
Nature of Illness

Relevant attribute	Primitive	Medical	Ecologic
I. Content of illness	An autonomous, amorphous being that attacks and kills = a force	Anatomical changes in tissues and cells classifiable into syndromes = a condition	An interaction between the environment and man's inherent disposition = an effect or result
II. Causation of illness			
A. Agent	Sin, evil spirits, wrongdoings	Microorganisms, toxins, germs, bacteria or trauma	Virulent disease or injury-producing agent
B. Host	Passive organism, attacked and punished	Active, resisting organism	Susceptible host
C. Environment	(Not recognized per se)	(Not recognized per se)	Poor or unhealthy environment (current or cumulative effects)
III. Intervention	Appease evil spirits, supplications to Gods, etc., to drive illness out of body	Identify, remove, counteract, neutralize, or correct aberration	Manipulate host, agent, and/or environment
IV. Identification of illness	Intuitive, speculative, and empirical	Scientific procedure—directly observable and measurable aberrations	Scientific procedure—directly observable and measurable aberrations

tion. Illness is associated with both physiologic and pathologic adaptation. It represents a balanced or an imbalanced relationship between the body's defenses and the aggressor. Signs and symptoms refer to the changes that exceed "normal" ranges for body structure and function. These changes may be both physiologic or pathologic.

Heavy reliance on signs and symptoms for the recognition of illness is one of the chief problems with the medical and equilibrium models of illness. Except for gross abnormalities, manifestations that distinguish between normal and abnormal or equilibrium and disequilibrium are vague and equivocal. The problem is to determine at what point a change in structure and subsequent function becomes a sign and/or symptom of illness. How far must a change extend beyond the normal range to become abnormal or to cause an upset in equilibrium? Normality may be defined in terms of a set

TABLE 1

Nature of Illness   (continued)

Equilibrium	Social	Nursing
An imbalance between aggressive and defensive forces = a process or reaction	Impairment of capacity to perform social roles and tasks = status	A phenomenon experienced by people in all societies
Stress (in form of internal and external stimuli)	(Not identified)	Aggressor that threatens to upset stability of the organism
Maladaptive host	(Not identified)	Susceptible host
(Implicit as part of stress)	(Not identified)	Poor or unhealthy environment (current and cumulative effects)
Support, encourage, nurture, reinforce, or strengthen body's defenses	Establish rights and obligations for the sick	Control the environment to restore balance and and assist body's defenses
Disequilibrium manifested by aberrations in structure and/or function	Feeling "bad" and deterioration of performance	Observable and/or felt changes in the body perceived as incapacitating

of norms or in terms of a statistical average. In other words, a change in structure or function can be assessed as abnormal if the change deviates from a normal standard or range or if it is found to be absent among the average members of a society.

Illness is culturally defined. What is diagnosed as illness in one society may be viewed as quite normal in another society wherein the assessed deviation is the rule rather than the exception for that society. Further, within a single society there can be lack of unanimity as to what signs and symptoms denote illness. For some persons the term *normal* is not a statistical concept but a personal judgment in which the individual uses himself as the standard from which to judge the presence or absence of deviations in others. Koos [1960] demonstrated in his study that the same symptom can be interpreted differently by different laymen depending upon their social stratification. In other words, among persons experiencing the same symptoms, some would seek medical care, whereas others would ignore the symptoms, failing to associate them with illness.

Even if the normal range for all structures and functions of the body were known, deviation from this range would not be a sufficient criterion of illness. The diagnosis of illness depends upon the kind of aberration, degree of severity, and amount of accompanying incapacitation. For example, localized infection of the index finger with signs of inflammation and pain may not be viewed as illness because it is confined to one small part of the body and does not incapacitate the individual. On the other side of the coin are persons who experience illness in the absence of identifiable aberrations. It is difficult to treat this individual as ill when his symptoms and the objective findings fail to conform to an established pattern or syndrome. We do not know precisely the normal range for thought, mood, or affect. Sometimes a response to one situation may be quite inappropriate for another situation. In other words, the response may be judged normal in one setting and abnormal in another setting. Until a clear-cut criterion of normalcy is available for every function of the body, sole reliance on signs and symptoms for the recognition of illness is impracticable. In addition, as stated above, the signs and symptoms must be accompanied with a feeling of incapacitation, since it is obvious that changes from normal structure and function alone are inadequate for a definition of illness.

The incorporation of the social model into our definition of illness presents a problem because of its relativity and subjectivity. There is no standard frame of reference for assessing the level of competence for a given set of occupations. In the first place, individuals vary as to their evaluation of performance. In addition, work requirements may be quite different in one situation compared to another. Some jobs demand heavy physical work, and others are sedentary. Thus an individual with a sprained ankle could be assessed as incapacitated in the former situation but quite capable of performing in the latter situation.

Hadley (1964) attempts to correct this deficiency of the social model by introducing minimal requirements for appropriate functioning in a given age-sex category and at a given growth or developmental level. Minimal physiological requirements for appropriate functioning are established by a physician, eliminating the relativity implicit in the earlier concept. For example, individuals who are unable to perform at the specified minimal level are assessed as ill. On the other hand, individuals who experience a disturbance in one or more spheres, but one that does not interfere with appropriate functioning expected at their age, sex, and developmental level, are not viewed as ill.

There is another group of individuals—those who are permanently disabled—that must be considered. Due to their disability they cannot perform at the minimal level for their age, sex, and development. They do not classify themselves as ill nor behave as ill persons. Should there be a separate set of requirements that takes into account such disabilities? The primary deficiency of the social model for nursing is its failure to distinguish between individuals experiencing illness and those experiencing permanent disability. A separate standard for evaluating minimal requirements for appropriate functioning must be developed for the disabled group.

In addition, the minimal requirements for "appropriate functioning"—which is the key to Hadley's definition—are not well defined to date. She has suggested that the physician should define the physiological requirements. She herself has attempted to define the psychosociological criteria (behaviors) that distinguish between the statuses of wellness and illness; e.g., in a normal adult male, trust and independence are associated with wellness, and mistrust and dependence are associated with illness. She fails to include any quantifiable measurement—e.g., frequency and degree of emission— to serve as an assessment tool. She does, however, state that the degree of frequency of emitting certain behaviors varies with age, sex, and developmental level. The amount that distinguishes illness from wellness is not made explicit. Therefore, the utility of this definition for nursing must await further delineation of its terms.

The social definition of illness is useful for the social scientist who is concerned with the smooth functioning of the social system. Defining the legitimate conditions under which an individual may withdraw from his usual role responsibilities and adopt the sick role is functional for both the person and his society. The advantage of the social model is that it allows for the recognition and acceptance of illness without medical confirmation. To define illness as "that which the doctor treats," is useless and inadequate for both the sociologist and the nurse. As Parsons (1960) states so clearly:

A person approaching death from old age is properly speaking no more "sick" than is a pregnant woman approaching the end of her term even though both may require special care, part of which may be defined as "medical care."

There will be persons under medical care who definitionally are not ill as well as persons who are not under medical care but because of their incapacity to perform social roles and valued tasks are considered ill.

Generally speaking, none of the models, individually, is found to be adequate for nursing. Their deficiencies can be attributed to the use of relative and imprecise terms and to a failure to distinguish illness from other dissimilar phenomena. What is needed by nursing is a model that identifies the common features of illness that set it apart from other phenomena.

A MULTIDIMENSIONAL APPROACH TO THE DEFINITION OF ILLNESS

It was stated at the beginning of this chapter that a definition of illness was needed to provide nurses with a base from which to predict behaviors associated with illness. Knowledge of the nature of illness should assist the nurse in recognizing the person experiencing illness and in developing measures that would facilitate his recovery.

The models discussed in this chapter have been reviewed in terms of their adequacy for nursing and have been found to be deficient. It appears that for the present a combination of ideas from several models, in spite of their limitations, will best satisfy the requirements for nursing. Perhaps we shall have to settle for something less than perfect for now.

The first criterion of illness that originates with the medical-physiologic model is the presence of observable and/or felt changes in the body. This is a necessary but not a sufficient condition of illness, since not all changes in the body represent illness. Limiting illness to changes in the body that the doctor treats or designates as ill health offers no solution. This solution eliminates the possibility of illness occurring among a group of people who do not visit the doctor. Likewise it implies that all persons seeking medical care for changes in the body are ill. The illogicalness of such deductions is obvious.

The criterion for evaluating whether the presence of observable and/or felt changes in the body is indeed illness should be the incapacity of the individual to perform at a level commensurate with his age, sex, and development. In other words, impairment of capacity to perform at a specified level due to observable and/or felt changes in the body can define the person as experiencing illness.

Impairment of capacity refers to the inability to perform certain physical, psychological, or psychosocial acts. The minimum performance expected should be established in accordance with socially prescribed expectations for a given age, sex, and developmental level. Allowances must also be made for handicapped persons and separate requirements identified so that the expectations established are achievable within the limits of the disabled.

But, what is the essence of illness? Is it a force, condition, or status? For nursing it can be all of these things. Illness is an event experienced by people in all societies. Whatever its essence it evokes a response congruent with the person's interpretation of the experience. For example, recognizing that illness is a being that attacks and kills will elicit a certain class of behaviors. Viewing illness as a process in which the forces of aggression are interacting· with the forces of resistance in a battle to restore health elicits a different class of behaviors. The former carries negative connotations and the latter, positive and constructive actions. The latter view alerts the nurse to a dynamic, changing phenomenon that influences and is influenced by many factors, bio-psycho-socio-cultural in nature. This view is inconsistent with a simple stimulus-response reaction.

What precipitates or initiates the experience of illness? Usually illness is triggered by an aggressor that activates the body's defenses. However, a stimulus that precipitates illness in one person may not be capable of eliciting the same response in another organism. This is the notion set forth by the ecologic model. Whether or not illness is experienced is directly related to the sensitivity and resistance of the organism as well as to the intensity, frequency, and character of the stimulus. Once illness is experienced, its termination can be delayed by overreactive defenses, which is sometimes a complication of illness. When the aggressor has been subdued and other influencing factors controlled, recovery follows.

In summary, illness is an event experienced by people that manifests itself through observable and/or felt changes in the body, causing an impairment of capacity to meet minimum physical, physiological, and psychosocial requirements for appropriate functioning at the level designated for the person's age, sex, and development, or handicapped state.

The behavioral response to illness is dependent upon intermediary processes that serve to interpret the changes experienced or communicated to the person. This chapter examined the nature of illness and proposed a definition. The next chapter will dissect illness for its phenomenalistic and denotable features in order to discover *how* illness appears to the person experiencing it vis-à-vis *what* illness actually is.

REFERENCES

BAUMAN, BARBARA "Diversities in Conceptions of Health and Physical Fitness," in *Social Interaction and Patient Care,* eds. J. K. Skipper and R. C. Leonard. Philadelphia: J. B. Lippincott Co., 1965, pp. 208–18.

ENGEL, GEORGE L. "Homeostasis, Behavioral Adjustment and the Concept of Health and Disease," in *Midcentury Psychiatry*, ed. Roy R. Grinker. Springfield, Ill.: Charles C. Thomas, Publisher, 1963, pp. 33–59.

HADLEY, BETTY JO "A Review of Current Concepts of Health and Illness for Becoming Well: A Study of Role Change." Unpublished manuscript, U.C.L.A., January, 1964, p. 16.

HINKLE, L. E. and H. G. WOLFF "Ecologic Investigations of the Relationship between Illness, Life Experiences, and the Social Environment," *Annals Internal Medicine,* 49 (1958), 1373–88.

KOOS, EARL LOMAN "Illness in Regionville," in *Sociological Studies in Health, and Sickness,* ed. Dorian Apple. New York: McGraw-Hill Book Company, 1960, pp. 9–14.

MENNINGER, KARL *The Vital Balance.* New York: The Viking Press, 1963, p. 401.

PARSONS, TALCOTT "Definitions of Health and Illness in Light of American Values and Social Structure," in *Patients, Physicians, and Illness,* ed. E. G. Jaco. New York: The Free Press, 1958, pp. 176–85.

——— "Toward a Healthy Maturity," *Journal of Health and Human Behavior,* 1, No. 3 (Fall, 1960), 163–73.

ROGERS, EDWARD S. *Human Ecology and Health,* Part III. New York: The Macmillan Company, 1960, p. 166.

SELYE, HANS *The Stress of Life.* New York: McGraw-Hill Book Company, 1956, p. 11.

SEQUIN, ALBERTO C. "The Concept of Disease," *Psychosomatic Medicine,* 8, No. 4 (July-August, 1946), 252–57.

SUCHMAN, EDWARD A. *Sociology and the Field of Public Health.* New York: Russell Sage Foundation, 1963, p. 65.

SWEETSER, DORRIAN APPLE "How Laymen Define Illness," *Journal of Health and Human Behavior,* 1 (1960), 219–25.

TWADDLE, ANDREW C. "Health Decisions and Sick Role Variations: An Exploration," *Journal of Health and Social Behavior,* 10 (1969), 105–15.

three | *The Perception of Illness*

Perception is said to have something to do with man's awareness of objects, conditions, and events about him. The act of perceiving is dependent upon the impression these objects or events make upon one's senses. However, perceiving is more than sense impressions, more than the way things look, sound, feel, taste, or smell. It includes the meaning or recognition given to objects and events. The perception of illness is concerned with *how* illness appears to the individual experiencing it vis-à-vis *what* it is. It is concerned with the patient's own concept of his illness and the meaning it has for him in terms of what he knows, sees, and feels.

A study of the perception of illness begins with a description of the objective features of the phenomenon to which the individual responds. The scientific procedure provides us with a careful description of the phenomenon and thereby allows us to draw generalizations suitable for an explanation or prediction of elicited behaviors. Any object or event, at least in principle, provides content matter for scientific observation and study. Some objects or events seem easier or more accessible to study than others. For example, the study of the reaction of plants to sunlight appears easier and more accessible for observation and study than the reactions of man to illness. In spite of the differences in accessibility, both events provide us with content matter for scientific observation.

The scientific method requires that observation be controlled so that error due to the activity of the investigator is reduced to a minimum, free from distorting biases. Three methodological rules have been developed to insure maximum objectivity in the description of all phenomena (Allport, 1955):

1. *Observer-detachment* refers to the degree of observer-involvement. It is necessary in any scientific procedure that the observer separate his interpretations, preconceived notions, and biases from his own observing activities and record only what he observes. The less involved the individual becomes with the experience he is describing, the more objective is the procedure. This is one of the reasons why investigators employ outside persons, not connected with the research project per se, to make observations and gather data. These individuals usually do not know the purposes of the project and therefore will not unintentionally bias the findings.

2. *Denotability* is the ability to physically contact or encounter some aspect of the event or object under study. Certain features of illness can be measured through touch, sight, and sound. Contact with any aspect of the phenomenon may be direct or indirect, requiring the use of instruments. Indirect observations may involve a chain of encounters between what is to be described and the observer. For example, visualization of lung pathology in situ is encountered only by means of x-ray machines following a series of minute encounters between cosmic ray particles, chemical interactions, and so on. Denotable columns of mercury record "thermal changes" and "pressure changes." The more data obtained from denotable sources, the greater will be the assurance that the description is objective and free from observer-involvement.

3. *Publicly performable* means the operations employed to describe the event should be capable of being duplicated by another person. Once the movements and manipulations involved in the operations can be learned and performed by others, they are said to be "public." Any study to be of scientific repute must be capable of replication by other experts in the field. For example, measurement of the body temperature by means of a thermometer can be performed by any person who has learned the technique. This aspect secures the support of observer-agreement.

Let us take these three standards of objectivity and apply them to the study of illness. What aspects of illness are denotable; that is, what aspects of illness can be physically encountered by the observer?

DENOTABLE FEATURES OF ILLNESS

In reviewing the characteristics of illness, it is possible to identify a class of denotable features generally referred to as the *signs* of illness. These are observable changes in the structure and/or function of the body that define illness. For example, a change in body temperature, in cell count, in urine composition, or observations of inappropriate behaviors such as jerky movements, inappropriate laughter, increased sleeping behavior, or a decrease in food ingestion—all of these are commonly regarded as denotable features of illness. *Symptoms* are known only by the person experiencing them and therefore cannot be included as denotable data since they cannot be physically encountered by the nonparticipant observer.

The signs of illness are recorded directly by gross observations or indirectly by the use of instruments such as recording machines, thermometers, x-ray machines, and by the use of biochemical, hematological, and/or bacteriological tests. These tests and measuring devices are indirect methods of gaining objective data about aberrations. Involvement in the mechanics or detailed procedures of the tests reduces the biasing influence of the observer on the results. In addition, the person conducting the tests generally has little or no vested interest in its outcome. Many times the person doing the test does not even see or know the person upon whom the test is being performed. The technician's primary goal is to carry out the technique correctly so that the results reported will be accurate. For instance, the person who wishes to administer a mental test for diagnostic purposes may ask another person to evaluate the test in order to insure objectivity. If he has no other recourse but to both administer and evaluate the test, he must discipline himself so that the possibility of introducing biasing effects to alter the results are minimal. Objectivity is further insured if another person is invited to duplicate the above operations. Anybody who has been taught the method can be asked to readminister the test, and other things being equal, he should arrive at similar conclusions.

In addition to the signs of illness, there are other objective features of illness that may not be denotable as defined herein but meet the test for gaining observer-agreement. Following years of clinical research and study, a science of medicine has evolved. The application of the scientific method supported by statistical techniques has enabled the medical clinician to classify or group certain signs and symptoms that occur and recur together as a recognizable clinical syndrome. For example, fever, cough, hemoptysis, and rales in the chest along with radiological confirmation of consolidation in one or more of the lobes of the lungs and identification of the pneumococcus organism from sputum examination form a recognizable clinical pattern that the medical clinician has labeled pneumonia.

In any population certain recurring illnesses lend themselves to systematic study and observation. The medical clinician can now predict with some certainty the course and duration, type of onset, incidence, prognosis, and communicability of pneumonia, hepatitis, diabetes, and many other such common recurring illnesses. Objective information on common recurring illnesses will change, of course, as advances are made in the fields of science and medicine. The discovery and application of improved diagnostic and therapeutic techniques can be expected to alter both the course and prognosis of the illnesses under study. For example, Myasthenia Gravis is considered today to be an illness with a fairly poor prognosis. This prognosis can be expected to change as knowledge is gained about the illness and as new drugs and techniques are discovered and implemented into the treatment regime. With the knowledge explosion and technological revolution affecting all aspects of society, nothing stands still. Generalizations and predictions accepted today may change tomorrow. But until research findings are reported and made available to the practitioner, yesterday's generalizations will provide the basis for the predictions necessary to control today's events.

Onset refers to the beginning phase of illness. The onset may be described as gradual and/or insidious or deceptive in its early phase, or it may be described as sudden and obvious or so evident that it is nearly impossible to deny its presence. Cancer is said to begin gradually and often insidiously, whereas an infarction or ruptured appendix may be quite sudden and unexpected. Illnesses that are known to begin suddenly without any warning period are usually limited to accidents or injuries and acute overwhelming infections. Most illnesses provide some kind of warning that may or may not be recognizable to the individual. Cancer is said to have warning signals, which if recognized early and treated properly, could alter the entire course of the illness. Many chronic illnesses begin insidiously; i.e., the early signs are not recognizable unless special tests are performed regularly to detect the unfelt aberrations. Certain illnesses like the communicable diseases have an incubation period wherein the individual harbors the organism but displays no overt signs of the illness. Precautions are taken based only on known exposure to the disease. In addition, although the onset of a given disease may be known to be gradual and accompanied with warning signals, it may be experienced as sudden by the patient who denies the presence of the warning signs or fails to realize their significance. Knowledge of this factor helps explain the oft-reported discrepancy between what the nurse or doctor knows about the illness and what the patient experiences. For example, although an illness may be known to begin gradually, it may be experienced as sudden and shocking. This discrepancy occurs most frequently in patients who are unwilling to accept the illness or are fearful that the felt aberrations portend serious or fatal consequences and so avoid reporting the symptoms to their doctor.

Most illnesses follow a certain *course* or path, which may be described as smooth, even, and uneventful or rough, stormy, erratic, and quite unpredictable. Certain chronic illnesses run a course that is marked by periods of exacerbations sandwiched between periods of remissions. A rough course usually refers to an instable situation, often life-threatening, in which there are varying degrees of physiological and psychological fluctuations. In the case of some systemic infections, the course is marked by severe fluctuations in the vital signs. The course of an illness is determined, in part, by the virulence of the organism, the resistance of the host, and environmental circumstances. For example, the course of an illness can be altered significantly, depending on the time at which therapy is instituted. If the course of an illness is known to be marked by crises, such as severe temperature elevations, it may be helpful to advise the family of this so that they do not become unduly alarmed. Most parents or others caring for the sick would rather know what can be expected, even though the facts may not in themselves be comforting, rather than be left with the unknown. However, the course of an illness cannot always be predicted correctly owing to individual idiosyncrasies. Thus, the prediction of the course of an illness may have less heuristic value because of its relativity. Certainly this is reflected by many authors of medical texts who are reluctant to describe the course of many illnesses.

The *prognosis* or outcome of certain illnesses can also be predicted. The prognosis may range from excellent, with full recovery expected, to poor, terminating in death. For certain illnesses the aberrations are irreversible but not necessarily terminal, in which case the prognosis is said to be "guarded" in that not enough is known about the illness and the effects of therapy to make a more definitive prediction. The prognosis in any illness is dependent upon proper care and adherence to the prescribed therapeutic plan. The predictions, when made, are usually based upon these assumptions.

The *duration* or length of an illness, imprecise though it may be, is also predicted for us by medical science. Certain illnesses are classified as short-term and others as long-term. It is known, for example, that the degenerative diseases, by definition, are long-term, lasting many years. This disease process is usually found to be irreversible, and thus the outcome for full recovery is dim. Some authors describe the short-term illness as covering a period extending anywhere from two or three days to several months, and a long-term illness as extending over a year or more in time. There is no agreement on the exact period that distinguishes a short-term from a long-term illness.

Two words, *acute* and *chronic*, are often used to describe both the severity and duration of an illness. Smith (1936) suggests that an acute condition should be defined as one in which there is a rapid state of change. The term *acute* does not refer to the seriousness of the illness per se, but rather it describes the rapid nature of the onset and progress. An example is the common cold, which is often described as an acute condition, and yet its consequences usually are not serious. The term *chronic* describes the lengthy, sometimes endless persistence of a condition without much change for the better. It too does not necessarily indicate the degree of severity or threat of the illness. A chronic skin condition could be more discouraging and upsetting than deadly, whereas a chronic heart condition is often a serious threat to life.

The frequency or *incidence* of an illness is another denotable feature given to us by medical science. When an illness is known to be common, routine, and familiar, it is experienced as less of a threat than an illness that is said to be rare and unfamiliar. Again, an individual through ignorance may experience a certain illness as rare and unusual when in fact it is known to be quite common and familiar. Incongruency between what is known and what is experienced elicits unpredictable behaviors. The individual will behave in a manner inconsistent with what is generally known about the illness.

Finally, the *communicability* of an illness, whether it is contagious or noncontagious, is denoted for us by medicine. The restrictions and limitations imposed by the contagious nature of the illness force the individual to behave in a manner congruent with this aspect of his illness.

In summary, the denotable features of illness are the signs, or objective manifestations and deviations, from normal structure and/or function of the body and/or psyche. Additional objective data given to us by medical science include the course and duration, characteristic onset, prognosis, frequency, and communicability. These are the features that can be observed with minimum observer bias. Let us now examine the phenomenalistic, subjective features of illness, i.e., those features that are known only to the person experiencing the illness.

PHENOMENALISTIC OR SUBJECTIVE ASPECTS OF ILLNESS

How does one know that he is experiencing illness and not some other phenomenon? The question seems absurd in view of the fact that many, if not most, illnesses are obvious and readily distinguishable. However, there are situations in which the individual is unsure as to whether or not he is indeed experiencing illness. How does he distinguish illness from other dissimilar phenomena? Theories of perception attempt to explain why things or happenings appear or seem to appear as they do. Perceiving is phenomenological; that is, the act of perceiving is private. The investigator of illness cannot encounter the same discomforts as the patient who is ill; these discomforts are privately experienced and are known only to the person experiencing them.

The phenomenalistic aspects of illness regulate behavior. How the individual experiences his illness is the important determinant of his behavior and as such becomes content for nursing. When the individual's perception of his illness is incongruent with the objective data given to us by medical science, efforts may be directed, when appropriate, towards changing his perception so that it is more consistent with reality.

The denotable aspects of illness are essential to the practice of medicine. This does not mean that doctors ignore the symptoms or subjective experiences of illness, for this knowledge is necessary to arrive at a diagnosis and a plan of therapy. However, the primary source of data for doctors is the objective signs, the observable changes in tissues, cells, body fluids, and so on in which observer agreement can be secured. On the other hand, the nurse bases her care on an assessment of the individual's behavioral responses to the above changes. These responses are directly related to the patient's perception of his illness.

How then is illness perceived? How is anything perceived? According to Floyd Allport (1955), there are six different but interrelated ways in which things or events appear or seem to appear.

Sensory Quality

The sensory quality of an experience is given to us by means of receptors. Exteroceptors include the organs of reception for vision, audition, gustation, and olfaction; interoceptors include receptors for pain, touch, cold, warmth, and pressure (kinesthesia); and proprioceptors transmit impulses for movement, position, and tension. Illness can be experienced as a change in the quality of sound, sight, odor, and in the degree of cold, warmth, and pressure. It can be experienced as pain, nausea, fever, pruritus, heartburn, and so on. The sensations experienced have at least four dimensions:

1. *Extension* refers to the site or location and extent of the discomfort experienced. Where is the pain or pressure felt? How extensive is the discomfort? Is it a generalized feeling involving the whole body or one involving only parts of the body? Cold and warmth tend to spread out, whereas pressure, pain, and sometimes pruritus are isolated or confined to one area of the body.

2. *Intensity* is the second dimension. It refers to the strength or magnitude of the discomfort. How severe or intense is the pain or pruritus or the buzzing in the ear? Each sensation experienced can be measured in terms of intensity, that is, in terms of being bright or dull, hard or soft, severe or mild, heavy or light, sharp or dull, loud or faint.

3. *Duration* refers to the fact that a sensation is experienced through time. How long does the discomfort remain or persist? Is it brief, intermittent, or constant? The duration perceived is relative to the sensory quality being experienced and to the surrounding environment. When one is busy and relatively content, time flies; whereas when the individual has nothing to do and feels relatively miserable, time seems to go by slowly—the discomforting sensation may seem never-ending.

4. *Clarity* is the fourth dimension of experiencing. A sensation may be experienced as clear, vivid, well-defined, and self-delimited or as diffuse and amorphous with an inability to pin-

point the precise location of the discomfort or to describe the exact odor, sound, and so on.

The sensory quality of things and events tell the individual how they appear by their intensity or strength, extensity, duration, and clarity. These qualities and their dimensions are, in turn, modified by the conditions under which they are experienced. Certain sensory qualities are experienced less intensely under conditions of reduced consciousness, such as in semi-conscious states, or in distracting surroundings.

Frame of Reference

Ordinarily the intensity or duration of a sensation can be estimated with reference to some objective standard. It is possible to measure the intensity of heaviness, brightness, loudness, and so on by comparing each sensation against a standardized scale; for example, a prescribed number of decibels determines the loudness of sound. This is not as easily done with the sensations of illness. What is the standard for measuring the severity of pain, nausea, and pruritis? At the present time there is no known objective standard for drawing comparisons. The act of comparison may be performed against one's own personal subjective frame of reference, based on past experiences with the sensation, or it may be measured against some outside objective frame of reference that carries meaning for both the patient and the investigator of illness. The former has meaning only for the patient. The latter provides the nurse with an opportunity to "get under the patient's skin," so to speak, and to more or less co-experience the event with him. In response to a question concerning the intensity or character of his pain, the patient may state that it is not as severe as the pain he had with his last illness. In this case, the patient is using a frame of reference that has no meaning to the person asking the question. The observer has gained no further insight into the quality or character of the pain unless he knew the patient during his previous illness and had elicited some acts of comparison at that time. If the patient had said that the pain felt like a "burning sensation," then the investigator might have had a better idea of what the pain felt like.

Patients do not usually engage in acts of comparison without prompting. As long as something hurts or itches, the patient's chief concern is to get some relief. If the individual has never experienced the sensation before, he will encounter difficulty judging its dimensionality; he has no standard from which to judge its intensity. If he encounters someone who is suffering the same illness or who is facing the same operation, he may use this person's experience to evaluate whether his own suffering is greater or less than "normal." Frequently a child is unable to describe the severity of his pain because he has never experienced something like this before. The nurse may help an individual establish a frame of reference by suggesting comparable sensations or similes, imaginary or real, that both may have experienced before. For example, does the pain feel like needle pricks, a toothache, or labor pains? One patient described his sciatic pain as the "kind of pain one feels when a dentist hits a nerve while drilling." Frequently a patient finds it difficult to identify the "thing" from which a meaningful comparison can be made and thus is dependent upon the nurse for suggestions. If the nurse is interested in gaining greater insight into the experience of illness, she will ask her patients to compare their sensations with some objective frame of reference that offers meaning to both parties concerned.

Perceptual Constancy

Although illness is experienced in different settings and under a variety of conditions, especially as a consequence of changes in the growth and development of physical and mental faculties, certain cues given by the illness itself and/or by the environment surrounding the experience help us to recognize it as illness. When an individual attempts to confirm an experience as illness, he will rely upon the presence of cues previously associated with the percept, i.e., the thing(s) being perceived. When the sensation fits his idea of illness, he will decide he is sick and engage in actions congruent with his perceptions. Thus, recognition of illness is made when the cues agree with past experience. Failure to recognize the thing or event being perceived (the percept) may be due to the lack of past experience with it or to the need to deny the presence of familiar cues.

Cues include sensations as well as verbalizations, facial expressions, and actions. For example, a word, a diagnostic label, or a test may recall for the individual a past experience that he will begin to associate and to liken to the present experience. Familiarity due to perceptual constancy can minimize or increase the fears associated with illness. The cues may recall an alarming situation previously experienced by the individual, or they may reassure him of the benign nature of the illness. For example, the swelling in the abdomen was recognized by Mr. S. as an enlarged spleen, which he had experienced once before. He expressed confidence that, as previously, therapy would be instituted to return the spleen to its normal size. There was little or no evidence of fear demonstrated. Another individual who had never experienced such a swelling before might have responded quite differently. Thus, manifestations of apprehension may be predicted based on the absence of familiar (reassuring) cues. Apprehension can also be elicited by the presence of familiar (fear-arousing) cues. For instance, the term *cancer* often carries certain connotations that elicit fears of pain, mutilation, and even death. How the individual deals with these feelings depends upon his usual mode of coping. Some persons will be immobilized with fear, whereas others will deny what they have been told or rationalize that the situation really is not as bad or as serious as some are led to believe.

Configuration

Configuration refers to the overall form or shape of the thing(s) being perceived. It implies interrelatedness; i.e., the parts or elements that make up the configuration are interrelated and interdependent. The existence or action of each part affects the existence and action of the other parts in lawful ways (Allport, 1955).

What then is the form or shape of illness? The spatial configuration of illness is least well understood. We know that illness is made up of many factors, such as deviations from normal structure and/or function in the body or psyche, including incapacitation, incidence, prognosis, communicability, and so on. The unifying principle that joins these elements into a whole called illness can be attributed to the proximity of each of the parts to each other, the similarity of the elements, the simultaneous occurrence of the parts, or the common meaning shared by all of the parts; e.g., together they may represent a threat to life. The content of each part varies from illness to illness. Thus the aberration may be a gastric ulcer or a fractured femur, the incapacity may be partial or total immobilization, the incidence may be frequent or rare, and the prognosis may be good or bad. However, the relationship between the parts, i.e., the way one part affects the other part, remains the same regardless of the change in content.

Although the parts or elements of the configuration are interrelated and interdependent, they are not all experienced with equal intensity. Certain features of the illness configuration may be experienced more intensely or more vividly at any given point in time than other features, depending on the situation in which the person finds himself. Thus the individual whose father died of a heart attack might experience a change in heart rate with more alarm than one who does not have this kind of a history, or an aspiring young athlete might view the incapacitation aspect of the illness with greater perturbation because of its possible impact on his career. In any event, the form that the illness takes is dependent upon central organizing processes within the individual. Cognitive meaning is said to be the central process that gives organization and coherence to experience. This will be discussed in greater detail in the section on concrete object character.

The temporal configuration of illness, comprised of onset, course, and duration, is described as triphasic: there is a beginning, a middle, and an end. The length of each phase varies with the illness, but again the sequential nature of the relationship remains the same. The salient features of illness vary from phase to phase. The most outstanding aspect in the beginning of an illness may be of no import in the middle or final phase. Certain illnesses appear to have no temporal configuration, no perceived beginning, and no perceived end. In this case illness is viewed as a way of life; the temporal configuration of illness coincides with the temporal configuration of life itself, which is also triphasic: birth, followed by maturation and decline, and consummated by death.

Illness thus has spatial components that distinguish it from other phenomena. It also has temporal components that are described as triphasic in character. Does the individual respond to the whole configuration of illness or only to certain salient parts at any given point in time? Recognition of the configuration of illness helps us to understand the meaning, i.e., the concrete object character of illness.

Concrete Object Character

Concrete object character refers to the meaning attached to objects and events. Perception almost always carries with it an awareness of the identity and characteristics of what we are perceiving. Things do not appear to us as mere qualities, dimensions, and forms. We interpret what we see, hear, and touch, and give meaning to it. The hard, square, or round object with a flat surface and four legs is perceived as a table. Likewise the peculiar and discomforting sensations associated with alterations in body structure or function appear to us as illness. Furthermore a table is perceived as something useful and functional. What about illness? Is illness viewed as something useful and functional or as a nuisance and a bother?

The meaning of illness may be associated with the whole aggregate or with one or more salient parts of the configuration. Moreover, earlier meanings carry over through time and affect the present situation. Each part achieves independent character and meaning from past experience, associations, interpretations, cognitions, and understandings. Thus the sudden pain in the chest, the diagnostic label, the accompanying disability, and the attending doctor each carries a meaning of its own. Also, the forces that emanate from the whole configuration can either accentuate or suppress the meaning of the parts. Frequently the meaning of the illness as a whole is superseded by the significance of one or more very important part(s). For example, the loss of a part of the body or the dysfunction of a specific organ system may carry more meaning at any given point in time than any of the other parts of the configuration.

The picture the person has of his body is of extreme importance, as is the factor of how much of himself is invested in this image. The heart is usually looked upon as the source of life; it has to beat permanently if life is to be sustained. The body has no provision for taking over this function if it (the heart) should fail. Thus almost every cardiac affliction is directly experienced as a severe threat to life. The act of breathing is so closely connected with feelings of living that any impairment of respiration causes anxiety. Respiratory embarrassment is an extremely threatening experience; the face expresses the terrific struggle between life and death.

The male associates the chest with ideas of virility, strength, and endurance. The female associates the chest with the breasts and attitudes that relate to feminine attractiveness and the maternal feeding function. Illness associated with the chest or reproductive organs may mean a loss of sexuality, femininity or masculinity.

Meanings may change as events and circumstances change. The aspect of illness that provides meaning for today may be displaced by something else that is more dominating and compelling tomorrow. Then, too, some parts carry lasting meaning, or sometimes the diagnostic label carries meanings associated with past experiences. Cancer is associated with feelings of suffering and death, and tuberculosis tends to evoke fears about family relationships and status. Diseases affecting bowel and bladder control evoke feelings of humiliation, shame, and embarrassment. The type of aberration, whether it is overt or hidden, also affects the meaning given to the illness. For example, an obvious deformity may mean humility, shame, ostracism, and social isolation. In the absence of overt manifestations the meaning of illness may also involve the fear of being accused of faking or malingering.

Studies of the upper and middle social classes in American society suggest that illness as a whole is viewed as an obstacle to goal achievement, an interruption in the rhythm of life (Sigerist, 1960). Illness may be viewed as a personal crisis, a situation of strain, a frustration of expectancies of normal life patterns, or a disruption in social relations, of being cut off from many normal enjoyments. Illness for some children is viewed as punishment for misdeeds. For example, children have been overheard to say, "I got sick because I was bad," or ". . . because I ate too much sugar," or ". . . I ran too much."

Thus, illness means different things to different people depending upon situational factors and what the individual is set to perceive (defined by Allport as "perceptual set").

Perceptual Set

Perceptual set differs from the other five variables in that it exerts a selective influence on the kind of sensory quality and meaning given to illness. It represents a different level of analysis. Perceptual set is defined as the tendency to perceive phenomena in a certain way. It recognizes individual differences and the changing physical and emotional states of the person. Individuals perceive in accordance with their needs, motives, attitudes, and preoccupations. The particular attitude of the individual, whether it be longstanding or momentary, affects the selection of the object to be perceived and to some extent the readiness with which it is perceived.

The perception of illness is selective and determined. The individual hears and sees only what he wants or what he is prepared to hear or see. Sometimes, however, the structural properties of the phenomenon are so compelling that it is impossible to selectively ignore their presence without resorting to irrational behaviors. For example, the size of the lump in the breast may become so large that the individual can no longer ignore its presence. The meaning assigned to the illness also depends upon current needs and motivations of the individual. Sometimes the symptoms are so severe and compelling that the need to get rid of the symptom takes precedence over all other aspects of the illness. Other times it may be fear of such factors as the expected outcome of the illness, the isolation of illness, the cost of illness, or the treatment plan that influences the perceptual set.

The physical and emotional states of the organism determine not only *what*, but also *how*, things are perceived. Perception under excitement and emotional stress is more likely to be incongruent with reality than when the organism is calm and confident. Fear is an affect of great potency in determining what the individual will perceive, think, and do. It is the most constricting of all affects. It can produce thinking that is slow, narrow in scope, and rigid in form. Fear tends to reduce the number of behavioral alternatives available to handle the situation. Moreover, a person with disturbances in physiological stability is likely to have altered perceptions of his world. An individual experiencing advanced kidney failure with consequent uremic poisoning is seen to behave in a confused manner, talking incoherently and hallucinating. Things have become distorted in his perceptual field owing to serious biochemical disturbances. Some authors suggest that the patient who is defined as "psychotic" may also be experiencing a biochemical imbalance.

Age, sex, race, occupation, and religious affiliation are other variables that influence perception. Children's perceptions are more susceptible to the influence of emotions than adults. They perceive more strongly in terms of their own expectations, their own inner promptings, which seem more real to them than those coming from the outside. This is due to the fact that the child lacks experience with the world of reality and therefore falls back on autistic mechanisms to interpret his perceptions. Children, according to Gellert (1962), assess the seriousness of their illnesses in terms of the perceived importance or relative indispensability of the affected part. In her study the most indispensable part of the body was identified as the heart; then the sense organs, such as the eyes, head, and brain; and then breathing. Adults perceive their illnesses not only in terms of the affected part but also in terms of their sexual and occupational roles. The individual who views his role as indispensable will experience his illness as more of a threat than those who place less emphasis on their respective roles. Individuals who believe in God and the power of prayer behave in a manner consistent with their beliefs. In the face of danger they seem to appear confident. Sometimes that is attributed to ignorance, but many times it is an expression of faith in an omnipotent being.

Personality characteristics of the individual predisposes him to perceive things in a manner consistent with these characteristics. If he tends to be suspicious of people, he will tend to view things and events in a suspicious manner. Illness-prone persons are set to experience illness more readily than persons who have never experienced the phenomenon before. Familiarity with a percept increases the likelihood of it being perceived. Thus an individual who has frequently experienced illness will recognize ambiguous cues as illness more readily than one who has had little or no prior experience with illness.

Many studies have been conducted to demonstrate the relationship between the state of the individual and what he perceives. For example, a food or water-deprived person is asked to identify what he sees in the amorphous drawings or inkblots presented to him, and predictably he will visualize food and thirst quenchers more frequently than other objects. If these same cards were presented to a food and water-satiated individual, the responses would be quite different. Thus, the prevailing set or state of the individual determines *what* objects or events are perceived or ignored and how these objects and events are perceived.

SUMMARY. These five qualities, then—sensory quality, frame of reference, perceptual constancy, configuration, and concrete object character—represent the characteristic *ways* of perceiving. The sixth variable, perceptual set, determines *what* is perceived. (See Figure 1.) Illness may be experienced as an unusual sensation or change in feeling state; as something relatively serious or not serious (depending upon the frame of reference used to judge the dimensionality of the signs and symptoms); as something familiar and recognizable or unfamiliar and strange; probably as something triphasic, although only one phase is experienced at a time; and as representing something beyond mere form and sensations. Different individuals attach different meanings to the experience of illness depending upon the individual's prevailing set and his state of well-being. No two individuals, even in the same diagnostic category, will perceive their illnesses exactly alike.

CASE ILLUSTRATIONS

Case One

Mrs. F. is a 26-year-old mother of two young boys, ages two and three. She was admitted to the hospital immediately following a fire in her sister's home. She had third-degree burns over 25 percent of her body (arms and chest), which were the denotable signs of her illness. The onset was sudden, the course was rather "rough" in the beginning, and the expected outcome was recovery with some scarring. The condition was not communicable, but because of the danger of infection the patient was placed in protective isolation to

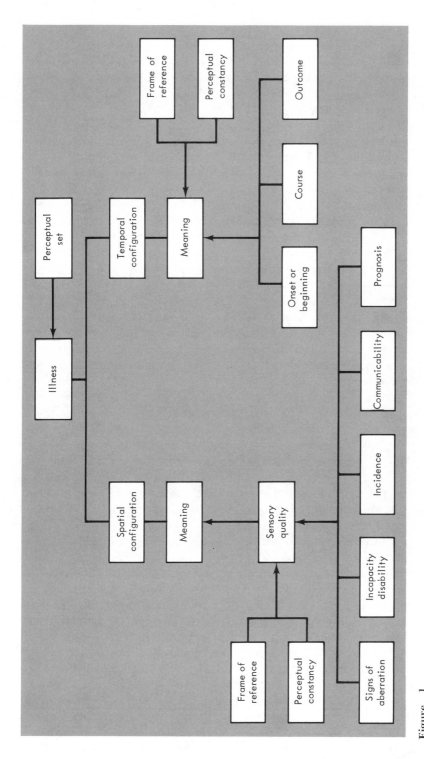

Figure 1
Experience of Illness

41

protect her from visitors and care-givers who might be harboring some pathogenic organisms. The incidence of burns is not uncommon, and the mode of treatment is fairly well defined. Mrs. F.'s knowledge about her illness is congruent with what is known by the nursing staff.

Subjectively, the illness was experienced as severe pain extending throughout the burned areas of the arms and chest, relieved only by medication. Mrs. F. apparently was unable to establish a standard for comparing the severity of the pain. She could only state that "nothing has ever hurt so much before!" In order to gain a better understanding about the pain she was experiencing, the nurse might have suggested certain similes for comparison. For example, the nurse might have asked if the pain felt like a black-and-blue (bruised) spot or like a severe sunburn. The burns and accompanying pain and incapacitation left little doubt in the patient's mind that she was indeed experiencing illness.

The configuration of the illness, as described on the day of the interview, was without shape or form. Although there was an abrupt beginning, there was no forseeable end. The patient envisioned an endless period of restructuring surgery to eliminate the scars and restore her health.

The meaning of the illness for Mrs. F. was the realization that she could "no longer wear a bathing suit to the beach or a low-cut dress to dances," because of the location of her burns. Furthermore, she expressed deep concern over her family and the future of her marriage. She was afraid to go home because she didn't know how her husband would respond to her now disfigured body. This illness represented a threat to her body image and to her feminine role as wife and mother. Mrs. F. faces a real challenge in her adjustment to the consequences of her illness.

The overall picture painted by the patient was one of gloom and depression. What factors (perceptual set) contributed to her pessimistic outlook? For one thing, Mrs. F. was only 26 years old and she had been married for only four years. Femininity, sexual appeal, and beauty are very important attributes at this age and especially in this culture that places so much stress on physical attractiveness. One of her comments was, "I guess everyone has their time. I am just sorry it had to happen when I was so young."

Another factor that influenced her perception of her illness was the fact that she was in protective isolation, feeling lonely and ignored. An artificial distance had been created and maintained with the doning of mask and gown by all who interacted with her. In addition, she expressed a lack of communication with the doctor. "They don't tell me enough. I think they ignore me on purpose.

They try to be sympathetic but no one can possibly understand what it is like in here."

The fact that she was a woman and mother also obviously influenced how and what she perceived. For example, she stated, "I try not to complain to the doctors and nurses because I don't want to irritate them, but it sure hurts." In addition she expressed the fear that if she complained the doctor might find something else wrong with her, and then she would not get to go home as soon as she wanted.

Here we have a young woman experiencing the phenomenon of illness. It is experienced as severe pain and evidenced by the sight of the burns and possibly by a peculiar odor that frequently accompanies burns. The patient had difficulty comparing these sensations with past experiences, real or imagined. Obviously she had no difficulty recognizing that she was ill. Furthermore, there seemed to be no form to the percept, except for a beginning, and there was no foreseeable end. The predominant meaning of the illness seemed to be associated with the part of the body that was most directly affected, the breasts. To Mrs. F. the illness meant a loss of femininity and a threat to her role as wife and mother.

Case Two

Mrs. R. is a 26-year-old mother of two children, a girl, five, and a boy, six years of age. She is a pale, thin, and debilitated woman with a diagnosis of acute ulcerative colitis. The signs of her illness include the presence of diarrhea, dehydration, fever of 103 degrees, occasional vomiting, inability to eat solid foods and recently a 30-pound weight loss. The onset had been gradual, lasting for three months before Mrs. R. consulted a physician. The course had been chronic, extending over a period of one and a half years with no improvement. In fact, Mrs. R. describes the course of her illness as progressively worse. The prognosis is guarded. She is scheduled for a colostomy. The illness is not contagious, although Mrs. R. was unsure about this.

This patient experiences her illness as "quite severe," and "beyond control." The sensory quality of the illness is described as a "painful burning feeling all along her lower bowel," due to tremendous pressure in her rectum. In terms of a frame of reference, Mrs. R. compares the pain to the "laboring" experience of childbirth. The cues for her were the recurrent experience of diarrhea and lower bowel pain, which she had already learned to associate with illness.

Mrs. R., like Mrs. F., experiences her illness as endless, without shape or form. She will have to cope with the change in her usual eliminative pattern for the rest of her life, and this is what dominates her conscious thoughts.

The meaning of her illness is presently influenced by the anticipated surgical procedure. Mrs. R. expressed disgust with the entire idea of having a colostomy and stated, when she was told about the operation, "It hit me like a ton of bricks." She anticipates having a "complex" about the colostomy for a long time to come. Furthermore the illness means that she will be unable to give her young children the care they need. She expressed concern that they had been "deprived" and stated it was her fault. She also stated that her husband had become tired of her sickness and was fearful that he was "going to leave me now for sure." Actually the illness Mrs. R. is experiencing is contributing to her guilt feelings about her role as an inadequate mother and wife and to her altered body image.

The factors responsible for the way she perceives her illness may be attributed primarily to her young age and young marriage. It is difficult to assess her perception of her illness as the forthcoming surgery has taken precedence and colors everything else she sees and hears. The factors that might be contributing to her perception of the surgical procedure include not only her age and sex, but also ignorance about the procedure and its consequences, erroneous preconceived notions, past associations, cultural background, and so on.

Case Three

Mrs. D. is a 60-year-old Caucasian female with a diagnosis of chronic emphysema. The sign of her illness is shortness of breath. The onset was gradual, beginning with asthma and progressing to emphysema. The course has been uneventful with gradual deterioration. Emphysema is not uncommon nor communicable. It is a chronic condition with no known cure. The prognosis is guarded. The individual will be handicapped with this condition for the rest of her life.

Mrs. D. experiences the illness as extreme shortness of breath and pain in her chest muscles when she breathes. She compares the pain she now has with her past experience with pleuritic pain and suggests that the present pain is much worse because "she can't get her breath" and "is afraid she will die." Unless the nurse has herself experienced pleuritic pain or knows the character of such pain from conversations with other patients, the frame of reference used by her patient will have no meaning for her. Therefore she will want to ask the patient to compare the present pain with something that has meaning for both of them.

Recognition of her illness was not difficult since it was an extension and exaggeration of previous symptoms. The inability to catch her breath was sufficiently compelling and incapacitating so that no other cues were necessary to convince her of the illness.

As far as configuration is concerned, there again seems to be no form or shape since the patient sees no end in sight. The predominant meaning associated with her illness is the threat of death, especially during severe respiratory embarrassment. In between times the patient complains that her illness does not allow her to "do chores or live a social life." In addition to age and sex, the primary contributing factor to her perception of illness is the disturbance to her respiratory system. The act of breathing is associated with life itself. Interference with this act is experienced as a real threat to life.

Case Four

Mr. G. is a 39-year-old male Caucasian with a diagnosis of low back-injury with secondary irritation of both sciatic nerves—acute L-S disc syndrome. The only signs reported were a voluntary muscle guarding on the left lower back and x-rays indicating a displaced disc. The onset of the illness was sudden. To date the course has been without crises, and the outcome is expected to be full recovery with the possibility of recurrence. It is fairly common among men who engage in heavy lifting, and it is not contagious.

The patient first experienced the illness as lower back-pain following work involving a lot of bending over. A couple of days later he found he could not move his legs without an excruciating sharp pain. He compared the pain to the kind of pain one feels when a "dentist hits a nerve while drilling." He recognized these symptoms as "sciatica" since he had had these same symptoms eight years before, after slipping on an icy sidewalk.

The configuration of the illness is viewed as triphasic. The patient is presently experiencing the recovery or terminal phase. He expects to be discharged in a few days. The illness with its consequent hospitalization has been experienced as a time to relax and read. He is financially well-off and states he is not worried about the time spent away from his job. He is a Ph.D. candidate and seems to welcome this period of rest and relaxation. He is extremely well informed about his condition. All of these factors seem to contribute to his optimistic outlook and easy adjustment to his illness.

REFERENCES

ALLPORT, FLOYD H. *Theories of Perception and the Concept of Structure.* New York: John Wiley & Sons, Inc., 1955, pp. 17–20.

GELLERT, E. "Children's Conceptions of the Content and Function of the Human Body," *Genetic Psychological Monographs,* 65 (1962,) 293–311.

SIGERIST, HENRY E. "The Special Position of the Sick," in Milton I. Roemer and J. M. Mackintosh, eds., *On the Sociology of Medicine.* New York: M. D. Publications, 1960, pp. 9–22.

SMITH, DOROTHY W. AND CLAUDIA D. GIPS *Care of the Adult Patient.* Philadelphia: J. B. Lippincott Co., 1963, pp. 59–60.

four | The Perception of Treatment and Hospitalization

A discussion of the nature and perception of illness would not be complete without a discussion of the perception of treatment and hospitalization. These two events, when superimposed upon the experience of illness, may exert a more powerful influence on behavior than the illness itself. Treatment and hospitalization are viewed as stimuli or stressors that the individual may have to deal with in addition to the illness itself. Sometimes they become the figure, that is, the central focus of attention against the background of illness.

Treatment as defined in this text shall be anything performed upon, or by, the patient for purposes of diagnosis, cure, prevention of disease and its complications, and/or relief of its symptoms. Diagnosis embraces not only the initial identification process whereby the nature of the disease process or illness is determined but also the continuing assessments required for monitoring the progress or decline of the patient's condition throughout the course of his illness. Care-giving activities are not considered as treatments per se. Treatments are, however, carried out with care, providing support, reassurance, and comfort both mentally and physically whenever possible. Care permeates everything a nurse does.

OBJECTIVE FEATURES OF TREATMENT

What are the denotable or objective features about treatment? What is known about treatment that is reliable or measurable; that is, what features can be observed by different people and yet be described similarly by all of them? Mrs. Minna Field in her much used book, *Patients Are People,* described the plight of people undergoing treatments as follows:

> The patient is subjected to examinations and tests, the purpose of which he does not understand and the results of which are not explained. A nurse comes in and sticks him with a needle, another puts a thermometer in his mouth; a strange looking machine is wheeled to his bedside and connected with his arms and legs; he is put on a stretcher and wheeled through long corridors and passageways. Some of the tests to which he is subjected are unfamiliar, some are painful, many are frightening, but nobody tells him what they mean. And nobody tells him whether the results are favorable or unfavorable. The patient is afraid to ask questions because everyone seems so busy, so intent on what he is doing, or perhaps the patient is afraid to ask because he is afraid to know the answer. Whatever the reasons, the unasked questions remain unanswered, and uncertainty and fear prey on his mind. [Field, p. 64]

In analyzing the behavioral responses described above, we note that the patient is responding to three aspects of the examinations and tests: (1) the purpose, or objective, and the results of the tests, (2) the acts or actions (sticks, puts, connects, wheels, etc.), and (3) the equipment and the solutions (needle, thermometer, machine) necessary to carry out the treatment. Let us examine in greater detail each of these objective features of treatments.

Purpose and Results

There is enough knowledge about many of the tests and therapies performed upon the human body for the investigator to predict, other things being equal, what the outcome will be or what the treatment is expected to accomplish. For example, it is known that Mercuhydrin, because of its chemical composition, can be expected to induce diuresis resulting in a decrease in the amount of fluid retention in the body. The effect of this treatment may contribute to a larger goal such as the relief of congestion in the cardiorespiratory system. In other words, a treatment may have a specific purpose that contributes to the achievement of a larger, more global purpose.

For example, one objective in the care of the postanesthetized patient is to prevent the accumulation of fluid in the lungs and subsequent development of pathologic processes. To achieve this goal the doctor prescribes an expectorant and oral-pharyngeal suctioning. In addition, the patient's position is changed regularly from side to side until he has regained consciousness. When he has awakened, he is encouraged to cough and to participate in deep breathing exercises at regular intervals. The purpose of the expectorant is to help liquefy bronchial secretions so that mucus can be coughed up or suctioned out. Turning the patient from side to side minimizes the possibility of pooled secretions that could lead to the development of a pneumonic process. Deep breathing exercises encourage expansion of lung tissue and decrease the possibility of atelectasis. All of these activities contribute to the primary goal—prevention. Thus the purpose of a treatment may be achieved singularly or in concert with other treatments.

Sometimes predictions about the outcome of certain therapies are not borne out. Individual differences and specific immunological response systems may inhibit certain biochemical reactions in the body, resulting in an unpredictable effect. For example, one individual may react more strongly or with more vigor than another individual being subjected to the same treatment. Current biochemical assays of body fluids are now providing medicine with greater predictive power to control the outcome.

Inherent in many treatments is an element of risk. There is much that is still unknown about the human body and mind, and extrapolations drawn from experiments on animals can involve a risk. In many ways human beings and animals do not respond in like manner, although similarities are known to exist.

Medical progress depends upon an adventurous and explorative approach to unearth the secrets and mysteries of the body. As knowledge about the human body and about the relationship between the physiology of an organism to its environment is gained, risks of incurring further damage, unpredictable side effects, and untoward reactions will be correspondingly reduced. A case in point is the recent reported research in the area of "biological or circadian rhythms." Who would have suspected a few years ago that a treatment given at one time in a monthly cycle, could be quite ineffective and even deadly when given at another time in the cycle? Stephens (1965) suggests that certain treatments may be effective during one aspect of a cycle, e.g., the menstrual cycle, and be less effective or totally ineffective if given at some other time within this cycle. The temperature and adrenal hormone rhythms are known to affect the body's schedule of wakefulness and activity. She suggests that perhaps there is a best, safest time for x-ray and surgical procedures, that a sampling of rhythms may determine the time for optimal therapeutic and minimal toxic effects. As research continues, other variables will be identified as significantly influencing the outcome of tests and treatments and may provide a clue for the previously mentioned unexplained and unpredicted results.

When the treatment successfully achieves the goal for which it is intended, it is assessed as functional. When it fails to achieve the goal intended, the treatment is assessed as nonfunctional. In the latter situation the disease process continues unabated owing to individual idiosyncrasies inhibiting a favorable response, or it may result in complications due to overtreatment.

Following are five general purposes of treatments as defined herein:

1. *To diagnose or measure the progress or decline of the illness.* Vital signs, electrocardiograph recordings, x-rays, and laboratory tests of all sorts are prescribed to determine the nature of the illness and the effect of treatment upon the disease process. For most tests a normal standard or range is known from which to compare the individual's test results. The therapeutic plan is based upon these findings and is modified as changes are observed and recorded. In addition, tests are performed to measure the rate of growth and development, as in well-baby clinics or in the progress of pregnancy and labor. These are normal physiological processes, and the tests are performed to insure that things are progressing normally. The purpose may also be prophylactic, which is another objective of treatments and tests. Whether or not an individual is informed about the purpose or results of his test(s) is at present the physician's prerogative. This decision is based in part on the prognosis and tolerance of the individual for stress.

2. *To support and to facilitate the body's defenses of resistance and repair; to establish and maintain normal physiologic and mental processes.* When illness is viewed as a process (i.e., a

fight against disease or a fight to restore health, both mental and physical) medical-nursing interventions such as treatments are prescribed to assist the body in this battle between aggressor and defender. The purpose of antibiotics, intravenous fluids and electrolytes, blood transfusions, cardiotonics, central nervous system stimulants, hot and cold applications, and oxygen therapy is to assist the body's defense reactions and to facilitate a return of normal physiologic processes. Traction, splints, and casts are also devices to assist the body in its repair process. The goal of psychotherapy is to make the patient better able to cope with future problems and to deal with future stress.

3. *To replace or substitute a structure or function lost by the body owing to congenital absence, disease, or trauma.* This includes the use of prosthetic devices, hormonal replacements, and supplements such as insulin and pituitrin, dialysis, organ transplants, valve insertions, and pacemakers.

4. *To suppress or remove the manifestations of disease and its byproducts; to inhibit overactive defenses.* Abnormal structures that cause a disturbance in normal body function must be removed or their growth suppressed if the individual is to survive. In addition, abnormal secretions such as excess gastric acidity or excess hormonal secretions must be suppressed. Bladder irrigations and wound debridements are frequently prescribed to assist the body in the removal of necrotic tissues and abnormal secretions so that the healing process can proceed more quickly. The prevention of lung pathology in the care of the postanesthetized patient was discussed earlier. Other treatments are performed to prevent the development of complications, such as contractures, and decubiti. Suppression by the use of various medications, and removal by surgical manipulation or other mechanical devices such as suctioning machines, contribute to the achievement of this goal. Other techniques include the use of certain anticancer drugs, which are administered to suppress the production of white blood cells; and with the increased practice of organ transplants, drugs must be invented to suppress the body's natural defenses, which reject implanted foreign objects and tissues.

5. *To protect the body from unnecessary stressors.* Many treatments are prescribed that are of a prophylactic-protective nature, e.g., injections to immunize against diphtheria, pertussis, tetanus, smallpox, measles, poliomyelitis, and typhoid fever. The injection of attentuated bacteria and viruses is to strengthen

the body's immunological defenses. The injection of the anti-bodies themselves is to supplement the body in its defense against the pathogenic organism. Associated with the perform-ance of any treatment is the possibility of introducing stressors. The individual with poor aseptic technique could conceivably introduce organisms into the bladder during an irrigation pro-cedure, resulting in a genitourinary infection. Thus, there exists the need to be scrupulous in carrying out proper tech-nique with all treatments. The goal of the treatment could be thwarted through negligence and inattentivenes to the details of the procedure.

SUMMARY. Thus a treatment may be administered for diagnostic, curative, replacement, suppressive, or preventive purposes. Individ-uals will respond according to their assessment of the treatment, in the light of *its* purpose and *their* goals. Some individuals may dem-onstrate little or no concern about the tests they must undergo, ex-pressing the hope only that "they will hurry up and find out what's wrong so they can treat me and get me well." Other more informed patients may express interest in the results of specific tests: e.g., a patient with a cardiovascular problem may express interest in the test that measures prothrombin time; a patient with a chronic infec-tion may inquire about the blood test measuring the sedimentation rate; or a person seeking confirmation or denial of cancer may be more anxious about the biopsy results than either the sedimentation rate or prothrombin. Each test carries with it certain meaning for the individual experiencing it. An increase in body temperature, blood pressure, or pulse rate may serve to alarm some and be ig-nored by others, depending upon a host of factors including past experience and present evaluation of their health/illness state.

The range of responses to the results of diagnostic tests and measurements varies from little or no concern, to shock and a feeling of incredibility, to a sense of relief. According to Janis (1958) if the individual has been prepared for the expected consequences, es-pecially for negative unfavorable consequences, remote though they may be, his chances of behaving in a disorganized, shocked, dazed, and incredulous way upon hearing the "bad" news will be greatly decreased. The tendency for most people is to deny the possibility of having to undergo treatment, especially if it carries with it the threat of pain, suffering, and even annihilation. Janis states it is much better to help the person think about the possibilities of what might happen, so he can build up certain behavioral devices that take into account the potential danger. This new set of reassurances, taking into account the possibility of the feared or unwanted object or event, is much more effective in helping him cope when the dreaded diagnosis or results of the test are given.

When the perceived efficacy of the treatment is congruent with the patient's goals, other things being equal, behavior will be supportive and cooperative. When the perception is incongruent with goal achievement, behavior elicited may be negative and uncooperative.

Acts or Actions

For every treatment there are acts carried out by the patient himself or by another person assigned to perform the treatment. In other words, the patient is either actively involved in the act or someone is acting for him. The basic purpose is generally the same, regardless of who carries out the act. The acts may include poking, probing, listening, rubbing, immersing, looking, feeling, and so on. There are acts of taking in, involving input, and acts of taking out, involving output. There are also acts that involve a rearrangement of parts, without adding or subtracting anything to the existing system of inputs and outputs. Thus any single treatment may include acts of input, output, and/or rearrangement by manipulation.

INPUT. When a deficit is present in structure or function, such as an absent part or deficient glandular production, input is prescribed to correct the deficit and restore the balance. For example, blood may be injected to correct a deficit in plasma volume or cell count, or a heart valve may be inserted to correct a defective valve and restore a balance in the cardiopulmonary exchange. Acts of input include inhalation, intubation, ingestion, instillation, insertion, and injection.

Sometimes an injection of a solution is made in the absence of a corresponding deficit. This is most clearly demonstrated in procedures performed to rule out the presence of an aberration. Usually these solutions are absorbed quite quickly into the bloodstream and are thereby eliminated, and thus they do not appreciably upset the balance. If the individual responds to the acts at all, it will be in terms of the input, since the fact that eventually the injected material is eliminated (or removed) is generally of no consequence.

OUTPUT. When there is an excess in body structure or function, such as overproduction of cells or overstimulation of secretions, acts are taken to remove the excess or to suppress the excessive production so that a balance is restored. For example, excess tissue can be removed by cauterization, radiation, or excision. Excess fluids can be removed by gravitation through the insertion of a drainage tube, or mechanically through the use of suctioning devices. Removal can also be achieved indirectly through the administration of drugs that induce diuresis, catharsis, or emesis, or by inhibiting or depressing the frequency of stimulatory impulses.

Sometimes removal is performed in the absence of excess structure (tissue) or body secretions. In such situations an imbalance results until the body is able to compensate for the loss or until a substitute is introduced to replace the lost part. For example, the removal of a benign tumor caused by abnormal proliferation of body tissue represents the restoration of a balance in the human system, whereas a leg amputation or eye enucleation results in a temporary imbalance. Although both acts involve removal of body tissue, one results in a return to a balanced state and the other leads to an imbalanced state until some device is added to take over the function of the lost part.

One might add to this group, occasions when acts of input and output are carried out sequentially. Thus, the net balance is not appreciably disturbed by the acts themselves. For example, the quantity of fluid removed may be equalled by the quantity injected, so that the net balance at completion of the treatment is essentially the same as at the start of treatment, as in bladder, gastric, colonic, and wound irrigations, or dialysis treatments or gastric washes. Other internal and external factors could create an imbalance, independent of, although partially attributable to, the treatment.

REARRANGEMENT. Some acts involve a rearrangement of parts, without adding or subtracting anything to the existing net balance. The rearrangement may involve a redistribution of energy, although no additions or subtractions are made to the usual exchange of inputs or outputs. Passive and active exercises and eye exercises are examples of acts that rearrange parts or alter function without adding or subtracting to the overall structure of the organism.

Treatment also involves the manipulation of behavior to effect a change. New behaviors are learned and are incorporated to replace less efficient ones. Old, outdated, and no longer useful forms of behavior represent a deficit or lack in the behavioral repertory, and therefore newly internalized behavior can serve to fill a void and correct an imbalance. For example, certain behaviors can be changed or shaped through operant conditioning. If the nurse knows that a certain stimulus, e.g., praise, evokes certain behaviors, she can present or withdraw the stimulus, depending on whether she wishes to reinforce or extinguish the behavior(s). Reinforcement is contingent upon the organism emitting the correct response.

The normal physiologic processes of elimination and other defense reactions such as vomiting and coughing are not viewed as treatment unless they require outside assistance. Forceful evacuation induced by the body's internal mechanisms is not a treatment. Childbirth is a normal physiologic process. The birth process may be assisted by treatments such as the injection of Pitocin to increase uterine contractility and application of forceps to facilitate delivery of the infant, but the birth process itself is not a treatment.

Up to now we have talked about input, output, and manipulations in terms of an individual's body or mind. Perhaps acts should be extended to include the control of input and output in the patient's environment. For example, the nurse may prescribe the introduction of certain stimuli into a patient's environment to resolve a problem of sensory deprivation previously diagnosed by her. Equilibrium of the person and of the system of which he is a part is dependent upon the balance of input and output. Too much input relative to output or too much output relative to input results in an imbalance unless manipulations within the system cause the parts to compensate for the overload or deprivation experienced.

The acts involved in any treatment are multiple. The quest is for a classificatory scheme of acts that provides a basis for the prediction of behavior. The question is whether patients respond to the different acts involved in a treatment per se, or whether they respond to the acts only in terms of the purpose or consequences of the treatment. Does the removal of a "thing" from the person's body represent something quite different symbolically from the intake of something, independent of its expected consequences? It is a curious fact that most individuals, if given a choice, will prefer to have a decayed tooth repaired than to have it pulled and removed. Acts have meaning independent of the whole of which they are a part. For example, the purpose of a treatment may be to protect the person against a known illness, but the acts involved in meeting the goal of the treatment may carry separate meaning, e.g., the threat of pain. The person's behavior will differ depending upon the meaning he associates with the acts. Some acts are inconsequential and carry little or no meaning by themselves. In such cases the patient is probably responding more to the purpose or results of the treatment.

Tentatively acts have been classified into four categories according to meaning. This assumes that it is possible to gain observer-agreement on the meaning of different acts that comprise a treatment. In other words, we know that certain acts carry specific meaning, and therefore we can predict with some degree of certainty the behaviors that will follow. These acts may be classified as follows:

1. Acts that involve intrusion or forceful entry into body orifices, such as intubations and injections.
2. Acts that involve an "invasion of privacy," such as vaginal and rectal examinations.
3. Acts that elicit a threat of pain, suffering, or annihilation, e.g., needle injections, surgical procedures, etc. This includes acts that threaten to destroy, distort, or alter the body image or the person's concept of himself, such as disfiguring surgery.
4. Inconsequential acts that carry little or no threat, such as taking routine vital signs.

Any treatment may include acts belonging to one or more of the above classes. The acts will carry meaning derived from past experiences, associations, understandings, and cognitions.

Carmenali (1966) identified six common concerns of patients about to experience an operation. These included pain and discomfort; not knowing what to expect and the fear of not being told the truth; disturbances over changes in body; cuts, incisions, and removals representing a threat to one's body image; fear of death; disruption of life plans, recreational as well as occupational; and fear of losing control under anesthesia. The meaning of surgery was related not only to the acts but also to the specific part(s) of the body involved. For example, it is more socially acceptable to have an appendectomy than a hemorrhoidectomy. For the former person the operation may mean something to talk about, whereas for the latter the operation may represent embarrassment. Individuals respond not only to the purpose of the acts but also to the equipment and personnel required to carry out the act.

Equipment, Materials, and Solutions

Equipment, materials, and solutions become the tangible, concrete evidence of treatment. The presence of a syringe and needle, oxygen tent, cardioscope, bottle of intravenous solutions, and so on confirms the patient's belief that he is receiving or is about to receive a treatment. According to Anna Freud (1952), the array of medical paraphernalia introduced into the patient's environment (not necessarily pointed or pain-producing) may arouse feelings of apprehension; and for young children such an array may even imply threats of mutilation and castration.

Perhaps the most useful approach to the classification of equipment for our purpose is to group it into two large classes: common or familiar, and uncommon or unfamiliar. It is again assumed that for a given culture it is possible to gain observer-agreement on the equipment that can be classed as common or familiar objects in any hospital setting vis-à-vis uncommon, unfamiliar or rare pieces of equipment. Individuals will respond according to their past experiences or associations with the objects. The individual may pick up certain cues that recall "danger," or the cues may recall for him no suffering and pain. Equipment that is strange and unfamiliar tends to evoke feelings of apprehension. People do not like to be left with the unknown. They begin to imagine all kinds of things because of their need to rid themselves of the unknown. An individual will grasp for any cues, words, or expressions to support or cancel out his self-conceived ideas about the event. Placing unfamiliar, strange equipment in a patient's environment without explanation is adding unnecessary stress to an already precarious situation.

SUMMARY. Most persons would agree, thus, that treatments as defined herein are made up of three denotable or observable parts: purpose, acts, and equipment. The individual may respond to one, two, or all three parts. Understanding the purpose of the treatment may be an important determinant of the individual's response to the acts that are introduced and to the equipment that is brought into his environment. According to Field (1958), when the purpose of the examinations and tests are not understood and when the results are not explained and the patient is afraid to ask questions, whatever the reasons, "uncertainty and fear prey on his mind." Given this kind of a situation it is possible to predict with some degree of certainty the kinds of behaviors that will follow.

THE SUBJECTIVE ASPECTS OF TREATMENT

Having examined the denotable aspects of treatment, let us now examine the phenomenalistic aspects, *how* treatments appear to the person experiencing them. Like the phenomenon of illness, treatment too is perceived in characteristic ways.

Treatment is experienced as sensory quality. Things and events are experienced through the five senses: touch (pressure), taste, smell, vision, and sound. For example, the insertion of a nasogastric tube may be experienced as feeling hard or rigid (pressure), cold (if the tube has been pre-iced), and painful (if forced against tissue containing pain receptors). There may also be the odor and taste of rubber and the sight of the tube. A needle injection into the gluteal muscle may be seen and felt as painful owing to pressure exerted by the fluid against nerve endings.

Patients describe the sensory quality of an experience in dimensional terms, based on some subjectively established frame of reference, real or perceived. For example, one patient described the feeling of the dye injected intravenously for a cardiac catheterization as "like a bed of hot coals." She further stated that the catheter insertion was not painful, but she felt pressure "like a tooth being pulled." Another patient stated that the tube insertion was the most uncomfortable part of the gastric wash. He described the sensation as "like having a piece of food lodged in the throat which he could get neither up nor down." The patient compares the sensation he experiences with anything that he recalls produced or is capable of producing similar sensations.

In preparing a patient for a treatment sometimes it is instructive to help him establish a frame of reference for the event he is about to experience. For example, he will want to know how painful, how long, or how cold it will be. It is helpful to prepare the patient for the kind of pain he can expect. A case in point is a 13-year-old boy who visited a specialist with the complaint of postnasal drip and nasal congestion. During the office visit he was prepared "physically" for a nasal cauterization; i.e., cotton saturated with some local anesthetic was inserted into the nostril. He was, however, given no "psychological" preparation such as information as to what was being done and what he might expect to experience. He described the cauterization, which was sudden and unexpected, as very painful and said that it "felt like my head was on fire." Following the treatment, he repeatedly stated that "if the doctor had only told me it would feel hot and be painful, it would not have hurt so badly." I am certain that unnecessary stress was placed on this child because of not being prepared for the pain he would be experiencing.

Unless the frame of reference provided by the nurse has meaning for the individual, it will not serve its purpose. In an attempt to give young children a frame of reference from which to judge the expected intensity of a needle injection, the nurse is often heard to say, "It's just like a bee sting." The question is, How many children have ever experienced a bee sting before, or how many children are able to conceptualize how a bee sting might feel? Unless the individual has experienced a bee sting or "knows" what a bee sting is like, it serves as no useful frame of reference for judging the expected intensity of a needle injection.

Anna Freud (1952) has suggested that children two to three years of age react with almost identical distress to the experience of injections and to one of sunlight treatments, although the former involves pain (plus anxiety) and the latter is merely anxiety-raising without any pain involved. How can we account for this almost identical response to two essentially different kinds of treatments? One explanation is based upon the constancy factor. Words, actions, persons, equipment, and so on may act as cues so that the object or event is recognizable even under changed conditions. Since children have vivid recollections of sensations, one small cue may readily recall a painful sensation. Small children recall, not ideas or words, but sensations. It is possible that the few cues that they respond to recall for them a painful experience and consequently elicit a similar response. Perhaps the person administering the treatment is viewed as similar to someone else in appearance, and so the patient generalizes the feelings he had toward that individual and applies these feelings to the present operator, even though the treatments differ. For example, both persons might have been wearing white uniforms, and thus the identical response. Maybe it is the approach, the expression, or the tone of voice that recalls the past painful situation, and thus the patient responds in similar fashion. We can only speculate as to the reasons for the similarity in responses, but individuals do bring their past experiences to bear in their interpretation of present experiences.

The constancy factor is an important aspect of perception because it provides structure and removes some of the unknown. Sometimes the cues picked up are helpful in interpreting the event, and other times they only serve to distort the event. A case in point is the five-year-old girl who was to have her temperature taken rectally. Her behavior was inappropriate and out of proportion to the degree of threat or pain associated with such a procedure. She screamed and continually cried, "No shot!" It was hypothesized that the thermometer represented a needle and syringe and the position she was asked to assume was similar to that assumed when given an injection. No amount of explanation or manipulation of equipment seemed to change her erroneous perception. In this situation there were cues that recalled for her the injection experience, and as long as she interpreted the cues in this way, her behavior remained unchanged. In contrast, 23-year-old Mrs. C. stated that the breast biopsy she was about to undergo reminded her of "the removal of a mole she had had excised about a year ago." Recognizing similarities between the two incidents was helpful to this patient in removing much of the unknown with the present experience.

All treatments have a form or outline that is described as triphasic; this includes the prelude, the act, and the postlude. In surgical jargon this becomes: the preoperative phase, the operation, and the postoperative phase. The content of each phase may differ, but the relationship between each phase is the same. In other words, the acts and equipment involved in each phase may differ, but the temporal relationship between phases remains the same. The individual may react more strongly or more violently to one phase than to another. For some, the postlude, which includes news of the outcome or the results, is the most important aspect of the treatment; whereas for others, the act itself, especially if it involves humiliating, uncomfortable, and painful procedures, is the most important; and for still others, the prelude with its associated apprehension is the worst.

Kassowitz (1958) in his investigation of children's attitudes and responses to the use of hypodermic needles observed that during the first six months of life the prelude was absent, and that the act and postlude involved a moderate emotional response; whereas for children six months to and including the fourth year, all phases involved an intense reaction. The children appeared to respond to the entire configuration rather than to individual phases.

Janis (1958) conducted a large research project on the effect of preparatory communication during the prelude (preoperative phase) upon the behavior of individuals during the postlude or postoperative phase. He stated that making correct predictions of what one can expect during the prelude, when confirmed, helps the individual gain confidence and trust in those who care for him in the postlude. When realistic information is given in the prelude before the operation, the individual is better able to relax during the act and the postlude, knowing that events are not proceeding in a random, whimsical, or unforeseen fashion. Treatments extending over time, like surgical operations, seem to be experienced in phases, whereas short, brief treatments tend to be experienced as one unit. The individual responds to the entire configuration rather than to each phase.

As stated earlier, the meaning given to the percept, whether it involves illness or treatment, is an important determinant of behavior. Meaning may derive from the whole treatment or from one or more of its parts that are independent of the whole meaning, such as the acts, and/or equipment. The three-to-seven-year old is said to associate certain medical-surgical procedures with fear of mutilation, castration, alteration of body functioning, and disfigurement. When seven-year-old Allen entered the examination room, he immediately screamed that he didn't want a "shot." He had been forewarned by his mother that this might happen. To allay some of the fear and anxiety built up by the anticipation of the feared event, the doctor gave the child a disassembled syringe and needle to manipulate. The child cautiously took hold of the needle and syringe and began to pull in and out on the plunger. Some of the fear began to dissipate as he became familiar with the equipment. In addition, the doctor promised some candy if the child would let him give the injection. The treatment now took on different meaning; it now represented reward for good behavior, and the child quickly agreed to the treatment and was rewarded as promised. As soon as the treatment took on different meaning, the child's behavior changed.

The meaning of a treatment, as a whole, is usually given in terms of the expected consequences. Treatments are perceived by many persons as routes to important life conditions, as leading to the remission of symptoms and a return to a state of good health. Mr. B., a 58-year-old male patient, was scheduled for a renal biopsy. He had a fatal collagen disease and was advised by his physician of the importance of the operation. When asked if he understood the purpose of the treatment, he replied, "The purpose is for my life; if it doesn't work, I won't be around." Following the treatment he stated, "It didn't bother me at all. There was no pain, but even if there had been, it wouldn't have bothered me. I'm willing to undergo any treatment that might help me get well. My life's too important." The meaning he placed upon this treatment was an important determinant in his perception of the event. He cooperated with the physician and followed instructions exactly and without hesitation. Another patient viewed her treatments as an attempt "to help her, and so she tried to cooperate by not complaining during the treatment."

Can the nurse predict behaviors based on the denotable and phenomenalistic features of treatments? A perusal of the literature reveals little or no research on the identification or recognition of any particular class of behavior that is associated with any given treatment. Janis (1958) has probably carried out one of the most comprehensive pieces of research on patient reactions to surgery, but we have little or no material on the reactions of patients to other treatments.

Familiarity with the procedure is an important determinant of behavior. For example, the general reactions to nasogastric insertion vary considerably from the first insertion to the third or fourth insertion, especially when these procedures follow each other closely in time. By the third or fourth time the tube-insertion act is no longer experienced as "intrusive," since the patient has "caught onto" the knack of swallowing a tube and participates willingly in its insertion. The act of insertion in this case becomes inconsequential, and the purpose of the treatment now takes precedence in meaning. If the act is intrusive, does this elicit a certain class of behaviors different from nonintrusive acts? How is knowing that an act is intrusive or painful helpful to the nurse? Could she apply this information toward the improvement of patient care? These are questions that have no answers today. Hopefully they will have answers tomorrow.

SUMMARY.   In summary, then, there are both denotable and phenomenalistic features to every treatment. (See Figure 2.) The denotable features that become part of the spatial configuration include the purposes, acts, and equipment. The purposes of treatments have been identified through systematic observation, recordings, and experimentation, both in animals and in humans. The acts and equipment are observable and can be encountered physically. Individuals experience treatment, like all other percepts, via the five senses. They judge the dimensions of treatment by a subjective frame of reference and by perceptual constancy. Treatments also have a temporal configuration that is triphasic: the prelude, the act, and postlude. Individuals give meaning either to the contents of each phase or to the total configuration. In other words, they may respond in terms of the meaning associated with the purpose, the acts, or the equipment; or they may respond to the meaning assigned to the whole treatment, to the whole configuration. Behavior is consistent with the meaning that is perceived.

PERCEPTION OF HOSPITALIZATION

Hospitalization shall be defined as confinement of a person to an institution with separation from one's immediate family for a protracted period of time for the purposes of diagnosis, care, and/or cure. Under the rubric of hospitals we shall consider both privately and publicly supported hospitals, mental institutions, homes for the aged and the unwed mother, convalescent homes, and sanitariums.

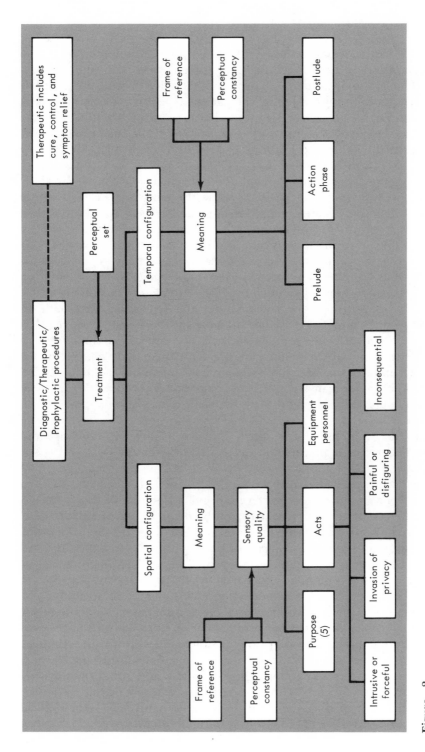

Figure 2
Experience of Treatment

63

When the experience of illness is moved from the home into the hospital, illness takes on new dimensions. Both the physical and social environments change dramatically. From the familiar secure surroundings of home, the patient is thrust into a strange and unfamiliar world where strangers begin to rule his life. Dr. Leo Simons describes perceptively the contrasts in "the culture of illness" between the home and hospital (quoted by E. L. Brown, 1961):

> In the hospital, the patient rings the bell and waits prayerfully for nurse or doctor, while at home the nurse and doctor ring the bell and wait patiently on the threshold. In the hospital the patient is "admitted" and "discharged" and all the relatives are visitors, while at home the physician is "on call" and can be "changed" and even the nurse is a visitor. "Orders" are written in the hospital, while "prescriptions" are expected in the home. In the hospital, patients are "pushed" around from place to place with not much time for explanations, but at home they are "led" about with both explanations and persuasions. In the hospital a nurse is "assigned" to the patient, while at home she may be "hired" and "fired." In the home, nurses come and go while the patient stays on, but in the hospital it is just the reverse, with the nurse holding tenure. Perhaps for many people there are few moves in life which are more ominous than the move from the home to the hospital. [Pp. 123–24]

Thus, Dr. Simons depicts the hospital as strange, foreboding, and disquieting for many, to say the least. Both the physical and social characteristics of hospitals tend to elicit a considerable amount of dread and apprehension on the part of the patient.

Today most of the mystery behind hospital walls has been removed via direct visits or vicariously through the media of television and movies. People now are familiar with the long corridors and large open wards, replaced in many hospitals by four-, six-, and eight-bed rooms and by a series of private and semiprivate rooms. Stripped "aseptic" rooms and barren walls have been replaced with pastel-colored walls, harmonizing draperies and bedspreads, television sets, and private baths, and there are solariums or lounges for both patients and guests to enjoy. Scattered throughout the hospital in different rooms and corridors are pieces of furniture and equipment, such as "guernys" (stretchers), side rails, wheelchairs, oxygen tanks, respirators, suction machines, bottles and tubes, monitoring machines, special beds (Circo-electric and Stryker or Foster Frames), plus an array of diagnostic and orthopedic equipment that may or may not be familiar to the newly admitted patient.

The preceding discussion concerns the physical features of hospitals, but what about the social characteristics of hospitals? The social structure of hospitals is usually described as authoritarian and bureaucratic. More time is spent by hospital personnel keeping an elaborate system in operation than doing something directly with or for their patients. The physician usually occupies the top position of a fairly rigid hierarchical system. Within the physician group there is a hierarchy based upon rank: consultant, visiting staff, chief resident, assistant resident, internes, and medical students. In addition to this there is a hierarchical system within the nursing group: director, supervisor, head nurse, team leader, staff nurse, aides, and nursing students. Nurses generally occupy an intermediate position, with aides near the bottom, of this large hierarchy. Policies related to patient care are decided by persons furthest removed from the patient; such decisions are usually made on a hospital-wide basis with little regard for the individualized needs of patients. Uniformity is looked upon as desirable; it makes for smoother and more efficient operation.

It is a fact that today's hospitals are crowded with professionally and technically prepared people; yet, paradoxically, patients still complain of feeling lonely. In spite of many changes we hear complaints of hospitals being cold and impersonal. Where once the nurse and doctor comprised the hospital staff, now there is a team that in the course of a 24-hour period may change its membership several times. The patient's care is often subdivided among aides, practical nurses, nursing students, and team leader, all of whom are in turn overseen by the head nurse and the supervisor if the patient is sick enough to be labeled critical. With his care thus compartmentalized the patient has little or no opportunity to identify with any single person in the hospital. In the midst of many he feels lonely and isolated.

The same loss of identity is seen in the patient's medical care. Visited by various ranks within the physician group, he may begin to wonder just who his doctor is. In addition to the medical and nursing personnel, he may be visited by dietitian, social worker, physical and occupational therapist, inhalation therapist, laboratory technician, and a host of others. The number of hospital personnel entering a patient's room within a 24-hour period is unbelievable. There is constant intrusion, without knocking, by a variety of people the patient has probably never met.

Take the following case as an example. In a large university-affiliated hospital, ten-year-old Kay was suddenly surrounded by 25 medical students whom she thought were doctors. She had been admitted for a cardiac catheterization and "had been looking forward to her stay at the hospital for months now. . . ." Following the two-hour examination (in the presence of the 25 students), hospitalization took on an ominous overtone as she interpreted their presence to mean that her condition had worsened. She no longer cared if she got better. She just wanted to go home. Perhaps if the doctors had talked to her rather than about her, the trauma incurred might have been less. Certainly the large number of "doctors" gathered about her bedside without explanation and the incomprehensible discussion that ensued contributed markedly to her changed attitude.

Associated with the large array of hospital personnel is a loss of privacy that many people have come to expect, especially in the nation's large teaching institutions. For example, 30-year-old Mrs. S. said she brought a thick robe because of anticipating that there would be "many people milling about" in a teaching institution. She inquired about the surgical domes, expressing a desire to be unconscious during surgery so that if she was observed by students, she would not be embarrassed. She stated that she did not mind being watched, but that she did not want to be awake and hear any of the comments made. Furthermore, she said that since this was elective surgery (removal of a pilonidal cyst), she had chosen the spring as the best time, anticipating that there would be fewer people in the hospital, students as well as patients. One is led to suspect that the large number and variety of people that the patient encounters each day during his hospital stay might very well augment and intensify an already precarious condition.

Associated with the hospital bureaucracy are the rigid schedules and unvarying routines. Visiting hours are set, and mealtime, bedtime, and when to awaken are uniformly scheduled for all patients. The patient and his family are robbed of all responsibility for making decisions. Whether he will be permitted privacy or not, or permitted visitors should he desire it, is determined by the medical and nursing staff, hospital rules and customs, availability of beds, and whether or not the patient is a V.I.P. (very important person). Furthermore, parents are expected to relinquish their normal parental responsibilities in the course of admitting their child to a hospital.

The admission procedure itself can have a profound effect upon the patient's perception of whether he will be welcomed as a human being or as the bearer of a disease to be treated. Patients entertain doubts as to the interest of hospital personnel in their welfare. Will they be accepted by the personnel? The admission procedure is notoriously known for its efforts to strip the person of all individuality.

Anonymity is fostered as the patient is converted into a room number, bed number, a diagnosis, and tagged with a bracelet with his name and hospital number. Adding to the feeling of "non-being" is the assembly-line technique in which patients are moved like robots from one department to another for diagnostic and therapeutic procedures. The assembly line not only moves slowly but encounters frequent bottlenecks in which there may be a complete breakdown, and so the waiting becomes tedious and tiresome.

Patients feel lost and are unsure of hospital routines. Not only must they learn to adjust to a single ward but in today's hospitals it is not uncommon to have to adjust to several areas; e.g., from a medical floor the patient may go to surgery, and then into a recovery room for a period of time, and then to an intensive care unit for another period of time, and finally to the surgical ward before discharge. This frequent movement and change of environments can become an added stress for many patients.

Like illness and treatment, the physical and social environments of hospitals are experienced subjectively. The sights, sounds, and odors experienced by all who enter into hospitals are experienced in varying degrees of intensity, extensity, and duration. Hospitalization comprises the peculiar sounds of hoppers, autoclaves, suction machines, oxygen machines, public-address systems calling unfamiliar names and words, the clanging of bedpans, the laughter and talk of hospital personnel, the crying and moaning of fellow patients, the regular click of the monitoring machine, and the hurried shuffling of shoes. It includes the smell of antiseptics, of anesthesia, and of body excreta. It embraces the sight of sick people, injured people, disabled people, dying people, people in pain, patients' bodies exposed as bed clothes are changed or examinations are conducted, and the sight of people in different colored uniforms and unfamiliar equipment. All of these sensations are associated with being in hospitals.

As always sensations associated with any percept are usually judged against some frame of reference for their intensity, extensity, and duration. One patient may complain bitterly about the noise in the hospital, while his roommate may state, "It's nothing compared to the noise in that other hospital." As patients get to know each other and share their experiences they tend to shift their entire frame of reference for judging the loudness, brightness, and so on in terms of whether the particular feature is greater or less than "normal."

If the individual has experienced hospitalization before, he will come to expect certain kinds of people, things, and events to occur and to help make the environment less strange and more predictable. If he has never experienced hospitalization before, he may draw upon what he has learned from previous visits to a sick friend or relative, or through conversations, readings, television shows, and movies. Some of the strangeness of hospitals is mitigated by bringing things from home, symbols of one's values and individuality. For example, 52-year-old Mrs. K. brought her fancy nightgowns and wigs to the hospital so as not to lose her identity as a wealthy, private patient. Although she was acutely ill with leukemia, she asked to have her bed made and hair done before her husband and friends came, because this was expected of persons occupying her status in society. A middle-aged woman admitted for minor surgery brought her own soft, flowered bedspread and pillow and teapot for use at the bedside. She displayed family pictures on the bureau and a vase of flowers on an extra table in the room. She had brought along a radio, books, and cosmetics. She was intent on making her three-to-four-day hospital visit as comfortable and enjoyable as possible.

It is important that hospitals allow patients to retain their self-identities, by giving individualized care and taking into consideration likes and dislikes and the little things that really count in the world of the sick. Bringing personal possessions from home and familiarizing patients with hospital routines can help to provide some structure to an otherwise strange and unfamiliar situation.

Hospitalization, like treatment, can be described as triphasic in form. There is the preparatory phase in which the individual is told of the need for hospitalization, and this continues through hospital admission and orientation to the ward, staff, and hospital policies. The second phase, the period of treatment and/or confinement, follows wherein the individual settles down to the job of getting well; and finally, there is the discharge phase. This is the phase in which the patient prepares to leave the hospital and to return home. The length and content of each phase—i.e., what and how each phase is experienced—will vary from individual to individual. The temporal relationship between each phase, i.e., their sequence, always remains the same.

As with other percepts, the experience of hospitalization may be inconsequential compared to some other more compelling and urgent percept. For example, nursing students interviewing newly admitted adult patients about their expectations of the hospital found that inevitably conversation turned to a discussion of the impending surgery or diagnostic procedure. At the time of admission the experience of hospitalization was not nearly as threatening as the anticipated treatment, which took on compelling features to dominate the perceptual field.

Hospitalization for most people means separation from one's loved ones, that is, those whom the patients depend upon for care and for meeting their needs. Many patients express the concern that their families cannot get along without them. The experience of illness and the treatments in and of themselves do not carry this meaning. In fact, whenever possible, persons experiencing illness are cared for in the home to eliminate the added stress of hospitalization.

To the child, going to the hospital may mean abandonment and rejection by his family. Anxiety over separation is most intense between the ages of two and four. At this age there is a need for tangible evidence of home and family. In the mind of the preschooler, parents have achieved a degree of permanence. He is beginning to associate certain acts as necessary to retain his parents' approval and love. Therefore, a child hospitalized during this period is particularly vulnerable to a distorted interpretation of the meaning and purpose of his hospitalization. He may think of it as punishment for forbidden acts or as a loss of love. Many times parents make statements that lead a child to believe that his illness or hospitalization was caused by misdeeds, by disobedience of parental command; for example, "You will get sick because you are a bad boy."

Bowlby (1960) and Robertson (1958) have written several articles concerning the anxiety aroused in young children two to four years of age when separated from their parents. They suggest that in the process of adapting to the perceived loss the child goes through three stages. The initial stage of protest, characterized by much screaming and crying, is followed by a stage of despair in which the child withdraws, appearing to be dejected and miserable. The child then enters the final stage of denial or detachment in which he appears on the surface to have adjusted to the separation. He greets his parents and seems to enjoy their visits, but he maintains a cool, detached distance. He refuses to be fondled and hugged by them.

Robertson suggests that the quiet, calm period observed in the final stage is evidence of the child's need to regain some stability. The child is using unhealthy coping mechanisms to restore his stability. Robertson further states that such experiences can lead to serious adjustment problems in later life and thus has urged the adoption of unlimited visiting hours for parents of young children requiring hospitalization or institutionalization.

In addition to the separation factor, hospitalization for the young child who has never experienced anything like this before can be quite frightening. Due to his lack of experience and inability to conceptualize, the child is particularly vulnerable to all kinds of irrational and nonrational interpretations of the sights and sound that surround him. He relies on internal autistic processes to help interpret his new and strange environment.

Hospitalization may be experienced as lonely and boring for some, and busy, interesting, and curious for others. It may mean a loss of identity, or a feeling of worth. For example, one chronically ill patient described his hospital experience as "outside of the hospital you're somebody; in here you're nobody." Hospitalization may mean the unpredictable, not knowing what to expect and when; it may mean fear of retaliation for inappropriate behavior; or of separation from valued people and things; or of infliction of unwanted controls and forced conformity. Or it may merely signify a change in one's daily routine. Hospitalization may also be a source of relief; the patient feels secure, safe and close to emergency equipment and trained personnel.

Other people view the hospital as a death house to which hopeless cases are taken to die. In a study of hospitalized southern negroes, three major fears associated with hospitalization were expressed: fear of death, fear of the dark, and fear of being left alone. Isolation and confinement can increase feelings of alienation. Persons who formerly were part of the patient's social life are now on the outside. The patient must wait for them to come to him, for he cannot go to them. There is a feeling of exclusion, of "missing out on something," because of being taken out of circulation. For some, there is a fear of change, that "things won't be the same when I go home," or that "I might have changed," or that "my wife and family might have changed," or that people will begin to forget about him now that he is "out of sight, out of mind." There is the fear that the "job won't wait," or "the kids won't know me." Life outside of the hospital is viewed as utopia. The longer an individual remains in the hospital, the harder it becomes for him to focus realistically on the outside world. "Everything will be okay if I just get well and get out of here. I drank a lot before I came in. My wife and I never did get along, but after discharge everything will be different. I'll never be unhappy again."

The hospitalized patient is acutely aware of the passing of time. Time is now measured along new dimensions. For the long-term hospitalized patient, time is gauged by the next sputum report, or x ray, or blood test, or whatever he is dependent upon to tell him that he is that much closer to going home. The ability to see the end to an unhappy experience makes it possible to endure the experience.

Hospitalization for the patient in a sanitarium means endless waiting, slow passage of time, loss of productivity, and feelings of aimlessness and sameness day in and day out. It means the same routines, the same four walls, and the same personnel with their unchanging ways. Like prisoners confined to their cells, sanitarium patients feel that they too are "putting in time," only their lot is worse because they "don't know the lengths of [their] sentences" (Sorenson, 1967).

No two patients will view hospitalization in the same way. Our reactions to hospitalization vary as our values and situations change. People perceive things according to their predominant needs, motives, and emotional state. For example, the businessman about to complete a big contract finds it impossible to come to the hospital and "rest for a few months," or the newlywed is desperately lonely in the absence of his or her mate. On the other hand, the lonely widower may find hospital living better than outside, and the busy physician may find hospitalization a time to "catch up on his reading and to do some writing." Hospitalization for 36-year-old Mr. C. B. meant that "there was something real wrong with me." For ten-year-old Ronald it meant apprehension because he did not like hospitals—"They always hurt people." For the 18-year-old university student, hospitalization meant boredom and being cut off from social activities.

The perception of treatment and hospitalization, like that of illness, is selective and related to a host of internal and external factors operating at that time. Previous experiences with the treatment or hospitalization, the state of disturbance, the severity and type of illness, the particular level of personality development, the technical and psychological skill of the operator, the site of the treatment or part of body involved, and the presence or attitude of parents and relatives all affect how the experience is perceived and what is perceived.

As mentioned above, age is an important factor in determining what the individual is set to perceive, especially for young children. Fantasy takes on a more important role than communication for children up to age seven. The younger the child, the more primitive his thinking and the more radical his fantasies. Everything seems possible in the child's world of fantasy, and a lot is left to the child's imagination, which is vivid. The three-to-seven-year old shows an awareness of defects, injuries, and mutilations in others and is extremely sensitive to physical handicaps and anomalies. He compares his body with others and observes the anatomical sexual differences. The young child is often afraid he will be hurt and scarred by hospital procedures. He is said to fear anesthesia because he is afraid he will lose control of himself or not wake up.

SUMMARY. In summary, hospitalization, like treatment and illness, has both denotable and phenomenalistic features. (See Figure 3.) The denotable features are found in the physical and social environment of hospitals. For example, the physical characteristics of hospitals include typical floor plans with multibed rooms, long corridors, and special furniture and equipment to care for those experiencing illness. The social environment is made up of a variety of people, routines, and policies and sets of expectations associated with hospitals. To the extent that the patient's knowledge of hospitals is congruent with reality, his behavior will appear consistent and predictable. Conversely, if the hospital experience is incongruent with the patient's expectations, it will elicit behaviors that are inconsistent and unpredictable.

The phenomenalistic features of hospitalization include the sound, sight, and odors of hospitals. Individuals encounter little difficulty in recognizing the physical structures of hospitals, whether or not they have ever been in a hospital before. They encounter much more difficulty in recognizing the varying routines and expectations associated with hospitals. They, of course, will use past experiences and associations to judge the deprivations and satisfactions of the present hospitalization. Generally speaking, hospitalization is experienced in phases rather than as a total configuration. As noted earlier, it is possible to experience hospitalization as unending, especially when the individual is confined over months and years. Hospitalization also carries special meaning depending upon the age and occupational status of the patient. Finally, as with all percepts, the individual's state of health, both mental and physical, and his stage of growth and development, sex, role, culture, etc. determine what is perceived and how it is perceived.

Illness, hospitalization, and treatment are perceived in terms of motives, attitudes, and preoccupations occurring at that time, and in terms of the structural properties of the phenomenon that are so compelling that one cannot evade them. A particular aspect of the percept, one that offers the greatest threat to the individual, may outweigh all other factors. For example, the symptoms may be so severe and compelling that they take precedence; or the anticipated outcome of the illness, the treatment itself, or the separation from

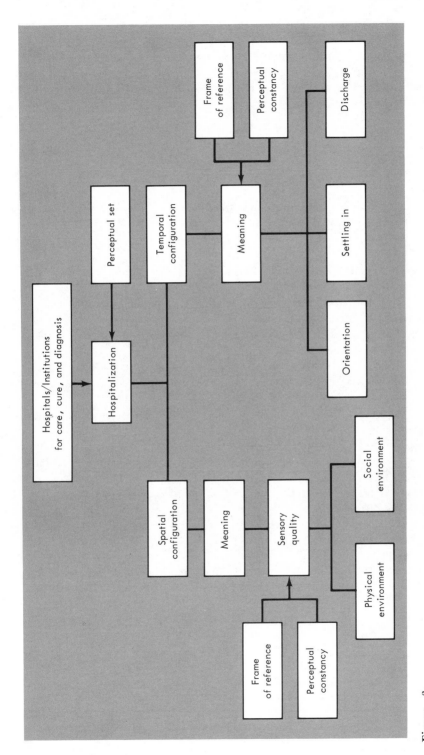

Figure 3
Experience of Hospitalization

the family—any one of these factors may become the focus of his attention at any given point in time. In sum, both treatment and hospitalization are stimuli that the person experiencing illness will be called upon to deal with.

REFERENCES

BOWLBY, JOHN *Maternal Care and Mental Health.* Geneva: World Health Organization, 1952, pp. 1–194.

———— "Separation Anxiety," *International Journal of Psychoanalysis*, 41 (1960), 89–113.

BROWN, ESTHER L. *Newer Dimensions of Patient Care*, Part I. New York: Russell Sage Foundation, 1961, pp. 123–24.

CARMENALI, DORIS L. "Pre-Operative Anxiety," *American Journal of Nursing*, 66 (July, 1966), 1536–38.

FIELD, MINNA *Patients Are People.* New York: Columbia University Press, 1958, p. 64.

FREUD, ANNA "The Role of Bodily Illness in the Mental Life of Children," *Psychoanalytic Study of the Child*, Vol. VII. New York: International Universities Press, 1952, pp. 69–81.

JANIS, IRVING L. *Psychological Stress*, New York: John Wiley & Sons, Inc., 1958, pp. 352–60.

KASSOWITZ, KARL E. "Psychodynamic Reactions of Children to the Use of Hypodermic Needles," *American Journal of Diseases of Children*, 95 (March, 1958), 253–57.

ROBERTSON, JAMES *Young Children in Hospitals.* New York: Basic Books, Inc., 1958. 103 pp.

SORENSON, KAREN M. AND DOROTHY B. AMIS "Understanding the World of the Chronically Ill," *American Journal of Nursing*, 67, No. 4 (April, 1967), 811–17.

STEPHENS, GWEN "The Time Factor: Should It Control the Patient's Care?" *American Journal of Nursing*, 65 (1965), 72–82.

five | *The Concept of Wellness*

Having examined the nature of illness and how it is experienced, our next task is to consider the concept of wellness and its relationship to illness. If illness is an event that is experienced by people in all societies, what is wellness? Is wellness the bipolar opposite of illness? In other words, if the individual is *not* experiencing illness, is he experiencing wellness? Is it possible to be both ill and well at the same time? The answer will depend upon how you define illness and wellness. If each is viewed as a condition or "state of being," can they be co-experienced? Can they coexist side by side, or must one be absent in the presence of the other?

Wellness, like illness, is an accepted fact of life. Unlike illness, wellness has provoked little investigation into its character and substance. Why then should nursing attempt to define wellness? First of all, nursing is concerned not only with the prevention of disease (illness) but also with the promotion of health-wellness or well behaviors. How can the nurse promote wellness if she does not recognize its manifestations? How can nurses support and facilitate behaviors associated with wellness if they cannot identify them? Second, it is important to distinguish between wellness and illness. Are the two concepts essentially the same thing, varying only in the quantity or amount of substance? For example, does wellness contain larger amounts and illness smaller amounts of the same components? Or is wellness substantively or qualitatively different from illness? A clear distinction between these two events must be made if nursing is to intervene appropriately.

If the concept of wellness is to provide us with a base from which to control behavior, it must be able to stand the test of reliability and utility. In the first place, then, different scientists observing an individual experiencing the event of wellness should be able to arrive independently at similar conclusions about its description. This is the test of reliability. However, if different scientists reach different descriptions of the same event, they have provided us with individual subjective opinions that are not reliable. In other words, can a definition of wellness be made that is sufficiently objective so that any person observing the same event will come forth with similar descriptions? Is there a set of criteria for wellness that can be measured objectively?

Second, does the description of the event observed serve a purpose for the person defining it? Can the nurse use the definition to help her recognize behaviors associated with wellness? This is the test of utility. Its success will be determined by the extent to which the concept enables us to understand how some event came to be, what conditions gave rise to the event, and what predictions we can make about the future.

Meeting the tests for reliability and utility does not mean that the definition cannot change as knowledge about the human organism is gained. In all sciences, terms that have been used at one time to describe events in nature have later been discarded as poor or erroneous conceptions and have been replaced by more appropriate ones. And so it is with nursing. The meanings of concepts and definitions of terms herein are subject to modification as new knowledge is gained.

DEFINITIONS OF WELLNESS

Let us now examine three definitions of wellness culled from the literature in light of their reliability and utility for nursing. Two represent a unidimensional approach, and the last one represents a two-dimensional approach: these are wellness as the polar opposite of illness, wellness on a graduated scale with illness, and wellness as a separate dimension from illness.

Wellness Viewed as the
Polar Opposite of Illness

Authors who view illness as a condition or state of being usually view wellness as the opposite state of illness.* When Romano (Engel, 1953) defined illness as "that phase of life in which there is a failure to adjust," he defined health as "that phase of life in which there is successful adjustment." Life as viewed by Romano consisted of these two bipolar phases, a phase representing successful adjustment, health-wellness, and a phase representing a failure to adjust, illness. Either the individual is able to successfully meet his needs through adaptation, or he fails to meet his needs and fails to adapt and thus to cope with the stresses of life. Definitionally it is not possible to both fail and succeed at once, and therefore both conditions cannot coexist side by side. In the absence of success there is failure and vice versa; and in the absence of health there is illness, and vice versa.

Parsons (1958) defines health as the "state of optimum capacity," and illness as an "impairment of capacity." The individual is either able to effectively (or optimally) perform the roles and tasks for which he has been socialized, relative to his status in society, or he is unable to perform to the expected level due to an impairment of capacity. Again it is definitionally impossible to be both "optimally able" and "unable" to "perform ones tasks and roles" at the same time. When an individual is "optimally able," he is experiencing a state of health; when there is an impairment and he no longer is "optimally able," there is illness.

Hadley (1964), similarly to Parsons, relies on the capability of the person to "meet minimum . . . requirements for appropriate functioning" to define wellness, and uses the phrase "disturbance in one or more spheres of an individual's capacity to meet minimum . . . requirements for appropriate functioning" for her definition of illness. Her definition implies that in the absence of a disturbance in one or more spheres of an individual's capacity to meet "minimum . . . requirements for appropriate functioning" there is illness. Thus wellness and illness cannot coexist.

---

*Sigerist (1960) defined illness as an interruption in the rhythm of life, and health as an undisturbed rhythm.

Most medical definitions of illness imply that health is the absence of disease and pathology. Where illness is represented by the presence of signs and symptoms of disordered function and "not feeling well," the absence of these indicators represents health.

The World Health Organization, on the other hand, has emphasized that health is more than the absence of disease and infirmity; in their view health represents a state of complete physical, mental, and social well-being. This definition implies that in the absence of a "state of complete physical, mental, and social well-being," whether or not there is disease or infirmity, there is illness. Thus, the absence of disease and infirmity may be a necessary but not a sufficient condition for health.

Are these useful and reliable definitions of wellness? All of the definitions could meet the test of reliability *if* the criteria for "successful adjustment," "optimal capacity," and "complete physical, mental and social well-being" were stated in behavioral terms. However, up to now these terms have not been operationalized adequately, and what one person would evaluate as "successful adjustment" or "optimal capacity" may be an entirely subjective opinion. Hadley has made an effort to close the gap with reference to certain "ideal types" she associates with wellness. These include among others, independence, integrity, industry, capability, feeling of well-being, identity, comfort, intimacy, and self-distantiation.* These behavioral descriptions of wellness provide a beginning framework for the assessment of wellness. As stated earlier, the chief deficiency of Hadley's "ideal types" is in her failure to provide a quantifiable scale for measurements, since all the attributes mentioned occur in varying degrees in terms of amount and frequency.

The utility of viewing wellness as the polar opposite of illness has one important limitation in that it does not seem to allow for degrees of illness and wellness. It views health as a static quality, which it is not. Health changes through time. According to the above definitions, the individual is either ill or well. There is no in-between state. The prediction of behavior requires a definition that includes the range of possible conditions from illness to wellness, since behaviors presumably differ depending upon the degree of capacity or incapacity, or degree of success or failure of the individual to adjust.

---

*"Self-distantiation" is a term Hadley borrowed from Erik Erikson (1950) to mean a readiness to repudiate or destroy anything that seems dangerous to oneself.

Wellness on a Graduated Scale

Dunn (1959) suggests that we should shift from a view of illness and wellness as a dichotomy and place them on a graduated scale. On the horizontal line of his health axis (see Figure 4) are represented degrees of illness and wellness, with death at one end and peak wellness at the opposite end. In between these two states are varying degrees of illness/wellness: serious illness, minor illness,

Figure 4
The Health Grid, Its Axes and Quadrants

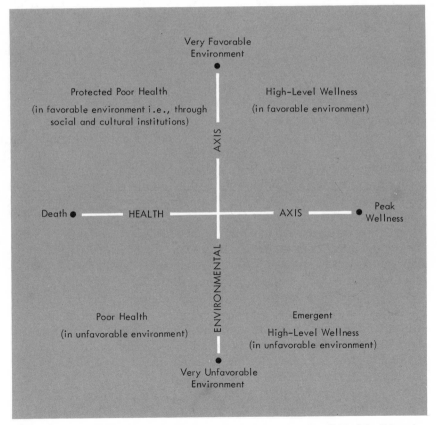

(From Dunn, 1959, p. 788. Original source: U.S. Department of Health, Education, and Welfare, Public Health Service, National Office of Vital Statistics.)

freedom from illness, and good health. Rotating around this horizontal line is the environment; the north pole represents a very favorable environment and the south pole, a very unfavorable environment. As illustrated in the diagram, the degree of illness or wellness is modified by environmental factors. In a very favorable environment one should experience a high level of wellness, whereas in a very unfavorable environment the same person would experience only emergent high-level wellness. High-level wellness, according to Dunn, (p. 791) is manifested in self-confidence and faith in oneself with growth of self-development toward fuller maturity and a balanced wellness of body, mind, and spirit.

Dunn retains the notion of wellness as the polar opposite of illness, but he extends the definition to include a range of conditions that fall between death or serious illness and peak wellness. He also recognizes that the severity of illness or degree of wellness is influenced by the environment. Although the environmental factor was not explicitly stated in the definitions discussed earlier, this idea does not contradict any of them.

The reliability and utility of Dunn's definition depend upon a set of criteria for each state or condition alluded to on the continuum. When health is viewed as a matter of degree, it presents a problem of exactness. How does one distinguish between lesser and lesser degrees of health? A definition cannot effectively include the gradualness with which health merges into illness, while still distinguishing between the two. In other words, how does one distinguish between a serious and a minor illness? One is just *more* serious than the other.

Dunn has provided us with some beginning criteria for identifying the person experiencing high-level wellness, but he needs to further operationalize his terms if they are to have utility for nursing. Since it is an extension of the bipolar approach to the definition of wellness, it suffers some of the same limitations. Illness and wellness are viewed as comprised of the same elements, varying only in quantity, so that there are maximum amounts at one end of the continuum and minimum amounts of the same elements at the opposite end. The confusion arises in the middle of the continuum. The individual is either more ill than well or more well than ill. The problem is whether to treat him as ill or well, or is it possible to treat him as both ill and well simultaneously? Can a person with signs and symptoms of disease experience wellness? Would it be useful for nursing to define wellness in such a way that it allows for the two events to occur simultaneously; so that the nurse could support and encourage the "wellness" aspect of the person while treating the "illness" aspect?

Wellness/Illness as
Two Separate Dimensions

Rogers (1960) made a beginning attempt to conceptualize illness and wellness as two separate entities. He used a spectrum to illustrate his concept of illness and health. (See Figure 5.) He states that each person possesses varying components of illness and also varying components of good health, and that the individual's total health status would be the net balance of these components. If the

Figure 5
Health Status Scale
A Theoretic Classification of Level of Health in
a Given Individual at a Given Time

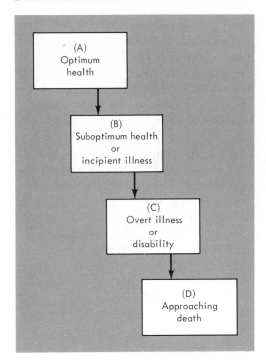

(From Rogers, 1960, p. 159.)

individual manifested more illness components than wellness components, his total balance might be assessed as "illness." If the reverse were true, the total net balance might be assessed as "health." Rogers' spectrum includes a range extending from a condition approaching death to one of optimum health. Since Rogers does not describe what he calls components of health and illness, the utility of his definition for nursing is limited.

However, the concept that health and illness are made up of different components and that both conditions can occur simultaneously in varying degrees is a useful notion because it allows for assessment of both conditions in a single person. The idea of a net balance is a more difficult concept to implement because it implies that the end result is some degree of either illness or wellness, a problem encountered with Dunn's definition. For example, if a person has eight health components (pluses) and four illness components (minuses), his net balance would be plus four, which may be interpreted as suboptimum health. If he had all health components and zero illness components, his net balance might be assessed as optimum health. The similarities between Rogers' model and Dunn's model of health-wellness may be attributed to the fact that both authors are in Public Health where end states are very important. Nurses, however, are more interested in helping persons achieve a desirable end state than computing a net balance or positioning a person on a health/illness spectrum or continuum.

Jahoda (1958), like Rogers, suggests that health and disease are qualitatively different and represent two independent but contrasting conditions or types: i.e., she views health and illness on two dimensions. She says that every person has healthy and sick aspects simultaneously, with one or the other predominating. This is where she differs in part from Rogers. Instead of algebraically adding the positive and negative components to arrive at a net balance, she recognizes that they both can exist in different quantities and that one does not eliminate the other. She states that it is possible "to observe healthy potential in sick people and illness potential in well people."*

The unidimensional approach of Dunn, Parsons, Engel, and others defines health as a relatively constant and enduring function of the personality, leading to predictable differences in behavior and feelings, depending on the stresses of the situation in which a person finds himself. Thus, the individual is assessed as more or less healthy; whereas in the two-dimensional approach espoused by Jahoda, the

---

*Marie Jahoda, *Current Concepts of Positive Mental Health* (New York: Basic Books, Inc., 1956), p. 75.

actions (of the individual) are assessed as more or less healthy. According to Jahoda, an individual can be both well and sick at once. One aspect may appear well and another aspect, ill. She gives an example of this when in reference to a patient confined to a psychiatric hospital, a visitor is overheard to say, "There's nothing wrong with him except he thinks he's Napoleon Bonaparte." Thus the patient may exhibit well behaviors in eating, sleeping, and physical activity, but show sick behaviors in inappropriate affect or thought processes.

A similar approach has been adopted by Kaufman (1963) who suggests that it is possible for the handicapped person, who she defines as ill, to achieve varying levels of wellness by capitalizing on his "well" features rather than by focusing mainly on his handicap. For example, a paraplegic patient may be ill in one part of his body but may be well in other parts. Rather than deriving a net balance of the ill and well components, as suggested by Rogers, Kaufman suggests that the nurse should not only place emphasis on care of the disability but should also place emphasis on developing the person's remaining well potentials.

Although Hadley (as stated earlier) views illness and wellness as polar opposites on a single dimension, it is possible to interpret her definition so that both illness and wellness occur simultaneously. In other words, it is conceivable that a disturbance in one sphere could result in little or no disturbance in the remaining spheres, depending on the definition of each sphere. She is presently attempting to incorporate the notion of two dimensions in her definition of wellness.

How does the two-dimensional approach to health and illness reconcile the notion that man responds as a unified whole? Martha Rogers (1970) maintains that "human beings are more than and difference from the sum of their parts (p. 46)." Man acts as a whole. One cannot view man's mind apart from his body. Thus, from the perspective of the perceiver, only one event can be experienced at any given point in time. In other words, when an individual is experiencing illness, he cannot simultaneously experience wellness. Illness components may dominate to control his behavior at one time, and wellness components may control his behavior at another time. Furthermore according to Jahoda it is possible for a person with a medical or psychiatric diagnosis to experience wellness, as well as for a person without any medically known disease to experience illness; whether an individual experiences illness or wellness at any given point in time is dependent upon both personal and situational factors.

Whenever an individual experiences illness or wellness, his behavior will change accordingly. For example, when the mental patient mentioned previously (p. 83) is eating, his behavior may be assessed as "healthy," since this behavior predominates at this point in time. When he begins to call himself Napoleon Bonaparte, his behavior may be assessed as ill, since the delusions characteristic of illness are now predominant. The unidimensional approach would say, regardless of the patient's behaviors, that if he has been assessed as ill, he is ill; whereas the two-dimensional approach states that he is ill only when his behaviors are assessed to be ill, regardless of a prior medical diagnosis.

In a similar fashion, a person who is defined as ill may *perceive* himself as well. Thus the mental patient who exhibits bizarre behaviors in affect and thought may be diagnosed as medically ill, but he may perceive himself as well. His capacity to function in accordance with his age, sex, and developmental level is impaired, but he does not perceive himself as incapacitated. His well components, such as the ability to eat and eliminate according to normal standards, should be supported at the same time as treating his illness components. Also the handicapped patient may experience illness when he perceives himself incapacitated, and wellness when he perceives himself capable of performing to the best of his ability. Thus, some authors have suggested that wellness is a state of mind. Certainly the disabled person controls to some degree whether he experiences illness or wellness.

What then shall be nursing's definition of wellness? Illness you will recall has been defined as an event experienced by man that manifests itself through observable and/or felt changes in the body causing an impairment of capacity to meet minimum physical, physiological, and psychosocial requirements for appropriate functioning at the level designated for the person's age, sex, and development, or handicapped state.

Consistent with the definition of illness, wellness shall be defined as an event experienced by man that manifests itself through his behaviors; i.e., individuals experiencing wellness will exhibit a class of behaviors congruent with the event. In an interview conducted by Twaddle (1969), men in their early and middle sixties defined themselves as "well" if they had no medically defined condition of illness or if they were told by a physician that they were in good health. However, since the presence of aberrant changes in structure and/or function is not a necessary attribute of illness, the absence of such changes does not necessarily denote the presence of health-wellness. What then, are the objective and/or subjective features of wellness?

The attributes of wellness, as set forth by Jahoda, include the following:

1. An ability to perceive in accordance with reality, free from need distortion. In other words, no matter how much the individual wishes that things were different, he is able to take in these matters without distorting them to fit his wishes.
2. An ability to adjust actively to varying situations in one's family, peer group, occupational group, etc. The individual is able to engage in problem-solving techniques when he encounters obstacles to goal achievement. Environmental frustrations to which some persons respond in ways considered unhealthy may be considered quite normal by these individuals. Health is not the absence of conflict and frustration but shows itself in the manner of handling these situations.
3. An ability to display a coherent and integrated personality, characterized by a wholesome, unifying outlook on life.

Each component of wellness, according to Jahoda, consumes energy. However, every component need not be maximized. The amount of energy vested in each component depends upon the psychological or situational context in which it is experienced. The optimal arrangement and the amounts of each component under a given set of conditions are not known. For example, if more energy is needed to actively adjust to a given situation, less energy may be available for the perception of reality. As long as the individual is able to maintain a balanced relationship between the various components, he is said to be experiencing wellness.

SUMMARY. Health-wellness has been defined as the opposite of illness by some authors and as something separate and distinct from illness by other authors. The dual-dimensional approach, viewing illness and wellness as two distinct entities, with a separate repertory of behaviors for each, allows for a more comprehensive assessment of the total organism and as such is a more useful concept for nursing. The nurse would look not only for illness components but also for the wellness components when caring for patients.

In the unidimensional approach, which views illness and wellness on a single dimension, composed of identical elements in varying quantities, the presence of the illness components would require that the person occupy some position near the illness end of the continuum. As such this approach would tend to focus the nurse's attention on the illness, and she would be motivated to ignore the potentialities for supporting well behaviors. In the long run, placing limitations on well behaviors because of narrowness of perspective and eagerness to modify the illness behaviors may prolong the illness to the detriment of the patient.

Like illness, health-wellness can also be viewed as an event in nature, a phenomenon that is experienced by the living organism. Health-wellness is manifested by a feeling of well-being, a capacity to perform to the best of one's ability; it is evidenced by an ability to adjust to and adapt actively to varying situations, to perceive correctly, free from need distortions, complemented with a wholesome outlook on life. In other words, health-wellness is not necessarily the absence of abnormal structure and function; it is something more than this.

Health-wellness, according to this view, is not some enduring characteristic of the personality. It may be, in fact, a momentary, fleeting experience that comes and goes in the life of an individual. The observer is able to distinguish between illness and wellness by means of certain behavioral manifestations that characterize or typify one or the other. When the nurse recognizes behaviors associated with wellness, she supports, facilitates, and encourages these behaviors. When she recognizes behaviors associated with illness, she intervenes to decrease the discomfort, remove or reduce the stressor, and support the body's defenses.

As long as the individual is experiencing wellness his total state is said to be in balance. Although energy may be distributed unevenly among the components that comprise wellness, the overall state of the organism is said to be in balance. If this assumption is correct, does an imbalanced state imply the presence of illness? Can an individual experience stability in the presence of illness? Let us next examine the concept of stability and its relationship to illness/wellness.

REFERENCES

DUNN, HALBERT L. "High Level Wellness for Man and Society," *American Journal of Public Health*, 49, No. 6 (June, 1959), 786–92.

ENGEL, GEORGE L. "Homeostasis, Behavioral Adjustment and The Concept of Health and Disease," in *Midcentury Psychiatry*, ed. Roy R. Grinker. Springfield, Ill.: Charles C. Thomas, 1968, pp. 33–59.

ERIKSON, ERIC H. *Growth and Crises of the Healthy Personality*, 1950, unpublished manuscript.

HADLEY, BETTY JO *Review of Current Concepts of Health and Illness*. Unpublished manuscript, 1964.

JAHODA, MARIE *Current Concepts of Positive Mental Health*. New York: Basic Books, Inc., 1956. 136 p.

KAUFMAN, MARGARET "High Level Wellness, a Pertinent Concept for the Health Professions," *Mental Hygiene*, 47 (1963), 58.

PARSONS, TALCOTT "Definitions of Health and Illness in the Light of American Values and Social Structure," in *Patients, Physicians and Illness*, ed. E. G. Jaco. New York: The Free Press, 1958, Chap. 20, pp. 165–87.

ROGERS, EDWARD S. *Human Ecology and Health*. New York: The Macmillan Company, 1960, pp. 155–78.

ROGERS, MARTHA E. *An Introduction to the Theoretical Basis of Nursing*. Philadelphia: F. A. Davis Co., 1970.

SIGERIST, HENRY E. "The Special Position of the Sick," in Milton I. Roemer and J. M. Mackintosh, eds., *On the Sociology of Medicine*. New York: M. D. Publications, 1960, pp. 9–22.

TWADDLE, ANDREW C. "Health Decisions and Sick Role Variations: An Exploration," *Journal of Health and Social Behavior*, 10 (1969), 105–15.

six | *The Concept of Stability*

In the beginning pages of this text it was postulated that a condition called behavioral stability can occur during experiences of illness as well as wellness. Furthermore, it was postulated that during periods of relative behavioral stability less energy is expended by the individual than during periods of relative behavioral instability. In light of this proposition it was suggested that during experiences of illness, when additional amounts of energy are needed for the recovery process, a primary goal of the nurse should be the maintenance and/or restoration of relative behavioral stability for her patients.

A similar notion was set forth more than a decade ago by Howland and Green (1958). They postulated that the role of the hospital in society was to help patients maintain their homeostatic levels. A patient was defined as "a person who is unable to maintain a desirable homeostatic balance unaided with respect to a range of variables." Is the nurse's role to maintain homeostatic levels and/or behavioral stability? What is the difference between the two terms? If they refer to the same condition, then for parsimonious reasons one of the terms should be eliminated. This chapter proposes that, although the two terms are interrelated, they actually represent two different perspectives of man and therefore should be retained. The latter views man from a psychosocial perspective, and the former views man from a biological perspective. Both perspectives conceptualize man as a complex adaptive system.

COMPLEX ADAPTIVE SYSTEMS

The concept of man as a complex adaptive system suggests that man possesses not only self-regulatory properties characteristic of a simple homeostatic system but also qualities of self-direction and self-organization unique to high-level adaptive systems. The chief distinction between a homeostatic system and a complex adaptive system, according to Buckley (1967, 1968), is that the former is geared principally to the maintenance of structure within preestablished limits (self-regulation), whereas the latter is geared not only to maintaining structure through compensatory acts but also to extending or changing a system's given form when necessary as a condition for survival (adaptation). Greater dependence on information exchange makes it possible for complex adaptive systems to engage in high levels of flexible and dynamic interchanges with the environment. The hormone and nerve impulse and the sound or gesture are chief transmitters and bearers of information to and from the organisms and their subsystems. These transmitters evoke adaptive behaviors that maintain the entity or modify it in conformity with environmental demands (Gerard, 1968). Biological evolution and learning are examples of structural modifications or elaborations imposed by the environment.

A complex adaptive system, like all systems, is comprised of a group of elements or components that are directly or indirectly related to each other in some kind of causal network (Buckley, 1968). The parts are connected with each other by means of information flows and energy exchanges. The biological and physical sciences stress energy transfer, and the social sciences stress information exchanges. At least some of the components of a system are related to some other components in more or less stable ways at any given time. The maintenance of this more or less stable interrelationship involves the interplay of many variables—physiological, sociological, psychological, and economic. Disturbances in the system may be limited to a group of related parts (subsystems) or extended to encompass the total complex of elements that comprise the system. Disturbances that upset the balance of the system are indicated by the appearance of abnormal physiological and/or psychosocial behavioral patterns.

In order to distinguish between the different kinds of disturbances that can occur to complex adaptive systems, we propose that the following terms be used to describe the various states:

1. *Homeostasis* shall be used to describe a physiological balance; and (*homeostatic*) disequilibrium, a physiological imbalance.
2. *Stability* shall be used to describe a behavioral balance, and *instability*, a behavioral imbalance.
3. *Steady state* shall be used to describe the equilibria of both forces, physiological and behavioral; and an upset in the steady state shall be denoted by *system imbalance*.

The presence of stable interrelationships among parts of a complex adaptive system, then, is known as a steady state. A steady state, by definition, requires the presence of both physiological homeostasis and behavioral stability. Behavioral stability may occur in the absence of homeostasis, and conversely homeostasis may occur in the absence of behavioral stability, if not prolonged. But the absence of either one destroys the steady state. (See Figure 6 for a diagram of these relationships.)

The view of man as a complex adaptive system represents an effort to present a unified model of man incorporating all of the critical variables in proper perspective. The approach taken in this book is to study man first from a physiological perspective and then from a behavioral or psychosocial perspective. In actuality, no sharp distinction can be drawn between physiological homeostasis as opposed to behavioral stability; the distinction is only a conceptual one.

PHYSIOLOGICAL PERSPECTIVE OF MAN

Howland and Green's (1968) perspective of the patient as a person who is "unable to maintain a desirable homeostatic balance unaided with respect to a range of variables" is based on Cannon's concept of homeostasis. In his study of the physiological processes of living organisms, Cannon (1968) noted that the equilibrium achieved by these processes differed from the equilibrium observed in closed physical systems. Closed systems do not have feedback mechanisms or other systematic self-regulation or adaptive capabilities. These systems take in nothing and put out nothing, being isolated from

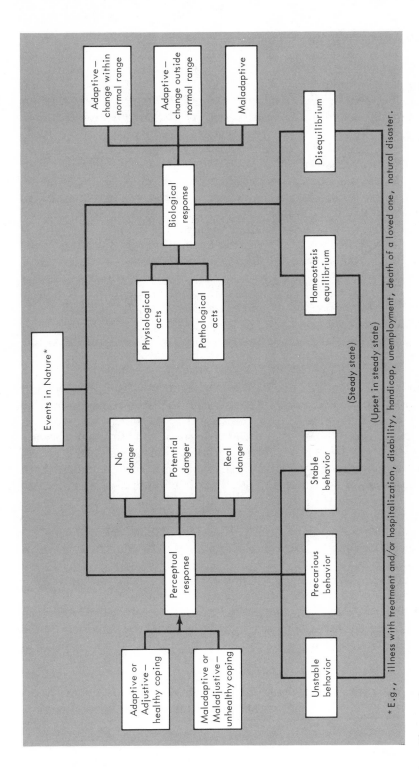

Figure 6
Stability, Homeostasis, and Steady State

*E.g., illness with treatment and/or hospitalization, disability, handicap, unemployment, death of a loved one, natural disaster.

their environments. Equilibrium is achieved when all known forces within the system are balanced. Energy is distributed randomly throughout the system. Examples of physical systems in equilibrium include the pendulum hanging vertically, the cube resting flat on its face, and the watch with its mainspring run down (Ashby, 1965). A system in equilibrium cannot do any work because there is no gradient or concentration of potential energy to be released.

In contrast, open systems have both input and output of matter and energy. Living organisms maintain themselves in a dynamic or flux equilibrium by mobilizing internal resources to cope with environmentally imposed changes (Gerard, 1968). The intrusion of outer energy is prevented from disrupting internal form and order by means of self-correcting (feedback) mechanisms. In order to distinguish this type of stability or constancy from the equilibria of closed systems, Cannon introduced the term *homeostasis*. This term describes a condition that may vary even though it remains relatively constant.

Other authors have described various kinds of equilibria similar to Cannon's notion of homeostasis. Koehler (1968) described the equilibrium of open systems as a steady state that he likened to the flame of a candle. As long as there is a continual supply of energy that the flame receives as "food" through the wick and oxygen from the air, it remains the same in size and shape unless disturbed by radical or abrupt changes in the environment. A steady state, according to Pringle (1968), is a type of equilibrium in which the rate of formation within a system is equal to the rate of destruction. Each unit appears to be constant or steady only because it is being formed and destroyed at the same rate. Organisms thus are capable of maintaining dynamic equilibrium in the face of continual disturbances from both external and internal sources. Homeostatic devices or compensatory mechanisms in the organism help neutralize or repair the disturbance.

Although the concept of homeostasis has been recognized for many years, the process or mechanism by which this condition is achieved was not well understood until recently when an interdisciplinary group composed of mathematicians, engineers, and physiologists applied their knowledge of regulation and control of machines to the study of organismic systems. This team extended the concept of homeostasis by incorporating it into *cybernetics*, the study of "control and communication in the animal and machine" (Weiner, 1954). This group observed that the control of function, the storage of information, and the principle of feedback in machines have much in common with the human system.

The feedback principle provides us with the key for understanding the nature of the self-correcting adjustments responsible for the maintenance of homeostasis. This principle states that certain portions of the system's output are fed back into the system's input to affect succeeding output (Hall and Fagin, 1968). Whenever future performance is adjusted by past performance, the feedback principle is involved (Weiner, 1954). Feedback that causes an increase in the deviation of output from the steady state is positive, whereas feedback that causes a decrease in the deviation of output from the steady state is negative (Buckley, 1968). The automatic correcting devices in the body act as rate regulators to speed up or slow down body processes.

Selye (1956) identified two kinds of hormones in the body that operate on the principle of feedback: those that stimulate (speed up) defensive reactions and those that inhibit (slow down) excessive defensive reactions. These devices may be viewed as compensatory mechanisms that neutralize an impending imbalance. For example, the body compensates with an increase in pulse and respiration following a run upstairs. An increase in energy expenditure requires an increase in energy intake to compensate for the loss. When the outside atmospheric pressure drops too low for optimal oxygen absorption by the red blood cells, the body compensates by increasing its production of red blood cells so that the amount of oxygen delivered by the cells remains unchanged even though each cell is delivering less oxygen per cubic millimeter than normal. Negative feedback maintains the current structure of the system providing insight into the mechanisms underlying simple homeostatic processes. Positive feedback, by increasing the deviation of output from the steady state, alters the parts or components of the system. This is the mechanism underlying structural change or elaboration, a characteristic of complex adaptive systems.

From the physiological perspective, man is viewed as a complex adaptive system comprised of biological subsystems. Through the function of these subsystems the body is able to maintain a favorable state of its fluids and thus of its cells. The electrolyte pattern is maintained with remarkable constancy in the fluid compartments: the body maintains a proper fluid balance; the hydrogen-ion concentration is maintained within certain limits; and the temperature is maintained at levels favorable to cellular function (Jensen, 1953).

The maintenance of this constancy is made possible by means of automatic self-correcting, self-maintaining feedback loops. These feedback loops are described as pseudofeedback by Buckley (1968) because they do not really "control" the system. What happens is that the original variables react blindly to the forces that they helped to create and that are now reacting back on them. By and large this is the mechanism that regulates and controls all physiological processes.

Man, however, is more than a biological homeostatic organism; he is a human being with purposeful, adaptive, and psychological properties. Purposeful behavior is different from automatic self-regulating behaviors in that it involves the internal representation of a goal and/or norm that may or may not have been previously experienced by the individual. Purposeful behavior is regulated by true feedback loops that go beyond the homeostatic principle. Deviations from the goal or norm direct the behavior of the system. Mechanisms measure or compare feedback input against a goal and pass the information to a control center that activates the behavior required to correct the error or mismatch. The maintenance of a steady state in complex adaptive systems involves true feedback, i.e., both self-regulatory homeostatic mechanisms and self-directing adaptive mechanisms. Since Howland and Green based their model of patient care on Cannon's concept of homeostasis, it seems logical to deduce that they are referring to the kind of balance that is regulated by means of automatic self-maintaining devices. In other words, their model in its current state views man from the physiological perspective. Illness represents a breakdown in the mechanisms that maintain homeostasis, and the hospital's role is to help restore the patient's homeostatic balance to the level required for survival.

When the changes in the body are excessive relative to the strength of an aggressor, or a shifting of energies fails to meet the exigencies of the situation, then a state of homeostatic disequilibrium results. Forces that are capable of upsetting the homeostatic balance include environmental stimuli such as bacteria and chemicals; sociocultural stimuli such as societal norms, values, beliefs; and psychological stimuli such as interpersonal conflict. So long as the external variations are not excessive in degree nor too sudden in development, the constancy of the system can be maintained.

Every human system contains a repertory of biological and mental acts to help maintain and/or establish homeostasis. As long as the acts contribute to the maintenance or reestablishment of homeostasis, they are described as physiological or adaptive. In Chapter 3, you will recall, we attempted to clarify some confusing points about the equilibrium model of illness by suggesting that man was capable of attaining varying homeostatic levels that were compatible with survival. One level, usually associated with the experience of health-wellness, is reflected in what has been called the "constancy of the internal milieu."* On this level, homeostasis is maintained within a range that is considered normal and compatible with health. The other level of homeostasis that is usually associated with the experience of illness lies outside the range of body functioning associated with health. In this case, changes that are required to deal with the stimuli exceed the "normal" range. Since any change that exceeds the "normal" range is by definition a sign or symptom of illness, a homeostatic balance associated with illness is attained. Such a response of the organism is described as "physiological" in that the body's defenses and adaptive processes are responding appropriately. Conversely, actions that contribute to an upset in the homeostatic balance by overreacting or underreacting to noxious stimuli are described as pathologic or maladaptive.

If man can obtain what is required and convert or eliminate what is in excess, he can maintain homeostasis. When the self-regulating mechanisms of the system fail to correct the imbalance, outside aid must be brought to bear. Many times, through careful manipulation of the environment, the organism can be helped to restore the balance. Prolonged homeostatic disequilibrium is incompatible with life.

To summarize then, the physiological perspective views man as a complex adaptive system comprised of biological subsystems that work together to maintain the constancy of the body's fluids and cells. Negative feedback or pseudofeedback operates automatically to correct any deviations in output that tend to cause homeostatic disequilibrium. Physiological acts are adaptive in that they contribute to the maintenance or restoration of homeostasis, either within or outside the "normal" range. Pathologic acts are maladaptive in that they fail to maintain or restore homeostatic balance, or they create homeostatic disequilibrium. Processes contributing to homeostasis should be supported as well as regulated so that they do not exceed the range compatible with adequate body functioning. The maintenance and restoration of a homeostatic level compatible with optimal body functioning are the primary concern of medicine.

---

*Julius Jensen, *Modern Concepts in Medicine* (St. Louis: C. V. Mosby Co., 1953), p. 43.

PSYCHOSOCIAL (BEHAVIORAL) PERSPECTIVE OF MAN

From a psychosocial perspective, man is conceptualized as a complex adaptive system comprised of behavioral subsystems that work together to achieve behavioral stability. (See Figure 7.) These behavioral subsystems are regulated by true feedback loops that not only maintain structure according to preestablished limits but also elaborate structure according to environmental demands imposed on the system. Social mores, values, motives, norms, and reinforcers influence the structure of the system.

Behavioral stability means different things to different people. Traditionally the term refers to the continuity and consistency of behavior over time. With maturation and experience, the human system develops preferred ways of behaving that keep interference and conflicts to a minimum and preserve the balance of the organism. With the passage of time these behavioral responses become automatic and increasingly resistant to change. Automaticity means a great saving of energy, since the individual does not have to go through an original process of thought and effort each time. Rigid adherence to these preferred ways, however, operates against the principle of stability. Flexibility is a necessary condition for the maintenance of stability. In other words, the system must be able to modify and adjust its responses to stimuli if it is to remain stable.

Although habits, traits, cognitive styles, and so forth provide continuity to behavior, they are not the sole source of stability in individual behavior. The locus of stability and change, according to Secord and Backman (1961), is in the interaction process. The essential condition for consistency in individual behavior is dependent upon stable patterns in the interaction process. An individual interacting with another person is always trying to shape the interaction process in accordance with certain requirements; i.e., he is always attempting to produce certain patterned relationships. He strives to maintain interpersonal relations that are characterized by congruent matrices. The fact that individuals do maintain intrapersonal structures, such as habits, traits, and styles of thinking, is due to the fact that the behavior of others toward the individual in question is consistent with such maintenance.

Vickers (1968) describes a similar phenomenon in which regu-

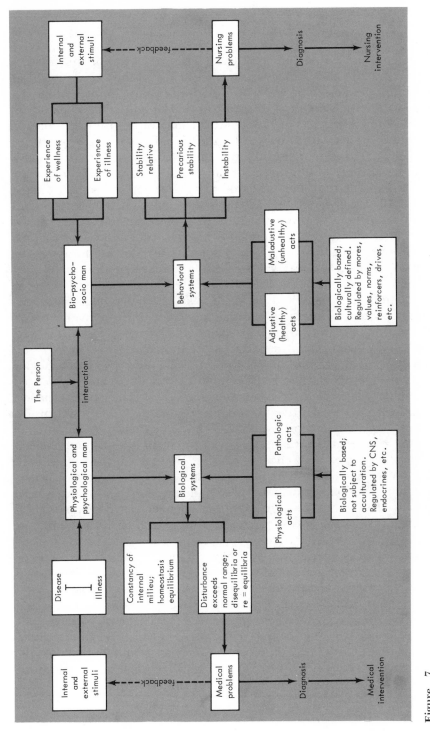

Figure 7
Physiological Equilibrium and Behavioral Stability

latory processes are constantly at work adjusting man's behavior (thoughts and actions) in accordance with the norms or limits established by the individual as a consequence of his own biological evolution, experience, and cultural conditioning. When usual behaviors are unavailable or cease to work, the individual experiences a breakdown or a loss of order and predictability in himself and/or in his relations with others. The individual must choose a way of behaving that will neutralize the disturbance. Each person has a limited number of alternatives from which to choose. He may alter himself by learning new skills or reorganize himself so as to make new behavior possible; he may alter the environment; he may withdraw from the environment and seek a more favorable one; or he may alter the norm that previously governed his behavior. In essence, man must regulate his behavior so that the relationships essential to the system's survival are kept within acceptable limits, i.e., stable.

Similarly, Secord and Backman (1961) state that man must regulate his system of interaction so that a balance is maintained between three components of his interpersonal matrix: the aspect of the person's self-concept, his interpretation of those behaviors that are related to that aspect, and his perception of the other person's behavior toward that aspect. The interpersonal matrix or system is balanced or stable when all three components are in a state of congruency. Congruency is a cognitive phenomenon achieved only by systems capable of internal representation. This congruency is continually being threatened by changes in the system of interaction. Societal norms and rules may change, causing changes in the behavior of those with whom the individual interacts, such as changes in behavior due to normal growth and development or to a change in occupation or marital status; or fortuitous changes may develop, such as death of a parent, loss of a friend, illness, and induction into the armed forces; or situations may arise in which the person's usual means of achieving congruency do not match the other's expectations. Whatever the cause, incongruency constitutes a stress that causes a certain amount of strain or tension within the system.

Secord and Backman describe seven interpersonal processes that they say are directed at restoring congruency and thus reducing the strain created by the incongruency. Recognizing that in any interaction there are at least two persons—a self (s) and another (o)—the first five processes are focused on manipulating or transforming the behavior of the other (o), and the last two processes focus on transformations of the self(s).

1. *Selective interaction with others.* An individual will interact with those persons whose behavior reinforces his own beliefs about himself. For example, a person who views himself as intelligent will choose to interact with persons who respect and/or allow him to exercise his intelligence, thus reinforcing his own self-concept.

2. *Selective evaluation of others.* An individual may change his evaluation of others in the interaction process, depending upon whether these persons are acting congruently or incongruently with certain aspects of his "self" and depending upon the importance of their relationship to him. If it is important enough to him, he will increase his liking for those who behave in a congruent fashion and decrease his liking for those who behave in an incongruent manner. The latter persons' potentially disrupting influence will therefore be decreased.

3. *Selective comparison with aspects of other's behavior.* An individual will selectively attend to those behaviors of others that are congruent and selectively ignore those that are incongruent with certain aspects of his "self" and his behaviors.

4. *Evocation of congruent responses from others.* An individual may develop techniques that elicit behaviors from others that are congruent with his self-concept. For example, if a person perceives himself to be dependent and helpless, he will behave toward others in a manner that will elicit the help needed.

5. *Misperception of the other's behavior.* Congruency is sometimes achieved by means of cognitive distortion; i.e., he misperceives or misinterprets the other's behavior. Congruency achieved by this means is said to be less stable than a reality-oriented congruency.

6. *Selective behavior-matching.* An individual will select from his own behavioral repertoire those behaviors that are most congruent with his perception of the others' expectations. Thus, instead of manipulating the behavior of others, the individual may change his own behavior to achieve congruency.

7. *Misinterpretation of own behavior.* An individual may misinterpret his own behavior so as to achieve congruency with an aspect of his self-concept and his perception of the others' expectation. In this situation the individual chooses to misinterpret or rationalize his own behavior instead of the other person's behavior in order to avert behavioral instability.

Incongruency among the components of an interpersonal matrix is therefore resolved by either restoring the original (previously congruent) matrix, leaving self and behavior unchanged (although cognitive distortions may occur), or by structuring a new matrix in which self or behavior is changed. Factors that affect whether there is a change in one or more of the components in an interpersonal matrix include: role expectations learned through the socialization process, the ease with which the individual can remove himself from the interaction, the extent to which the individual's congruent relations are dependent upon misinterpretation and misperception, and the amount and value of support that undergird the behavior. In a radically altered environment where others behave toward the individual in new and strange ways, the individual would be compelled to modify his own behavior to produce a new set of congruent matrices. For example, aggressive behaviors would continue to appear only as long as these were congruent with certain behaviors of those interacting with the individual and with certain components of his self-concept.

Rigid adherence to old patterns of behavior that are no longer effective in dealing with the external challenge can lead to system disruption and dissolution. Instability is seen when the individual is confronted with marked and frequent changes in the behavior of peers and of adults that are incongruent with components of his self-concept and behavior. These changes lead to shifts in the individual's self-concept and behavior, and in turn new relations are sought in order to establish congruency with these modified aspects of self and behavior. Old matrices become less congruent and progressively weaker in affect.

A loss of order and predictability, which can precipitate behavioral instability, may be due to the nature of the event being experienced. Rapoport (1965) suggests that any event that is perceived as hazardous is likely to cause instability in the human organism. (See Table 2.) He makes a point of distinguishing this kind of an upset from disturbances associated with disease, by suggesting that such an upset can occur in the absence of any medical symptomatology. It is possible, for example, to become highly emotional and even hysterical over the sudden loss of a loved one, without being defined as medically ill.

In addition, illness, like any other event that is experienced, is capable of precipitating behavioral instability or an upset in the "steady state." When the individual perceives that his illness is preventing him from meeting his basic needs for food, fluid, oxygen, elimination, release of sexual tension, sleep, rest, and exercise, or

TABLE 2

The Concept of Stability

Person/Situation	Response Mechanisms	State of Stability	Behavioral Manifestations
1. Frequently encountered events perceived as nondangerous.	Usual self-regulating, self-maintaining, homeostatic devices and problem-solving activities; automatic, habitual.	Tension is at an optimal level. A balance is maintained. Energy is evenly distributed to all parts of body. Behavior fluctuates within a "normal" range, i.e., within physiological limits.	Feeling of well-being, comfort, pleasure; perception of order and predictability in himself and in his relations with his environment.
2. New, persistent, and intense events perceived as potentially dangerous.	Exaggeration and distortion of normal coping devices in order to deal with the event; evidence of struggle between forces of aggression and defense.	Tension exceeds optimal range as emergency devices are brought into play. Energy is redistributed through compensatory moves in an effort to avert an imbalance. Fluctuations increase and threaten to exceed limits of stability.	Efforts to maintain control with a new tenuous balance; moderate discomfort and apprehension. Threatened loss of order and predictability.
3. New, persistent, and intense events perceived as dangerous.	All emergency devices known to the organism have failed. Coping mechanisms are ineffective, inadequate or have over reacted. New measures unknown to the organism must be instituted.	Tension level has exceeded tolerable range for stability. An imbalance or upset in the steady state has occurred. Body has failed to compensate for the loss or overload incurred by the event. Outside intervention is necessary or death will ensue.	Perceives loss of order and predictability in self and in his relations with his environment; severe discomfort, displeasure, diffuse, purposeless behavior with total disorganization.

N.B. Illness, treatment, and/or hospitalization may be experienced as any one of these events; as familiar, as new and unfamiliar, as potentially dangerous, or as very dangerous.

when he perceives the loss of a valued part, or when he perceives that his self-identity is threatened or denied expression, he is likely to evidence behavioral instability. If the illness is not perceived as hazardous, the individual is less likely to experience instability. The tendency for congruency is greater when the signs and symptoms of illness are severe and compelling, lessening the chances of denying or rationalizing them away. However, it will be recalled from Chapter 3 that an individual's perception does not always coincide with reality. For example, even though there is no actual loss of a body part, if the individual perceives a loss, he will behave accordingly; his behavior will probably appear unstable.

From the above discussion it would appear that man is driven solely to achieve behavioral stability and homeostatic equilibrium. This is an erroneous assumption that has its origin in the "pleasure principle," which states that the primary goal of the organism is to get rid of tensions and drives and to achieve a state of equilibrium (nirvana). On the contrary, neurotic and psychotic behaviors, according to Freud, are man's efforts to restore equilibrium. Bertalanffy (1968) has since argued that the "equilibrium principle" misses the point that psychological and behavioral activities are more than a relaxation of tensions; far from establishing an optimal state, too much relaxation of tensions could be responsible for psychosislike disturbances. Sensory deprivation experiments have demonstrated that a flow of environmental stimulation is necessary for the maintenance of inner stability (Allport, 1968). Experimental subjects who were deprived of such stimulation over a period of time complained of severe discomfort, frequent episodes of hallucinations, and generally appeared agitated, irritable, and restless (Heron, 1961). In other words, not only stresses and tensions but also complete release from stimuli and the consequent mental void may cause homeostatic disequilibrium and/or behavioral instability.

Gordon Allport's "functional autonomy" (Hall and Lindzey, 1957) and Maslow's (1959) "self-realization," and White's (1959) "competence motive" all speak to the same point. The spontaneous activity of the bio-psycho-socio organism forces man to go beyond homeostasis or the steady state, to strive for an enhancement and elaboration of internal order at the cost of considerable disequilibrium and/or instability (Allport, 1968). As Cannon (1968) implied many years ago, some instability at stated intervals may be necessary for the stability of the organism. Thus, instability is sometimes sought after purely for the pleasure, thrill, and excitement it affords the individual.

Between the states of stability and instability there is a state, at least conceptually, that is neither stable nor instable called precarious stability. When the individual experiences a potential threat, such as the deprivation of one or more of his basic needs or the loss of some valued thing, he will appear precariously stable. He will mobilize his energies in an effort to thwart realization of such threats and thereby avert an imbalance. The tension increase associated with precarious instability is experienced chiefly as anxiety, the signal that alerts the organism and sets in motion the coping devices to deal with the situation and avert an imbalance. The individual appears somewhat nervous and uneasy. Outside intervention may be necessary to avert an upset in the steady state.

To summarize, behavioral instability may occur when an individual fails to maintain and/or establish congruency among the three components of his interpersonal matrix, when he perceives that an event he is about to experience is hazardous, and/or when he seeks high levels of stimulation (thrill) temporarily for its own sake. Because prolonged instability is incompatible with life the individual will make every effort to restore congruency among the components of the matrix and to remove the threat of a perceived hazardous event by any available means.

HEALTHY VERSUS UNHEALTHY COPING DEVICES

Up to now only brief reference has been made to the social acceptability or unacceptability of the mechanisms or means used to restore behavioral stability. We have refrained from imposing any value judgment on the action taken. The most important thing for the individual, we have said, is the restoration of stability regardless of the techniques used to achieve this goal, for prolonged instability is incompatible with life.

However, concern about the long-term as well as the short-term effects on the individual forces the nurse to evaluate the mechanisms employed in the light of future adjustment. Is the mechanism used to restore stability a temporary device, specific for the current crisis only, or will it help the individual deal with similar crises in the future? Does the coping device that the individual uses to help restore his stability better fit him to the conditions of his environment, resulting in a higher level of functioning, or does it result in a lower level of functioning and a lower level of mental health? The former describes *healthy* coping behavior and the latter *unhealthy* coping behavior. For example, the individual facing the loss of some valued body part may deal with it by denying the reality of the situation, engaging in magical thinking or in regressive behaviors. These are essentially unhealthy coping behaviors, which are used to deal with the present crisis and to avert an imbalance. They must eventually be replaced with healthy behaviors, compatible with the continuance and maintenance of life. Certain unhealthy behaviors may be supported temporarily in behalf of stability. Following the crisis they should be replaced by behaviors that help the individual deal with the changing demands of his environment. Coping devices that restore stability, both healthy and unhealthy, are adaptive. Coping devices that fail to restore stability are maladaptive.

An example of coping behaviors that are essentially unhealthy but adaptive is revealed in the study reported earlier by Bowlby (1960) and Robertson (1958) of the Tavistock Clinic in England. The study concerns the response of children two to two-and-one-half years of age who have been separated from their parents because of hospitalization. The authors conclude that there is a characteristic response of children ages two to two-and-one-half years to a perceived loss that is triphasic: the initial phase is described as protest, followed by a phase of despair, and, finally, a phase of denial (later described as detachment). During the phase of protest, the child maintains the hope that the mother will return and protests his condition vigorously and loudly with much crying and overt distress. In the phase of despair, there is increasing hopelessness. The predominant emotion is depression, described as part of the grief and mourning syndrome. There is increasingly withdrawn behavior and inactivity. The third stage is detachment, which Bowlby earlier called denial. It is a quiet period in which the young child seems to be making an "adaptation" to the perceived loss. He appears contented, whereas in reality his contentment is the result of resignation. In this phase, defenses are developed such as denial of the longing for the mother and detachment in relation to the nurturing adult. The child at best forms shallow attachments. He becomes increasingly self-centered and attached to material objects. He has restored his stability through the use of unhealthy coping devices. Assuming he is in the hospital for an illness, it may be said that he is experiencing stability in illness. Following the crisis, efforts must be directed towards helping the child develop healthy ways for dealing with the stress of separation.

Another example is the autistic child. He also utilizes unhealthy devices to restore his stability. Since he exhibits aberrations in thought and action that impair his capacity to perform at the level expected of him, he is defined as ill. By withdrawing into his own shell, he perceives his private world quite stable and orderly. As long as no one disturbs him, he experiences stability in illness. If restoring stability represents adaptation and failure to restore stability, maladaptation, then the child has adapted. As long as the devices employed impede future adjustments, they are assessed as unhealthy. Unhealthy devices serve the immediate need to restore stability, but eventually they become maladaptive as they impede further adjustments. The use of denial and withdrawal to maintain stability during a crisis become maladaptive in time. Like the rigid patterns held onto in old age, the continued misuse or overuse of mental mechanisms interferes with overall adjustment. The world does not stand still even for the autistic child. The human system must continually adjust in its efforts to better fit itself to the changing conditions of its environment.

SUMMARY.   In summary, man has been conceptualized as a complex adaptive system that tends toward a steady state. From the biological perspective he is viewed as a set of biological systems interacting to achieve homeostasis. Physiological homeostasis exists whenever there is an equalization of tension or a balance between the body's defenses and the stimuli that are continually bombarding the organism. Physiological homeostasis is possible during the experience of illness as well as during the experience of wellness. So long as the body's adaptive devices are able to restore a balance compatible with some survival state, physiological homeostasis is attained. This suggests the possibility of homeostatic levels lying outside the range normally associated with the experience of health-wellness. Such a balance may be considered physiological in the sense that it demonstrates the body's ability to resist and to defend itself. When the body fails to respond or overresponds, an imbalance results. Aberrations in body structure and function may represent successful defense (adaptation) or unsuccessful defense (maladaptation). In the former case, the process should be supported and regulated so that an imbalance does not occur. In the latter case, efforts must be directed towards stimulating and supporting the inadequate defenses and impeding or slowing down the overreactive ones so that a balance is restored. The primary responsibility for maintaining and restoring physiological homeostasis remains with medicine.

Nursing views man as a complex adaptive system comprised of behavioral subsystems that work together to achieve behavioral stability. The precise nature of these subsystems is under study. The assumption is that during a period of relative stability more energy is available for the recovery process. Thus, the goal of nursing care is the maintenance and restoration of behavioral stability.

Behavioral stability exists so long as the individual perceives order and predictability in himself and in his relations with his environment. Such a definition allows for periods of stability in illness as well as in wellness. So long as the individual does not perceive his illness as threatening or hazardous and/or perceives congruence among the three components of his interpersonal matrix, he will exhibit stable behaviors. Both healthy and unhealthy coping devices may be used to restore stability. Although nursing's primary goal is the maintenance and restoration of stability, with or without the use of unhealthy devices, another goal is to help the individual adjust to the world of reality. Thus, the nurse must also assist the individual to change to healthy behaviors that are compatible with adequate functioning in his society. Careful and continuous assessment must be made to determine the appropriate time to disturb the patient's stability in order to introduce him to more socially acceptable behaviors. The nurse may precipitate temporary instability in her efforts to move the patient towards more healthy behaviors; thus there is a need for an accurate diagnosis and proper timing of nursing intervention.

The maintenance of physiological homeostasis and behavioral stability during illness is the responsibility of all members of the health team. As the doctor works to achieve physiological homeostasis, the nurse supplements his efforts in her drive to maintain behavioral stability. It is hypothesized that the efforts of the doctor to restore and maintain physiological equilibrium can be made more difficult and sometimes futile if not supplemented by equal efforts to maintain psychosocial (behavioral) stability. Both efforts are necessary for ultimate recovery and survival. Efficiency of the curative process is enhanced when supplemented with stable behaviors. A loss of structure, not knowing what to expect, or a misunderstanding can upset the very "constancy" the medical profession is attempting to restore and maintain. Physiological homeostasis and behavioral stability in illness can be achieved only through the joint efforts of the entire health team.

A SYSTEMS MODEL FOR THE ANALYSIS OF PATIENT BEHAVIOR

A model designed by Howland and McDowell (1964) for the evaluation of patient care provides us with a basic framework from which a model for the analysis of patient behavior may be constructed. According to these authors, if homeostatic disequilibrium occurs, the hospital must provide the resources such as staff, equipment, and supplies to restore the balance. Patient care is viewed as a measure of the system's performance rather than as a component of the system. The level of patient care (or ability to restore homeostatic balance) that can be provided by a hospital depends on the state of the patient and the resources of the hospital.

Howland and Green (1958) identify the internal hospital system, i.e., the staff organization within a hospital, as one of three subsystems in the hospital suprasystem. The other two subsystems are the Community Medical Care System and the Community Hospital System.

Within the internal hospital system the authors have identified a basic subsystem that is responsible for maintaining patient states through direct patient care. This subsystem is the nurse-patient-physician TRIAD (Howland and McDowell, 1964). The patient is conceptualized as a process, generating signals to a monitor located in an information feedback loop. The paradigm attempts to specify tasks and missions that must be performed to achieve the goal of the system and to relate them to the resources necessary for their accomplishment. The goal of the hospital system is defined as the achievement of a general level of wellness [as per Dunn (1959)].

The nurse-patient-physician TRIAD is involved in three levels of monitoring. At the first level, patient "output" information is recorded by the monitor (nurse) and/or relayed to the comparator (M.D. or nurse). The comparator measures the difference between the actual and the desired patient states and transmits this difference to the regulator (M.D. or nurse) who makes the decision regarding the action needed to correct the error (difference). At the second level, the monitor assumes the comparator function and transmits the difference measured to the regulator. At the third level, the monitor serves as a comparator and regulator and takes the action needed to maintain the patient's condition within specified limits.

The variables of concern to the TRIAD may be physiological, psychological, sociological, and/or economic. The authors, Howland and McDowell, hypothesize that good patient care should be characterized by the ability of the hospital system to respond promptly and accurately to changes in patient conditions relative to any of these variables, while poor patient care would be the reverse. The crucial variables that must be regulated will depend upon the setting, whether in the operating room, recovery room, ward, or home.

The quality of patient care depends upon the kind of information the TRIAD obtains about actual and desired patient states. The nurse's action, guided by the physician's orders and her own professional judgment, is based on information she receives from the physician, from the patient's record, and from her personal observations and measurements of deviation (Chow, 1969). Thus, if a hospital is to respond quickly and appropriately to changes in patient conditions, the staff must be well informed about actual and desired patient states. Information about the patient with regard to all critical variables becomes a matter of primary concern. These authors predict that a high-information environment should lead to better patient care than a poorly informed environment. Knowledge about the mechanisms for maintaining homeostatic equilibriums and behavioral stability should contribute to improved patient care. Acting both as negative and positive feedback controls, the TRIAD can assist in the maintenance and restoration of a steady state.

The model, according to Howland and Green (1958), must state what functions or tasks are performed in the system and how its resources are utilized in performing these functions. If the goal of nursing care is behavioral stability and physiological homeostasis, the nurse should be able to manipulate the model to optimize this goal. Variables must be identified and relationships expressed. The utility of any model resides in its ability to predict the effect of changes in the independent variable on the system's performance. Howland and Green's model focuses on patient care. What is needed now is a model that (1) focuses on patient behavior, (2) predicts the effect of such variables as illness, treatment, and hospitalization upon patient behavior (dependent variable), and (3) can be manipulated to achieve a steady state while reducing the threat of subgoal optimization. This remains a challenge for nursing.

The remainder of this book is devoted to a discussion of the various behaviors that can be expected during the phases of health, illness, and disability. Chapter 7 on health behavior deals with the period when the experience of illness has not become a reality yet; it is only a possibility. Chapter 8 on illness behavior describes the time of life when the individual experiences peculiar sensations or observes changes in structure or function in himself, and Chapter 9 on sick role behavior deals with the period when the individual declares himself ill and is entitled to the rights and obligations accorded such a status. Finally, impaired role behavior as discussed in Chapter 10 includes a plea to remove this class of behaviors from under the rubric of illness. Instead of focusing on the disability, the plea is to emphasize the remaining potential and to capitalize on the positive features of the handicapped person so that he too is allowed and encouraged to work towards "peak wellness." The preceding material on the nature and perception of illness/wellness should serve as a basis from which it is hoped the reader will be better prepared to assess the behaviors accompanying these experiences.

REFERENCES

ALLPORT, GORDON W. "The Open System in Personality Theory," in *Modern Systems Research for the Behavioral Scientist*, Walter Buckley, ed. Chicago: Aldine Publishing Co., 1968, pp. 343–50.

ASHBY, W. ROSS "Principles of the Self-Organizing Systems," in *Modern Systems Research for the Behavioral Scientist*, Walter Buckley, ed. Chicago: Aldine Publishing Co., 1968, pp. 108–22.

BERTALANFFY, L. V. "General Systems Theory: A Critical Review," in *Modern Systems Research for the Behavioral Scientist*, Walter Buckley, ed. Chicago: Aldine Publishing Co., 1968, p. 25.

BEXTON, W. H., W. HERON, AND T. H. SCOTT "Effects of Decreased Variation in the Sensory Environment," *Canadian Journal of Psychology*, 8 (1954), 70–76.

BOWLBY, JOHN *Maternal Care and Mental Health*. Geneva: World Health Organization, 1952, pp. 1–194.

———— "Separation Anxiety," *International Journal of Psychoanalysis*, 41 (1960), 89–113.

BUCKLEY, WALTER *Sociology and Modern Systems Theory*. Englewood Cliffs, N.J.: Prentice-Hall, Inc., 1967, 227 pp.

———— "Society as a Complex Adaptive System," in *Modern Systems Research for the Behavioral Scientist*, Walter Buckley, ed. Chicago: Aldine Publishing Co., 1968, pp. 490–513.

CANNON, WALTER B. "Self-Regulation of the Body," in *Modern Systems Research for the Behavioral Scientist*, Walter Buckley, ed. Chicago: Aldine Publishing Co., 1968, pp. 256–58.

CHOW, RITA "Post-Operative Cardiac Nursing Research: A Method for Identifying and Categorizing Nursing Action," *Nursing Research*, 18 (Jan.–Feb., 1969), 4–13.

COBB, SIDNEY, G. W. BROOKS, S. V. KASL, AND W. E. CONNOLLY "The Health of People Changing Jobs: A Description of a Longitudinal Study," *American Journal of Public Health*, 56, No. 9 (Sept., 1966), 1477–81.

DUNN, HALBERT L. "High Level Wellness for Man and Society," *American Journal of Public Health*, 49, No. 6 (June, 1959), 786–92.

FREEMAN, VICTOR J. "Human Aspects of Health and Illness: Beyond the Germ Theory," *Journal of Health and Human Behavior*, 1 (1960), 8–13.

GERARD, R. W. "Units and Concepts of Biology," in *Modern Systems Research for the Behavioral Scientist*, Walter Buckley, ed. Chicago: Aldine Publishing Co., 1968, pp. 51–58.

HALL, A. D. AND R. E. FAGIN "Definition of System," in *Modern Systems Research for the Behavioral Scientist*, Walter Buckley, ed. Chicago: Aldine Publishing Co., 1968, pp. 81–92.

HALL, CALVIN S. AND GARDNER LINDZEY *Theories of Personality*. New York: John Wiley & Sons, Inc., 1957, pp. 269–73.

HERON, WOODBURN "Cognitive and Physiological Effects of Perceptual Isolation," in P. Solomon et al., eds., *Sensory Deprivation*. Cambridge, Mass.: Harvard University Press, 1961, pp. 6–33.

HOWLAND, D. AND ROBERT S. GREEN *The Development of a Methodology for the Evaluation of Patient Care*. Columbus: Ohio State University, 1958, 82 pp.

——— AND WANDA E. McDOWELL "The Measurement of Patient Care: A Conceptual Framework," *Nursing Research*, 13, No. 1 (Winter, 1964), 4–7.

JENSEN, JULIUS *Modern Concepts in Medicine*. St. Louis: C. V. Mosby Co., 1953, pp. 17–46.

KOEHLER, W. "Closed and Open Systems," in *Systems Thinking*, F. E. Emery, ed. Baltimore, Md.: Penguin Books, Ltd., 1969, pp. 59–69.

MASLOW, ABRAHAM H. *Motivation and Personality*. New York: Harper & Row, Publishers, 1954, 411 pp.

PRINGLE, J. W. S. "On the Parallel Between Learning and Evolution," in *Modern Systems Research for the Behavioral Scientist*, Walter Buckley, ed. Chicago: Aldine Publishing Co., 1968, pp. 259–80.

RAPOPORT, LYDIA "The State of Crisis: Some Theoretical Considerations," H. J. Parad, ed., *Crisis Intervention: Selected Readings*. New York: Family Service Association of America, 1965, p. 23.

ROBERTSON, JAMES *Young Children in Hospitals*. New York: Basic Books, Inc., 1958, 103 pp.

SECORD, PAUL F. AND CARL W. BACKMAN "Personality Theory and the Problem of Stability and Change in Individual Behavior," *Psychological Review*, 68, No. 1 (1961), 21–32.

SELYE, HANS *The Stress of Life*. New York: McGraw-Hill Book Company, 1956, 324 pp.

——— "The Stress of Life," *Nursing Forum*, 4, No. 1 (1965), 29.

VICKERS, GEOFFREY "Is Adaptability Enough?" in *Modern Systems Research for the Behavioral Scientist*, Walter Buckley, ed. Chicago: Aldine Publishing Co., 1968, pp. 460–73.

WEINER, NORBERT *Human Use of Human Beings*, 2nd ed. New York: Doubleday Anchor Books, 1954, p. 33.

WHITE, ROBERT "Motivation Reconsidered: The Concept of Competence." *Psychological Review*, Sept., 1959, 66 (No. 5) 297–333.

seven | *Health Behavior*

Earlier in this book it was stated that illness is experienced by people in all societies but that not all people in all societies experience illness. Differences in age, sex, race, and frequency of exposure to trauma or infection do not entirely account for this variability. For example, it has been found that people with similar ethnic and social backgrounds, living in the same general environment and sharing the same occupation over a period of time, vary in their likelihood of becoming ill.

Hinkle et al. (1958) suggest that there is a difference in general susceptibility to illness that appears early in life and can be said to be at least in part constitutional. Susceptibility to illness is measured in this report in terms of the number of episodes of illness experienced per unit of time. The authors suggest that the difference in susceptibility from person to person may arise from differences in the perception and evaluation of the environment, or from innate differences in reactivity, or both. In comparing the characteristics of persons who have experienced a large number of illness episodes with those who have been relatively healthy, the authors found that there appeared to be a relationship between frequency of illnesses and the manner in which life situations were perceived. Individuals who perceived their life experiences as more challenging, more demanding, and more conflict-laden experienced more disturbances of bodily processes and of mood, thought, and behavior. This was attributed to the need to cope with a greater number of perceived challenges.

Age is also an important variable in adaptability. Adaptive defenses are not well developed in the very young owing to lack of experience and maturity and are poorly implemented in the aged because of resistance to change and inflexibility.

Susceptibility to illness or frequency of illness episodes may also be influenced by the actions taken or not taken by an individual to avoid illness. Some persons make little or no effort, whereas others are extra cautious and highly protective in their efforts to avoid such an encounter. Any activity undertaken by an individual who believes himself to be well to avoid an encounter with illness shall be defined as *health behavior*. Included in this definition are activities that promote and maintain wellness, plus activities undertaken to detect aberrations in their subtle and covert states. Although the frequency of illness episodes is known to be influenced by genetic and environmental factors, it is also known that individuals may either voluntarily or involuntarily take action to minimize or prevent an encounter with illness.

DESCRIPTION OF HEALTH BEHAVIOR

Behaviors that are directed toward the maintenance and promotion of wellness range from regular hygienic practices and participation in well-balanced programs of rest, exercise, diet, and elimination to activities that are directed toward the attainment of self-actualization and "peak-wellness."

Activities undertaken to discover aberrations in their early asymptomatic states include physical, dental, and eye examinations, as well as participation in detection programs for PKU (phenylketonuria), cancer, diabetes, tuberculosis, and such diseases. These activities are based on the assumption that early detection will minimize the possibility of more serious consequences and sometimes, if appropriate action is taken, will prevent an actual encounter with illness.

Prenatal, postnatal, and well-baby visits to a doctor's office or clinic also come under the rubric of health behaviors. The purpose of these visits is not only to detect early aberrations but also to promote wellness in pregnancy, minimize occurrence of complications associated with pregnancy, and promote wellness in infancy and childhood.

Activities undertaken to minimize the possibility of an encounter with illness include participation in prevention programs such as immunizations, antiallergy treatments, fluoridation, and practicing techniques that protect one against certain communicable diseases or other environmental hazards. Wearing charms, observing taboos, taking vitamins, living "naturally" or in moderation, jogging, eliminating certain foods from one's diet, and performing rituals, magical and/or spiritual, are all examples of disease-preventing actions. Patent medicines are also used as preventive measures. A common example is the use of laxatives to "keep the bowels in good condition" or the taking of vitamins. Any of these activities may be initiated voluntarily or under pressure to fulfill specific requirements, for example, the health examination required of all students enrolled in certain universities or the schedule of immunizations needed to obtain a passport to a foreign country.

DETERMINANTS OF HEALTH BEHAVIOR

In the absence of forced compliance, what motivates a person to take health action? In discussing the determinants of health behavior, we will discuss first the factors that motivate a person to *decide* to take action and then the factors that determine in what *direction* the action will be taken. The following section is drawn chiefly from the work of Hochbaum (1960) and that of Rosenstock (1961 and 1969).

Decision to Take Action

Important determinants of all behavior are the individual's system of beliefs, values, needs, and motives. Subjective reality refers to how things appear to the individual, as opposed to objective reality that refers to how things really are. Objective reality is measured in terms of the three criteria of objectivity discussed earlier: observer detachment, denotability, and observer-agreement. Thus, objective health-needs correspond to the professional person's assessment of a client's state of health, whereas subjective health-needs are the individual's own perceptions of his health needs. A person's perception of his own health needs may agree completely with objective findings, it may agree only in part, or it may be totally incongruent with objective reality.

Behavior is determined by subjective reality. What the individual believes to be good or right for himself determines whether or not he will engage in a given activity. To the extent that one's beliefs about his health needs are congruent with objective reality, he will probably take the recommended action. As long as his beliefs are incongruent with objective reality, for example he does not believe himself susceptible to the threatened disease, he will probably not take the recommended action.

Rosenstock believes that an individual will not engage in health behavior unless he thinks that the action recommended is important for his present and future well-being. Furthermore, he states that motives to engage in health behaviors must compete against a host of other motives, any one of which may take precedence over other competing motives. Since motives tend to fall in an hierarchical order, when an opportunity arises to satisfy only one motive, the one that is most salient will be selected. After all, health-related motives comprise only a small portion of the vast array of human motives. Also the importance of health motives varies according to age, sex, occupation, education, cultural values, and disposition. For persons employed in occupations related to the health services, health may be a central motive in their lives. The average layman, however, may be much more concerned about finances, security, social status, and self-esteem, all of which constitute motives that take precedence and may in fact conflict with health motives. People who are deeply involved in their tasks or are worried about matters unrelated to health will be relatively insensitive to admonitions concerning certain dangers that threaten to alter their health status. In fact, individuals motivated to achieve at high levels have been known to purposely risk their lives or their health to attain these other goals. Thus, the less salient motives are postponed, unless a crisis of some sort occurs to alter the situation, such as a threat to one's existence or way of life.

If motivation is the drive or force that moves a person to take action in a certain direction, then the individual must be helped to believe that the recommended health action is as important to him as some of his most salient moves. The health motive will gain in importance to the degree that the individual perceives himself susceptible to the condition the health action is said to protect him against and to the degree that he perceives serious consequences for himself should he fail to engage in the recommended acts. The individual may be intellectually aware of his susceptibility to a serious disease and yet refuse to believe or accept the facts. It is what the individual perceives, based on his beliefs, that determines the kind of actions taken.

Individuals vary widely in their beliefs about personal susceptibility to a given illness. At one extreme are the individuals who deny any probability of contracting the illness. These individuals can accept the fact of susceptibility for all people except they themselves. They believe that everybody except themselves will contract the disease if they do not follow the recommended action. They believe they are endowed with a certain immunity that does not carry over to the population at large. In a more moderate position are persons who admit to a statistical probability; i.e., there is only a remote possibility that the event will happen to them. At the other end of the spectrum are persons who believe they are highly susceptible and will very likely contract the disease, and there are others who are fully convinced that they have already contracted the condition. Fear is suspected as a chief emotion responsible for this distorted view. Although we do not know how real the threat of contracting the disease must be to motivate action, we do know that those who perceive themselves highly susceptible feel more threatened than those who believe themselves less susceptible or immune to the condition.

Individuals also vary in their interpretation of the consequences for themselves or for others if recommended action is not taken. Frequently it appears that the individual judges the consequences in terms of the difficulties he believes contracting a given condition will create for himself, but he also may view the threat of illness in terms of the medical, economic, or social consequences it will have for others. For example, if he believes that detecting a given condition will create severe psychological and economic hardship for his family, he is unlikely to take action that might uncover such a condition. On the other hand, if he believes that taking precautionary measures now will prevent his contracting a disease associated with fatal consequences later on, he is more likely to take preventative action. In addition he will probably take action if he believes that detecting a given condition in its early asymptomatic state will result in a cure and that lack of such action could mean a prolonged and perhaps incurable illness. However, it is important to understand that individuals measure the consequences of action or inaction not only in terms of the medical condition and benefits of early diagnosis, but also and more importantly in many cases, in terms of the consequences for economic status, social status, and other statuses.

Perceived susceptibility and perceived consequences, if action is not taken, define the degree of threat experienced by the person. Thus, published reports of the serious danger and threat of lung cancer for those who continue to smoke will have no effect on promoting health behavior (i.e., discontinuance of smoking) as long as individuals perceive themselves to be nonsusceptible to the danger and refuse to believe that serious consequences to their health will ensue if recommended action is not taken. Individuals will not engage in health actions unless they believe that the condition they are asked to protect themselves against is a real threat to their own well-being and way of life.

From the above discussion one might conclude that the more susceptible an individual believes himself to be to a given condition and the more serious he believes the disease is for himself, the more likely he will be to take the recommended action. However, this is not necessarily true. It is true that when the individual sees no threat whatsoever, his tendency to act will be zero; and that as intensity increases moderately, the tendency to act increases accordingly. But, as the intensity of the threat increases still further, severe anxiety may be aroused, which can interfere with adaptive action. When fear arousal is used to stimulate preventive health action, the anxiety created may be more disturbing and painful than the thing that aroused it in the first place. Behavior becomes disorganized as anxiety mounts. The individual consequently is forced to deal with his anxieties rather than taking action to prevent the disease.

The defensive denial hypothesis explains in part the resistance to persuasion that occurs under conditions of fear arousal. It states that fear leads to defensive avoidance; that is, fear and anxiety motivate individuals to make responses to decrease the tensions created. A typical response of this type is to deny or to minimize the likelihood or severity of the threat.

Leventhal and Kafes (1963) suggest that fear not only inhibits constructive action but it also facilitates constructive action. If techniques can be found for eliminating the denial when fear is aroused, fear can facilitate adoption of recommended health action. They suggest that if anxiety is aroused and a means is provided to eliminate that which caused the anxiety, such as the availability of a chest x ray immediately after viewing a film on lung cancer, the individual is likely to take constructive action as defensive denial will not have had time to develop. If no action is available to protect against the thing that aroused the anxiety, results may be contrary to the intended ones. A case in point is the widespread fear of cancer. As long as people believe that nothing can be done to protect themselves against the disease, they are put into a position where they have to suffer intense fear without being able to do anything about it. When fear is sufficiently intense, the individual will develop psychological means to diminish the threat. He will avoid any communication that is likely to maintain or further increase the fear.

Persons afraid of cancer tend to avoid reading any health educational material about cancer. When the means to protect oneself against the dreaded disease is made readily available, constructive action usually follows.

Some authors report an inverse relationship between the level of threatening material used and a positive attitude change toward the recommended behavior, and others found that there was a direct relationship: the more threatening the message, the greater was the tendency to accept the recommendation. Radelfinger (1965) suggests that the different types of actions recommended may be responsible for the response discrepancy. In other words, when threat is aroused, the resistance or acceptance of preventive behavior may depend on the characteristics of the action that is recommended. Failure to follow recommended action in response to a highly fear-arousing appeal may be due to the fact that no provision has been made for taking immediate action. Thus the listener is forced to tolerate over a relatively long period of time the tension induced by the communication. Other causes for failing to take preventative measures may be due to the fact that the recommended actions are too complex or involve too much effort. In other words, it is not possible presently to draw generalizations as to the degree of threat necessary to motivate health behavior. Positive action depends not only on the health behavior recommended in the message but also on the listener and his perceptual frame of reference as well as the affective aspects or emotional tone of the message.

The question that remains unanswered is the degree of threat necessary to motivate health action without evoking psychological defenses that could interfere with these actions. Rosenstock suggests that moderately intense threat is most effective. But then, what distinguishes moderately intense from highly intense fear?

Janis and Feshback (1953) report the results of a study involving 200 high-school students and their responses to a lecture illustrating the dangers of inadequate dental care. The purpose of the lecture was to get the students to accept more adequate oral hygiene practices. Three different programs were presented, varying in the degree to which they provoked fear: low, medium, or high. The strong appeal used lecture and illustrations to emphasize the threat of pain, disease, and body damage. The moderate appeal described the same dangers in a "milder" and more factual manner. The minimal appeal made very little reference to the unpleasant consequences of improper dental hygiene. The investigators assumed that the threat of body injury would elicit a high degree of fear behavior and conversely that the absence of such threat would elicit minimum fear behavior. The subjects were divided into four groups: a control and three experimental groups. Each of the experimental groups was exposed to one of the programs. The results indicated clearly that subjects who were exposed to the least fearful program were most apt to accept the dental practices recommended and were least likely to believe proposals antithetical to that depicted in the program. There was some evidence that as the amount of fear-arousing material was increased, conformity to recommended practices decreased.

In another study, Leventhal and Kafes attempted to induce three levels of anxiety, low, medium, and high fear, through the use of a color-sound movie and a pamphlet on lung cancer. The preventive health action recommended was to stop smoking and to have a chest x ray. Free diagnostic aides were made available at the site. The pamphlet showed statistics linking smoking to lung cancer. The film was a highly emotional portrayal of the pain and mutilation of lung cancer, and it linked the disease with smoking. High fear-arousal was obtained by showing a complete operation for the removal of a carcinomatous lung. Medium fear was obtained by stopping the movie prior to the operation sequence. In the low fear group the movie was not shown. The pamphlet was distributed to all three groups. Both high and medium fear-arousal groups expressed more conviction than the low fear-arousal group that smoking caused lung cancer. There was a tendency, although not significant, for a direct relationship between the degree of fear aroused and conformity to recommendations; that is, the desire to have an x ray increased with the threateningness of the film. Unlike the Janis and Feshback study, the fear-arousing film did not arouse disbelief or skepticism in the audience. The authors also found that there was a significant difference between the levels of anxiety in the three groups.

It appears that fear appeal up to a point can motivate individuals to take recommended action. The problem is to define in operational terms the optimal level of fear and the recommended actions that will minimize defensive avoidance in a given group of individuals.

Determinants of the
Direction of Action Taken

Having made the decision to follow the recommended action does not necessarily guarantee that action will follow, nor does it guarantee that the action that is taken is the recommended one.

Depending upon the time interval allowed to elapse between decision and action, a variety of possibilities can occur.

As long as the conditions are the same as when the decision to take action was made, the recommended act will usually be carried out. However, if there is an interval between the time the decision is made and the time the individual can take action, conditions may change so that the individual is confronted with a new and more urgent problem. As a result of this change, he may lose interest in the earlier problem and vest his energy in dealing with the new and more pressing situation that now confronts him.

Thus, when there is a lapse of time between decision and action, the motivation to act tends to lose momentum. The longer the individual remains "safe" in the absence of action, the less he will believe that action is necessary. As stated earlier, health behavior is more likely to occur when the recommended action is readily available for quick and immediate implementation.

The direction that the action takes will also depend on the individual's beliefs about the relative effectiveness of the recommended action. Will the act reduce the degree of threat to which he feels subjected? His beliefs about the relative effectiveness of action may or may not be congruent with objective reality. For example, although there is evidence to support the fact that a given vaccine protects against contracting a certain disease, the individual may believe that the vaccine does not offer the protection it purports to give. His choice of action will depend on how well he thinks the various possibilities open to him will reduce his susceptibility to the illness. Will the vaccine really protect him from contracting the disease; or how well will it decrease the seriousness of the illness should he contract it? Again, will early detection, and therefore early treatment, really decrease the seriousness of the illness?

Not only does the perceived effectiveness of the action play an important role in whether there is follow-through, but also the convenience, attractiveness, pleasure, and effort required are determinants of action. If the action recommended is expensive, inconvenient, unpleasant, painful, or upsetting, these factors are likely to act as barriers to action. So long as the threat of contracting the disease is greater than the barriers the individual perceives, action is likely to follow, and vice versa.

When both the threat of the disease and the barriers or negative aspects associated with the recommended action are equally high, conflict occurs that is difficult to resolve. The individual will either seek alternative actions that are more acceptable to him, or if no alternative actions are available, he will resort to the use of unhealthy devices to resolve the conflict and avoid instability. For example, he may avoid the situation psychologically through displacement by engaging in activities symbolically related to the threat. He may participate in a cancer detection program advising others of the threat but be unable to "face the music" himself. If the individual cannot resolve the conflict, he will begin to lose control and become highly instable. His fears and anxieties mount. He is unable to think constructively or to behave rationally about the problem. The intensity of the threat and the fear of consequences, if action is taken, combine to immobilize the person. Like walking a tightrope, the problem of motivating persons to engage in health behavior by predicting dire consequences in the absence of such action is a delicate one. Too much fear-arousing communication can immobilize the person, creating more serious problems than the threat itself.

Thus, in order for action to take place, once a decision has been made, the individual must believe that the means to reduce the intensity of the threat are available and effective, and he must be aware of how to use these means and be able to resolve any conflict arising out of the situation such as inconvenience, cost, and discomfort. The probability of taking action is less if the recommended action cannot be acted upon quickly, if it is too complex, or if it involves considerable individual effort. If the individual must seek a qualified person, look up his office phone number, call for an appointment, cancel other conflicting engagements, and so on, all this may be viewed as too much "trouble," and therefore no action is taken.

CUES TO ACTION

In the absence of symptoms, what triggers a person to take action? What motivates a person to voluntarily participate in health promoting programs? Health behavior is said to be evoked more readily when a cue or stimulus is presented to trigger the action. The cues may be informal discussions with others, knowledge that someone they know has contracted the disease, or information obtained from the mass media, for example, the billboards, radio, and television. Knowing that behavior is a product of one's beliefs, values, and needs, persons with little interest in health matters will probably require intense stimuli to trigger action, whereas persons highly motivated towards the maintenance and promotion of health will require minimum stimuli to trigger action.

Mass appeals to the unmotivated group are usually ineffective. The appeal must be more direct and individualized. Studies have found that messages that stress personal and social consequences of health damage are more effective than those that stress bodily damage. For example, in a study on smoking behavior conducted by Swinehart (1960), he found that the reasons why smokers who knew they were more susceptible than nonsmokers to various diseases continued to smoke were because (1) the risk is not a certainty, and (2) the predicted disease, since it has not been experienced, lacks sufficient reality to have much impact on present behavior. Swinehart thus suggests that health educators should shift their focus from pathology (which has never been experienced) to things the individual has done and enjoyed and will be unable to do if the recommended action is not undertaken.

Swinehart also suggests that messages that are repeated too often can produce hostility toward the communicator, greater rigidity in attitudes, and forgetting or distortion of previously received information. In other words, there is an optimal number of times a message should be repeated beyond which limit it becomes ineffective. This is especially relevant in situations where individuals are trying to follow recommended action but encounter a great deal of difficulty. Further exhortations to those who have already made a decision, for example, to stop smoking, tend to undermine rather than to sustain the motivation that led to the decision.

Rosenstock's model of health behavior emphasizes the problem of motivation in stimulating persons to take advantage of health knowledge and facilities. The important factors are those that relate to the person and his situation. The readiness of the person to take action depends upon his own perception of his susceptibility and the seriousness of the threat, plus the convenience of the recommended action and the amount of effort required on his part.

Suchman (1967) suggests that there is another important factor that must be reckoned with to understand what motivates health behavior. He states that the health promoter must understand the social influences in the group and the social role definitions of the individual. He believes that this is an exceedingly powerful determinant of behavior, especially in today's society that is dominated by alienation or lack of psychic involvement and by feelings of powerlessness, all of which is associated with the social isolation of the individual and family unit. The roles, statuses, and organizational membership of individuals, e.g., those of family, club, and school, as well as the values, beliefs, and attitudes of one's social group, determine whether or not the individual will participate in community health action programs. Individuals have a great need to be accepted in their social group. Pressures within the group tend to enforce conformity. A group image is developed with expectations of its members of what entitles one to membership. If an action is acceptable by the group, the individual is more likely to follow the recommendation. This action must be consonant with customary behavioral patterns accepted by the group.

Clausen (1954) reports that the role definition of mothers participating in a study he conducted was a significant determinant in whether or not their child was permitted to participate in polio vaccine trials. Low-income family mothers, according to his report, took their children to be vaccinated, although ignorant about the disease, because they believed this was what was expected of good mothers.

Gray et al. (1966) conducted a study on the effects of social class and friends' expectations on oral polio vaccine participation. They reported that the reason why lower social class persons tend to have lower immunization rates is because there are proportionately more people in the upper and middle social classes who believe their friends expect them to be immunized than there are in the lower socioeconomic class. Perceived expectations served to motivate the upper- and middle-class groups to participate in the polio vaccine programs.

Morris et al. (1966) hypothesized in their study that "feelings of powerlessness or social isolation (alienation) might affect the amount of preventive health care a mother would seek for her infant." They found that in the medically indigent group feelings of powerlessness and social isolation were more prevalent than in higher socioeconomic groups and that these feelings adversely affected care-seeking behaviors.

Suchman has proposed a model of preventive health action that incorporates not only the factors of psychological readiness but also the need for social approval and the characteristics of the innovation or recommended health action itself. His model is an adaptation of the epidemiological model of host, agent, and environment. The model proposes that individuals and groups be assessed according to the following three factors: personal readiness factors (tendencies of the host), social control factors (influences of the environment), and situational or agent factors (attributes of the agent).

A. Personal Readiness Factors (Tendencies of the Host).
   1. Recognition of seriousness of the problem. The individual must be aware of the problem being attacked by the desired measure and believe that it is an important one.
   2. Acceptance of personal vulnerability. The individual must

be favorably disposed toward the desired action or change. His attitudinal set must be positive.

3. Predisposition to take action. The individual must be favorably disposed toward the desired action or change. His attitudinal set must be positive.

4. Motivation to act. The desired action must offer the promise of need satisfaction or reward, i.e., reduction of sense of personal vulnerability.

5. Ability to act. The individual must be in a position to take the desired action, physically and psychologically.

6. Knowledge of desired action. The individual must know how to act. He must be aware of and know the desired measure or what he is expected to do.

7. Belief in desired action. The individual must be convinced that the action or measure offers an effective solution to the problem, or at least one worth trying.

B. Social Control Factors (Influence of the Environment)

1. Social pressure to act. The individual must feel that his social group approves of the desired action and are, in fact, acting themselves.

2. Incorporation into role performance. The individual must define the desired act as expected and appropriate for fulfilling his role obligations.

3. Acceptability of the action. The act must be consonant with the existing values and customary behavior patterns of the individual and his group.

C. Situational or Action Factors (Attributes of the Agent).

1. Effectiveness of the action. The action or measure must produce the desired effect or the promised solution.

2. Pleasure of the action. The action must offer more pleasure than pain. It cannot create too much discomfort or interference with what the individual likes to do.

3. Effort of the action. The action or measure must be convenient and accessible without too much effort. It must fit into the individual's regular routine as much as possible.

4. Previous experience. The individual must have had positive previous experiences with the desired action or measure, or at least not negative ones.

5. Favorable environment. The action or measure must be presented in an environment or situation favorable to its completion or use.

6. Attractiveness. The action or measure taken must be offered in an attractive "package" or image.

The more the host, agent, and environmental factors listed above succeed in meeting conditions described, the greater will be the acceptability of the desired action or measure. [Suchman, 1967, pp. 207–8.]

SUMMARY. Thus, a person will decide to engage in health behavior when he believes such action is important to his well-being, when he believes himself susceptible to the conditions he is advised to take precautionary measures against, and when he perceives that failure to follow the recommended actions could result in dire consequences to himself and/or his family. His beliefs about the susceptibility and seriousness of the health problem under consideration will derive from and reflect the beliefs of his primary group orientation. Convenience, comfort, and effort required will determine whether the recommended action is followed.

Several studies provide support for the notion that belief in susceptibility to a disease and belief in the benefits of early detection are instrumental in determining whether the individual engages in health behavior (Leventhal et al., 1960; Kegeles, 1963; Hochbaum, 1958). The difficulty of any study is determining whether the stated beliefs preceded and therefore determined the actions taken, or whether a belief was stated so that it would be congruent with the individual's behavior. In other words, individuals may modify their perceptions after deciding to accept or reject a health service in order to bring their cognitions or beliefs in line with their behaviors. In spite of this problem there is sufficient data to suggest that prior beliefs are instrumental in determining subsequent action. To date only one study failed to support the above findings, and this study differed from all of the others in that no effort had been made to inform the public about the available services (Rosenstock, 1966). In addition, the absence of clear-cut cues to stimulate action as well as unequal opportunities to act could have accounted for the failure to replicate earlier studies.

DEMOGRAPHIC VARIABLES

Health behavior, like all of the other behaviors that follow, will be influenced by demographic and background variables. For example, in a comprehensive review of the literature by Kasl and Cobb (1966), persons in the upper socioeconomic group, young adults, and the more highly educated were found to participate most often in health promotion, illness prevention, and detection programs. Taking preventive action based on beliefs about susceptibility and benefits was found to be most prevalent among the high-income group, females, whites, the better educated, and the relatively young (Rosenstock, 1969). However, within every demographic (SES class) grouping those who held a belief in benefits were more likely to engage in preventive action than those not holding such a belief. Haefner (1967) found that a sizable number of people who could have taken preventive action did not do so and that this pattern tended to remain consistent across time for a variety of possible actions such as check-ups, chest x rays, and dental phophylactic measures.

In most of the studies reviewed, whenever income was controlled, education became an important variable. The less educated group appeared to be fearful and apprehensive of scientific advances. Rosenstock (1969), however, states that even when educational attainment is controlled, there is a positive correlation between income and the possession of correct information about health and science. He attributes this to the different values held by the different social classes. For example, he states that the lower socioeconomic class accords greater priority to immediate rewards than to the achievement of long-range goals. Their situation requires a choice between the necessities of today versus the contingencies of tomorrow. Expenditures of money or time to ward off disease or check on symptoms that are not disabling is a luxury that cannot take precedence over providing food, clothing, and shelter. Thus, income accounted for a larger proportion of variation in taking a Papanicolaou test than education (Kegeles, 1965).

Attitudes are important variables that must be considered in an analysis of health behavior. Persons who undergo periodic medical examinations believe that modern medicine can effect a cure and that the earlier the disease is detected the better the prognosis. In contrast to this is what Rosenstock (1969) calls the "culture of poverty." He recognizes that financial costs may serve as a barrier to obtaining health services, and states that for this low-income group the cultural dimensions associated with poverty are the controlling factors, including such attitudes as the tendency towards immediate gratification, the reluctance to use professional referral systems, the different values placed on knowledge and health, and the general feeling of powerlessness in what the poor perceive as a hostile environment. These are some of the problems that must be attacked if we are to alter the health behaviors of this low-income group.

To summarize, factors that influence health behavior, such as age, sex, race, religion, social class, and culture, are not well understood to date. Most of the reported findings are contradictory and inconclusive. Further studies are needed to identify the determinants and to develop intervention strategies that will elicit the desired behaviors.

SOME THEORETICAL EXPLANATIONS OF HEALTH BEHAVIOR

Why does one person in the absence of symptoms take health action, whereas another receiving the same cues refuse to take the recommended action? Are there any theories of human behavior that will help explain the behaviors observed? Are there some rules or laws governing behavior that can serve as a basis from which to predict the probable occurrence or nonoccurrence of health behavior? Theories of perception, learning, personality, and motivation all attempt to explain human behavior. Any of these theories are capable of providing some explanation for the health behaviors described. For example, theories on perception state that what the individual perceives is more important in determining his behavior than what the expert observer perceives. This accounts for the incongruence between subjective and objective reality. What the individual "knows" about his condition may be quite different from what the expert knows; but unless the expert understands the important role that beliefs, values, and needs play in behavior, he will be ineffective in evoking desirable health behaviors.

How does one explain the behaviors of persons who have been informed about the possibilities of their contracting a given disease and yet fail to take any action to protect themselves against an encounter? How does one explain the incongruence between what an individual knows or recognizes as reality and what he does? Leon Festinger (1957) offers a "Theory of Cognitive Dissonance" that may help explain some of this behavior.

Cognition, according to Festinger, is anything a person knows about himself, his behavior, and his environment. Such things include his opinions, beliefs, values, and attitudes, garnered from what others think, what others have told him, and what he has experienced himself. Dissonance occurs when the cognitive elements, that is, what he knows about himself, his behavior, and his environment, fail to fit together or are inconsistent. To experience dissonance, the two cognitive elements in dissonance must be related. For example, a doctor tells Mr. X. that he is sick and must be hospitalized. Mr. X. says he does not feel sick. These two facts are related. The individual's feelings deviate from what is expected as reality. Knowledge that he is ill will exert pressure so that the appropriate cognitive elements are brought into correspondence with reality; in this case Mr. X. begins to "feel" sick. On the other hand, trying to get Mr. Y. to stop smoking by telling him that safety belts can save lives will not create the desired dissonance since the two are quite unrelated.

Dissonance between related cognitive elements is experienced as unpleasant and uncomfortable. Festinger hypothesizes that the human organism tries to establish internal harmony, consistency, or congruity among his opinions, attitudes, knowledge, and values. The existence of dissonance being psychologically uncomfortable will motivate the person to try to reduce the dissonance and achieve consonance. This drive toward consonance among cognitions agrees with the overall drive of the organism for stability. When an individual knows that smoking is harmful, he must believe that this is true and take appropriate action or expect to experience cognitive dissonance. When an individual knows that detection of disease in its subtle and covert stage is beneficial in alerting oneself to early treatment and cure, he must believe that this is so and behave accordingly if he is to experience cognitive consonance. An individual behaves according to his beliefs and not necessarily according to what he knows; thus the urgency to bring into consonance what he knows and what he believes. Knowledge is assumed to be objective and in accordance with reality, whereas beliefs are subjective and may be incongruent with reality.

There are many situations that can elicit dissonance in an individual. Forced or accidental exposure to new information such as health recommendations may introduce ideas that are dissonant with the person's existing cognition. For example, if the individual believes that adults are immune to polio, exposure to information suggesting that polio strikes all ages may create dissonance. Open expression of disagreement in a group can create dissonance in the members of the group, particularly if these members identify with the person voicing the disagreement. Whenever an individual is faced with two alternatives for action, his susceptibility to dissonance increases. For example, he may be faced with the alternatives of smoking or not smoking. If he chooses to smoke, knowing that smoking is dangerous to his health and that if he stopped smoking he would feel a lot better, he will experience dissonance. If he stopped smoking, believing that his health will improve and that continued smoking can cause chronic lung disease, he experiences consonance. Belief in the negative elements of the chosen act creates dissonance, whereas belief in the positive elements creates consonance.

Offering rewards or threatening punishment to get an individual to take health action, when inconsistent with his private opinion, can also cause dissonance. If the individual follows the recommended action, knowledge of his behavior will be dissonant with his private opinion but consonant with the reward. If he fails to take the recommended action, knowledge of his behavior will be consonant with his private opinion but dissonant with the reward. Thus, although the individual may not believe that typhoid injections are really necessary to protect him during a trip to a foreign country, the trip itself may be sufficient reward to reduce the dissonance between his beliefs about the value or necessity of the injection and his compliance. If he fails to comply, the dissonance created will increase in magnitude according to the importance of the reward. If the trip overseas is not really important to him, it will not overcome the dissonance between the need for the vaccination and his beliefs that it is an unnecessary requirement.

Festinger further hypothesizes that the need to reduce the dissonance depends upon the magnitude of the existing dissonance or the degree of incongruity. In other words, the presence of dissonance does not necessarily elicit behaviors to reduce it. An important variable is the importance of the opinion being attacked. If the opinion is not very important, the disagreement introduced will create only mild dissonance. For example, an individual may not believe that fluoridating the city water supply will reduce the incidence of dental decay. However, when it comes to referendum, he may not bother to vote one way or the other because the outcome is really not that important to him. However, when the recommended health action is diametrically opposed to what he believes, the magnitude of dissonance increases. For instance, telling a person who believes that smoking is related to the incidence of lung cancer or that any smoking increases the probability of disease creates greater dissonance than a statement suggesting that disease is probable if he smokes more than one package per day. The latter is less opposed to his original belief than the former.

If one knows the magnitude of dissonance that pressures an individual to take action to reduce the dissonance, one could predict under given situations of dissonance that certain behaviors will follow. For example, one could predict with a fair amount of certainty that if a certain person's opinion is very important to an individual or very different from the opinions of the experts, that individual will experience sufficiently severe dissonance to cause him to take action to reduce the dissonance. Conversely, when the personal opinion being attacked is of little or no import to the individual, or when it differs little from the opinion offered by the experts, the individual will exert little or no effort to eliminate the dissonance.

An individual who feels pressured to reduce dissonance, especially incongruence between what he knows and believes and what he hears or is told, will do one of several things:

1. He will believe that the differences between what he knows and hears are not as great as they seem to be.
2. He will seek information or agreement from others to support what he already believes.
3. He will avoid situations that are likely to disagree with what he believes and thus increase the existence of dissonance.
4. He may change his own opinion and behaviors to agree with that being presented.

For example, a cigarette smoker has decided to give up smoking. He will seek out information to support this decision and avoid sources that encourage continuance of the habit. He will selectively seek out information to support the notion that smoking is bad, an offensive and costly habit, capable of causing serious damage to the lungs. Another cigarette smoker who decides to continue smoking in spite of warnings of dire consequences will selectively seek information that counters these warnings and avoid sources of information that suggest it is harmful. He will agree with fellow smokers that the linkage of cigarette smoking with lung disease has not been proven and will believe that its psychological value offsets any known detriments. If he cannot deny that smoking affects one's health in light of all the evidence bombarding him on all sides, he may reduce dissonance by believing that it will affect others but not himself.

Another way of reducing dissonance is to raise the level at which smoking is considered dangerous. In other words, if the experts say one package a day is dangerous, the smoker will say two packages per day is dangerous and so will continue to smoke. If he cannot avoid information suggesting the harmful effect of smoking, he may have to change his behavior, that is, stop smoking to reduce the dissonance. Misinterpretation or misperception of information can sometimes be attributed to the individual's need to reduce dissonance by distorting the message so that it is consonant with his opinions. The reduction of dissonance is a function of the personality and the susceptibility of the situation to reality testing. Once the dissonance has been reduced or eliminated, the question then becomes, For how long? Of course there is no guarantee that the person will be able to eliminate or reduce the dissonance. He may not be able to find the information or social support needed to change his cognition. If attempts to reduce or eliminate dissonance fail, the individual will show overt signs of discomfort, displeasure, and instable behaviors.

Berlyne's "Theory of Arousal" (1960) may help explain the contradictory reports concerning the effect of fear-arousing communication on health behavior. Arousal, according to Berlyne, is "associated with restlessness, heightened reactivity of the skeletal-musculature, and general agitation." So-called emotional states are, according to Berlyne, states of high arousal. The intensity of the stimulus is an important determinant of arousal. For example, Berlyne suggests that a rewarding condition can be sufficiently intense to provoke high arousal and thus can be experienced as distressing. Rewarding conditions that elicit high emotional tension can be as distressful as unpleasant, painful conditions.

Other important determinants of arousal include the degree of novelty, surprise, incongruity, complexity, and uncertainty associated with the stimulus. High arousal caused by curiosity is relieved through recognition. Uncertainty and conceptual conflict, like monetary rewards and social approval, are motivators of behavior. Even when uncertainty concerns something relatively minor, pressures to eliminate the uncertainty can be irresistible. One of the major sources of suffering in prison, reports Berlyne, is the uncertainty of how much time the prisoner will have to serve. Those prisoners who have hopes of a parole suffer much more than those who know they will never be released. Uncertainty increases as the range of alternative possibilities increases. Maximum uncertainty occurs when an event has a 50–50 chance of materializing or not materializing. The uncertainty of the consequences if the recommended health action is not followed causes an increase in the level of arousal, which may account for the ineffectiveness of the communication. Efforts are directed toward reducing the displeasure elicited by the uncertainty in the communication rather than attending to the recommendations.

Maximal vigilance coincides with *moderate* arousal. In other words, the relationship between level of arousal and some measure of efficiency is in the form of an inverted U. (See Figure 8.) In states of either extreme excitement or somnolence, the individual is un-

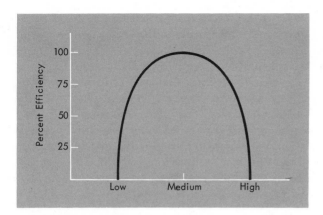

Figure 8
Level of Arousal

able to respond maximally to subtle differences between stimuli. Fear can be measured along the same dimensions as arousal, that is, low, medium, and high fear-arousal. Thus, according to Berlyne's postulates about arousal, a moderate degree of fear, equivalent to moderate arousal, should facilitate preventive health behavior; and a high degree of fear, equivalent to high arousal, should inhibit such action.

Strong fear-arousal or anxiety-laden appeals, according to Janis and Feshback (1953), generally result in three forms of resistance: inattentiveness during the communication session, rejection of the communicator's statements, and subsequent defense avoidance. The dominant tendency in most persons is to deny the probability of encountering danger. They attempt to bolster their sense of personal invulnerability by developing blanket immunity expectations and thus ward off the fear aroused by the communication.

A moderate level of fear, equivalent to moderate arousal, according to Janis (1958), generally produces a marked increase in conformity behavior, whereas the arousal of a high level of fear generally has a disruptive effect and gives rise to a decrease in conformity behavior. The amount of fear-arousing material plays an important role in determining the incidence of repudiation and hyperdefensiveness among normal personalities. For maximal effectiveness the communications should be devised in such a way as to elicit a gradual, stepwise increase up to but not beyond a moderate level of fear. If the threat content markedly overbalances the reassurance content within any given communication, the individual is likely to be left in a state of high emotional tension. As a result he may become strongly motivated to minimize the threat and to avoid thinking about it. He may adopt "magical," "wishful," or other types of reassuring beliefs that are opposite to those recommended by the communicator. Some individuals alleviate residual emotional tension through spontaneous interpersonal communication with members of the audience.

The interruption of an integrated response sequence, such as an organized plan of action, according to Spielberger (1966), can also produce a high state of arousal. Unless the individual is allowed to complete the sequence started, he will show signs of anxiety, fear, or distress. In other words, when attempting to change certain behaviors belonging to an organized plan or response sequence, it is important to provide the individual with a substitute response so that the response sequence can be completed. Thus when an individual wants to follow the recommendation made by the communicator and no provision is made for him to complete this sequence, he becomes disturbed and chances of completing the sequence at a later date are minimal. He will attempt to ignore or minimize the importance of the threat in order to reduce the level of arousal initiated by the interruption.

Berlyne (1960) attributes the decrease in arousal following continued or intensified exposure to the very stimulus responsible for its rise to habituation. He states that when an initially novel stimulus is repeated over and over without any special significance, it loses its novelty. Exceptions to this rule are high fear-arousal produced by stimuli associated with pain or danger to life. For some unexplainable reason pain and threats to life are highly resistant to habituation by repetition. They continue to provoke high fear-arousal.

Fear can inhibit or facilitate adoption of recommended health measures, depending on what actions are recommended (Leventhal, 1963). When a warning of dire consequences if action is not taken is delivered by a person believed to be an authority or expert on the subject, Janis (1958) suggests that there is an increased tendency to view the matter more seriously. Most persons begin to engage in an imaginative mental rehearsal that promotes the development of effective acts to deal with the threatened danger. When successful, this mental activity leads to action and mastery of the threat situation. The tendency for taking constructive action increases as blanket immunity defenses are dropped.

Theoretically, then, it is possible to predict that the use of high fear-arousal to motivate persons to conform to a set of recommenda-tions causes emotional tension that is generally unrelieved by the reassurances incorporated into the communication. The disturbed individual will try to reduce the tension by ignoring the threat or adopting "magical" or wishful beliefs generally antithetical to that recommended by the communicator. Conversely, a moderate degree of fear can stimulate constructive action and thereby facilitate pre-ventive health behavior.

There is no established theory that can be relied upon for de-pendable predictions as to how people will react under specified con-ditions of environmental stress. What is needed are more refined theoretical constructs to account for the attitude change and social conformity under conditions of exposure to fear-arousing stimuli.

The resistance to persuasive communication is explained, in part, by Festinger's Theory of Cognitive Dissonance and by Berlyne's Theory of Arousal. These theories apply to all of the behaviors that follow, but they seem particularly relevant to the understanding of health behaviors.

What happens when the individual begins to experience a change in body structure, impairment of customary functioning, or unusual sensations? What happens when an individual is told, fol-lowing a routine physical examination, that he has manifestations of an illness? Does his behavior change? According to Janis (1958), the presence of external signs increases a person's awareness of the proximity of a threat and thus tends to elicit an increase in denial tendencies. In the following chapter, we propose to deal with these issues.

REFERENCES

BERLYNE, D. E. *Conflict, Arousal and Curiosity*. New York: McGraw-Hill Book Company, 1960, 350 pp.

CLAUSEN, JOHN A. ET AL. "Parents Attitudes Towards Participation of Their Children in Polio Vaccine Trials," *American Journal of Public Health*, 44 (December, 1954), 1526–36.

FESTINGER, LEON *A Theory of Cognitive Dissonance*. Evanston, Ill.: Row, Pe-terson and Co., 1957, 291 pp.

GRAY, ROBERT, J. P. KESLOR, AND P. M. MOODY "The Effects of Social Class and Friends' Expectations on Oral Polio Vaccination Participation," *American Journal of Public Health*, 56, No. 12 (December, 1966), 2028–32.

HAEFNER, DON P. ET AL. "Preventive Actions in Dental Disease, Tuberculosis and Cancer," *Public Health Reports*, 82 (May, 1967), 451–60.

HINKLE, LAWRENCE E., W. N. CHRISTENSON, F. D. KANE, A. OSTFELD, W. N. THETFORD, AND H. W. WOLFF "An Investigation of the Relation Between Life Experience, Personality, Characteristics and General Susceptibility to Illness," *Psychosomatic Medicine*, 20, No. 4 (1958), 278–95.

HOCHBAUM, GODFREY M. "Why People Seek Diagnostic X-Rays," *Public Health Reports*, 71 (April, 1956), 377–80.

———— *Public Participation in Medical Screening Programs*, U.S.P.H.S. Pub. No. 572. Washington, D.C.: U.S. Govt. Printing Office, 1958.

———— "Research Relating to Health Education," *Health Education Monograph*, No. 8 (1960), pp. 10–20.

JANIS, IRVING L. AND S. FESHBACK "Effects of Fear-Arousing Communications," *Journal of Abnormal and Social Psychology*, 48 No. 1 (January, 1953), 78–92.

———— *Psychological Stress*. New York: John Wiley and Sons, Inc., 1958, pp. 359–60.

KASL, STANISLAV V. AND SIDNEY COBB "Health Behavior, Illness Behavior and Sick Role Behavior," *Archives of Environmental Health*, 12 (February, 1966), 246–66.

KEGELES, S. STEPHEN "Why People Seek Dental Care," *Journal of Health and Human Behavior*, 4 (Fall, 1963), 166–73.

———— ET AL. Survey of Beliefs about Cancer Detection and Taking Papanicolaou Tests," *Public Health Reports*, 80 (September, 1965) 815–24.

LEVENTHAL, HOWARD AND PATRICIA N. KAFES "Effectiveness of Fear-Arousing Movies in Motivating Preventive Health Measures," *New York State Journal of Medicine*, 15 (March, 1963), 867–74.

———— ET AL. "Epidemic Impact on the General Population in Two Cities," in *The Impact of Asian Influenza on Community Life*, U.S.P.H.S. Pub. No. 766. Washington, D.C.: U.S. Govt. Printing Office, 1960.

MORRIS, NAOMI, MARTHA H. HATCH, AND DISNEY S. CHIPMAN "Alienation as a Deterrent to Well Child Supervision," *American Journal of Public Health and the Nation's Health*, 56, No. 11 (November, 1966), 1874–82.

RADELFINGER, SAM "Some Effects of Fear-Arousing Communications on Preventive Health Behavior," *Health Education Monograph*, 19 (1965), 2–15.

ROSENSTOCK, I. M. "Decision-Making by Individuals," *Health Education Monographs*, 11 (1961), 19–36.

———— "Why People Use Health Services," *Milbank Memorial Fund Quarterly*, 44 (July, 1966), 94–127.

———— "Prevention of Illness and Maintenance of Health," in *Poverty and Health*, John Kosa et al., eds. Cambridge, Mass.: Harvard University Press, 1969, pp. 168–90.

SPIELBERGER, CHARLES D. *Anxiety and Behavior*. New York: Academic Press, 1966, p. 265.

Suchman, Edward A. "Preventive Health Behavior: A Model for Research on Community Health Campaigns," *Journal of Health and Social Behavior,* 8, No. 3 (September, 1967), 197–209.

Swinehart, James W. "Changes Over Time in Student Reactions to the Surgeon General's Report on Smoking and Health," *American Journal of Public Health,* 56, No. 12 (December, 1966), 2023–27.

eight | *Illness Behavior*

When an individual learns that he has manifestations of an illness, or when he begins to experience unusual sensations or impairment of customary function, his behavior will change correspondingly. He will begin to engage in activity either to deny the uncomfortable sensations or to define his state of health and to discover a suitable remedy. The way in which a person deals with pain, discomfort, or other signs of organic malfunctioning constitutes what Mechanic (1962) has coined as *illness behavior*. Mechanic suggests that the conditions surrounding the etiology of illness should be separated from those surrounding illness behavior. Whatever caused the illness behavior may have nothing to do with the illness per se. Therefore, it is necessary to identify the social processes that bring a person to a treatment facility. Many times, according to Mechanic, a doctor erroneously assumes that the reason a person visits his office is to obtain help for some illness, when the real purpose may be to seek relief of other symptoms through emotional complaints. An analysis of visits made to company dispensaries and student health services supports this fact. Illness is often used as a pretense to obtain help for social and interpersonal problems, such as feelings of loneliness, rejection, and resentment.

Illness behavior, as described by Mechanic, might better be called help-seeking behavior. Whenever an individual visits a doctor's office, he is seeking help with a problem he is unable to manage alone. The problem may not be related to an illness or injury. Another person might choose to visit a family counselor, social worker, rabbi, or minister for the same kind of problem. The person or facility one chooses to seek help from is determined in part by the kind of rapport the individual has previously established with one of the professional persons mentioned above. It is not the type of person from whom help is sought that determines whether the individual is engaging in illness behavior; rather it is the reasons for seeking help. Help-seeking behaviors permeate the very fabric of life, from the very first cry of the newborn soliciting help from his mother to the seeking of guidance and counseling by the adult. Nurses are concerned with help-seeking behaviors that are directed towards the identification, prevention, and alleviation of illness. Thus, although visiting a doctor's office is a form of help-seeking behavior, it does not necessarily constitute illness behavior.

Illness behavior, as contrasted with health behavior, shall be defined as behavior that is triggered by such cues as pain, discomfort, signs of malfunction, and/or by confirmation by word of mouth that the individual, although presently asymptomatic, is experiencing illness. It is the initial response of the person to aberrations of the body and psyche, which he perceives as incapacitating and therefore as a sign of illness. The individual can no longer, at least rationally, deny his susceptibility or avoid facing the consequences of the illness. Illness behavior includes any behavior triggered by the above cues, regardless of the stage, phase or length of illness, the purpose of which is to define one's state of health and to seek a suitable remedy. Thus, illness behavior is not necessarily limited to the early stages of illness. As long as the individual is searching for a better cure, or seeking a diagnosis for his present condition, he is engaging in illness behavior. It will be seen later that illness behavior sometimes will displace sick role behavior, which can be detrimental or harmful to full or early recovery. In the presence of signs and symptoms, what will the individual do and why will he do it?

DESCRIPTION OF ILLNESS BEHAVIOR

In response to the cues of illness, the individual may engage in one or more of the following behaviors: (1) take action to relieve the symptoms, (2) take no action, (3) remain in a state of flux in which he vacillates between taking and not taking action, or (4) take counteraction in opposition to the cues.

Taking Action

Taking action to relieve the symptoms and to restore one's previous state of health may be viewed as healthy and constructive, or unhealthy and even harmful to the individual. In response to the cues of illness the individual may immediately seek help from a qualified practitioner or he may go to a quack. He may engage in self-diagnosis, self-treatment, or self-medication and home remedies before seeking professional help. The outcome of self-treatment often determines the next acts to be taken.

Beatrix Cobb (1958) has identified four classes of people who tend to make detours to quacks in response to the cues of illness. First are the *uniformed*, and these comprise the largest group seeking out the services of a quack. They are unaware of the difference between licensed medical doctors and nonlicensed persons who operate clinics specializing in the treatment of certain diseases, such as cancer. Next come the *"miracle-seekers,"* those who are in search of a sure cure overnight; then the *"restless ones,"* those individuals who are impatient with existing modes of treatment and waiting periods; and finally the *"straw-graspers,"* a group that detours to quacks as a last resort, unable to accept the terminal nature of their illness.

Blackwell (1967) conducted a study in which she asked healthy upper-middle-class adults what was the first thing they would do if they experienced a symptom such as rectal bleeding. The most common response given by her subjects was that they would first attempt to find the cause. If they could hypothesize that the symptom was caused by something they did or did not do, they could then attempt to change whatever was done or not done to get rid of the symptom. If this failed, then her subjects stated they would seek professional interpretation of the cause. Blackwell further states that if the dysfunction is known to be abnormal, there is less delay in seeking professional help than when the abnormality is not made explicit. She reports that individuals tend to experiment more extensively with their symptoms when the cause defies solution or when the symptoms are vague and nonspecific. For example, it is difficult to identify the cause of indigestion, fatigue, malaise, or neurotic anxiety. Each of these symptoms may be due to a number of reasons, and so the individual experiments with various methods in an attempt to alleviate the symptom prior to seeking professional help.

Individuals who are able to use fear constructively will seek medical diagnosis and treatment promptly. Cobb found that patients who were "prompt in coming to the doctor were aware of the significance of their cancer, while delayers somehow suppressed or never had an awareness of the meaning." The fears of prompt patients operated to mobilize resources and overcome inertia, and these patients expressed their dependency needs through intelligent cooperation with the physician. Mention should also be made of another class of people—those who seem to be highly sensitive to physical symptomatology and seek medical care with the slightest twinge of pain or discomfort. Characteristics of this group that lead to a quick assumption of illness include such factors as general emphasis on matters related to health, hypochondriasis, sensitization, guilt, and dependency (Blum, 1960).

Another common form of illness behavior is complaining and seeking consultation from friends and relatives in an attempt to obtain "provisional validation" of one's state of health. These discussions are not only to gain advice and information but also to obtain permission to suspend normal obligations and activities. Seeking care and assistance from others must be done in a way that is acceptable to the group.

Taking action, then, is an illness behavior that includes such activities as self-treatment, seeking "provisional validation," soliciting help from medical or other professional care-givers or quacks, or any step that is directed toward the relief of signs and symptoms that the individual perceives as manifestations of illness.

Taking No Action

Taking no action usually results in a "wait and see" attitude. The individual procrastinates, rationalizing that the symptoms are benign and trivial and not serious enough to warrant medical attention.

The literature on delay in seeking diagnosis and treatment following recognition or appearance of symptoms is voluminous (see Kasl, 1966). The concept of delay is ambiguous and equivocal. In some studies delay is computed from the date of the first appearance of symptoms, whereas in other studies delay is computed from the time a complaint is perceived by the patient as needing medical attention. There is a wide discrepancy between the time of the first appearance of the symptom and the time when the individual recognizes that medical care is needed. According to one study, when the period from the onset of symptoms to the first attempt to seek diagnosis and treatment exceeds three months, the individual is described as having delayed action. Thus a person who waits two months before seeking treatment for a suspected illness has not "delayed" action. The problem of delay is a knotty one with little or no consistent findings, due to ambiguity and confusion in the operational use of the term.

It is a known fact that people do tend to avoid taking action in the presence of signs and symptoms for varying periods of time. This is attributable in large part to the inability or unwillingness of the individual to experience the distress of illness and to organize behavior to meet it positively. Fear plays an important role in inhibiting constructive action. The threat of disease, especially when accompanied with knowledge of danger signals such as cancer, can immobilize a person.

Often an individual will delay seeking help because he does not know whom to see. This is particularly true in this day of specialization, malpractice, and high mobility. From the small family doctor who treated everything, the field of medicine has grown to immense proportions and complexity. The referral system can be both costly and time-consuming. Individuals want to go to the right specialist from the beginning, and so they delay in their search for the right person, realizing that the final choice they make can be either disastrous or advantageous.

Others delay seeking help for their illness for fear of rejection or ridicule. This applies to the patient who too frequently (for him) has heard "It's nothing." Also, with the increased focus on psychosomatic illnesses, some individuals are reluctant to take their complaints to doctors for fear of being dubbed malingerers or hypochondriacs.

The person who chooses to take no action will ultimately have to take action if the symptoms do not subside. Factors contributing to a slow acceptance of illness include not only denial but also competition from more interesting and demanding events.

Remaining in a State of Flux

Vacillating between taking action and taking no action is just one small step above taking no action; at least the individual is considering taking action, even if he does nothing. He has ambivalent feelings about his inadequacy and the need for help. In the early symptom stage he wants to avoid bothering his family, friends, and the doctor, and yet he fears the consequences if he waits too long. This individual realizes that in the face of illness, diagnosis and treatment represent important steps toward a return to a state of health. However, diagnosis and treatment are viewed as expensive and time-consuming. Therefore the individual is in a state of conflict. On the one hand he wants to obtain medical care because he knows that it can lead to the remission of symptoms and a return to a state of good health; on the other hand not only is diagnosis and treatment painful, expensive, and time-consuming, but the illness that the diagnosis may uncover is associated with pain, helplessness, expense, dependency, and perhaps even death. Under these circumstances the individual is torn between the forces that impel him to take action—the desire to avoid his present discomfort and the desire to regain his health, and the forces that resist such action—the desire to avoid pain and expense of diagnosis and treatment and the desire to avoid the discomfort, cost, and danger of illness. Only when the combined strength of the former is greater than that of the latter will the person persist in securing medical attention and thereby resolve the conflict. The problem of conflict occurs repeatedly throughout the course of illness and is partly responsible for the lapses in treatment and interruption of care observed in many situations.

Taking Counteraction

The individual who takes counteraction to the cues of illness responds by trying to prove that "it is not so." He refuses to give in to the illness. He purposely increases his work load to prove to himself that the unpleasant discomforts are a figment of his imagination. He is unrealistically biased, confident that everything will be all right and underestimating the chances of his ever falling ill. Along with the denial and refusal to give in is "shopping" behavior. In keeping with his needs and preconceptions the individual tries multiple sources and a variety of medical practitioners, including quacks, to support his view that he is not sick or that his terminal illness is curable.

Taking counteraction represents a medical-nursing problem. It is an abnormal, unhealthy response to the cues of illness. Properly speaking it should not be classified as illness behavior because the behavior is in opposition to the identification and assessment of the discomforting sensations. However, since it is a response to the initial cues of illness, it shall be referred to as deviant illness behavior. This individual wants a definition of his state of health that denies the presence of illness.

The problem of assessing this kind of behavior is to separate psychological denial (that something is wrong) from real ignorance. For example, an individual may appear to be denying the existence of certain symptoms when in reality he is unaware of the fact that these are not part of growing up or part of the aging process, but are indeed signs of illness.

SUMMARY. In general, a person can do several things in response to the cues of illness: he can do something to relieve the symptoms, he can take a wait and see attitude, he can vacillate without taking any concrete action, or he can behave in ways that deny the presence of symptoms. What factors determine which form of illness behavior is followed? Some of the factors have already been alluded to in the preceding paragraphs, but let us now view each group of factors in a more systematic way relative to their influence on illness behavior.

BEHAVIORAL DETERMINANTS

Mechanic (1966) suggests that the general variables affecting help-seeking or illness behavior are similar, regardless of the type of disease involved. He has proposed seven major classes of variables, which will be discussed below:

1. *The amount, persistence, and recurrence of the aberrance.* The amount of aberrance does not refer to the degree of severity, which will be discussed later, but rather to the frequency with which the aberrant behavior is emitted. When it is emitted or displays itself only occasionally, it is likely to be ignored or viewed as an exception or something out of the ordinary. When the rate of emission increases or the aberration persists, it can no longer be ignored either by the person or by his significant others. The frequency or amount of deviancy affects how the behavior will be noticed, defined, and acted on. The more frequent the aberrant behavior the more annoying it becomes to the person or to the group, and thus the more probable it is that some action will be taken to control it. Increased social pressure is applied to seek help when the behavior deviates considerably from societal norms. If the symptom persists or

continues in spite of self-treatment, the individual is more likely to seek professional help. However, if the symptom subsides, he is less likely to seek professional interpretation of the symptom. Thus, amount, persistence, and recurrence of the aberrance are important determinants of the form of illness behavior.

2. *The visibility, recognizability, or perceptual salience of the aberrance.* Blackwell (1967) states that if the aberrance is external and observable, the patient will behave differently than if it is covert, ambiguous, and ill defined (for example, rectal bleeding as opposed to indigestion). In the former there is less experimenting with self-treatment since the alternatives are limited, whereas in the latter the alternative forms of treatment relative to causality are unlimited.

The size and form of a community can affect visibility and symptomatology, and hence the consequence and definition of aberrant behavior. In large, less intimate communities aberrant behavior is less readily defined. It is either ignored or tolerated. On the other hand, prejudice in our society toward those whose physical characteristics deviate from the majority and the high social value placed upon physical attractiveness may motivate many persons to seek help for an otherwise minor aberrance. The factor of visibility of the aberrance does not always elicit illness behavior. For example, MacGregor (1960) describes the seemingly paradoxical reaction of two individuals with the same deformity, one complaining vigorously about his deformity and the other appearing unconcerned and even ambivalent about the proposed corrective surgery. She attributes the differences in response to the aberrance to the varying social-psychological needs of each of the persons. When the visible aberrance is experienced as social prejudice, the individual is more likely to seek help regardless of the amount of aberrance. In fact in MacGregor's study, patients classified as mildly deformed tended to exaggerate the degree of the deformity, whereas those classified severely deformed were inclined to minimize the degree of the deformity. She suggests that individuals who seek help for minor deformities may be actually using this as a cover for difficulties that are unrelated to the defect.

According to many reports the role of visibility in seeking diagnosis or treatment for cancer is contradictory. For certain investigators delay increased with visibility of cancer signs, whereas for others there was either no difference between persons with visible or nonvisible signs or else the visibility prompted an early response. Perceived severity, regardless of visibility, seemed to be a more important variable of illness behavior.

Mechanic (1962) suggests that the type of medical diagnosis or its saliency will also influence whether or not an individual will seek help in response to the cues of illness. Realizing that certain individuals tend to seek help for whatever reasons more readily than others, he reports that illnesses defined as common, familiar, predictable, and usually nondangerous prompt a larger percentage of total visits made than those illnesses lacking such criteria. An important and well-known social-psychological principle is that familiarity or recognizability provides structure to an otherwise unstructured experience. Once the individual is able to reduce the fear associated with the unknown, he can mobilize himself to take action. When a symptom is recognized as something that he has experienced before, if the past treatment was successful, he is likely to repeat what was done at that time.

3. *The perceived seriousness of the aberration and the extent to which it disrupts the individual's ability to engage in family work and other social actitvities.* According to Suchman (1965) the more serious the symptoms and the more they interfere with the individual's ability to carry on his usual activities, the more likely will that individual be to show concern. Delay in defining illness is attributed to competition from more interesting and demanding events. People tend to underemphasize the importance of symptoms that are perceived as neither serious nor incapacitating, especially if these symptoms do not interfere with their social life.

On the other hand, if a person suspects that the symptoms signify the beginning of a serious illness, he will decide to take action and get in touch with a physician. Thus, most of the subjects in this study, when faced with frightening symptoms, seemed to think almost at once of seeking professional medical care.

Perceived seriousness of symptoms was an important determinant of the form of illness behavior observed in a study by Koos (1960). Subjects were presented with a list of recognizable symptoms and asked to check those symptoms that they perceived as important enough to warrant the attention of a physician. Although the perceived seriousness of symptoms (measured according to whether subjects indicated a need or no need for medical attention) varied along socioeconomic lines, over 50 percent of the subjects tested felt that symptoms associated with unexplained bleeding should be reported to a doctor, whereas persistent backache was least often checked as needing medical attention. Between these two points there was tremendous variation among the three social classes as to which symptoms were serious enough to warrant medical attention. Fear, according to Koos, seemed to be one of the most important factors influencing the form of illness behavior emitted. There were people in his study who were so fearful of the idea of "going under the knife" that they would ignore the most pressing of symptoms rather than face the possibility of an operation. There were others to whom the hospital represented the "end of the road." These individuals would deny the symptoms if they felt that hospitalization would be necessary.

Another factor suggested by Koos is the place that health holds in the person or group's hierarchical value system. Seeking help for some symptoms must compete with other needs and desires of the family. If some material need is more valued than health, care of the aberration or symptom will be delayed until that particular need is met.

The seriousness of an aberration is frequently measured in terms of the anticipated consequences of the behavior to the group. If the aberration results in serious or disruptive consequences to the group, action to control the aberrance is likely to take place. If there is stigma associated with the aberrance, the group may refuse to accept a definition of illness and will choose to ignore it instead. The anticipated consequences to the group if an individual fails to fulfill role expectations adequately or violates some legal or moral issue highly valued by the group, determines ultimately the seriousness assigned to a given aberration.

If the aberration is perceived as a threat to the person's life or to fulfilling one or more of his basic needs, he will respond as he does to all kinds of perceived threats. Like health behavior a moderate degree of perceived severity and serious consequences increases the likelihood that action will be taken. However, if the individual experiences severe threat associated with the symptoms, he is likely to become immobilized with fear. Behavior is thus directed toward dealing with the anxiety rather than taking constructive action to protect himself against the perceived threat.

4. *The tendency of the individual to be concerned with abnor-*

malities and tolerance for same. Individuals who place a high priority of attention on matters of health and show greater sensitivity to changes in body structure and function, sometimes known as "hypochrondiacs," tend to define themselves as ill more quickly than those who lack the above attributes.

Tolerance for an abnormality such as pain may be culturally defined. According to a study conducted by Zborowski (1969), Jewish and Italian patients were observed to be less tolerant of pain than the patients of Old American and Irish origin. Moaning, groaning, tears, and other manifestations of pain were most frequently observed among the former group of patients. Recognizing that the threshold of pain is the same for all human beings regardless of age, sex, and nationality, the author concludes that responses to pain are learned and patterned according to the norms of behavior accepted by one's cultural group. Another author suggests that Orientals tend to be stoical in their reactions to pain (Tao-Kim-Hai, 1965). Reports such as these need to undergo further study before generalizations are drawn.

Stress is said to be both a cause of illness and a determinant of illness behavior. Psychological stress tends to increase the individual's sensitivity to already existing symptoms. Mechanic (1964) reports that in a study he conducted there was a positive relationship between the amount of family stress and the tendency to be concerned with symptoms. As pressures increased, mothers tended to become more sensitive to the presence of symptoms in their children.

According to Kasl and Cobb (1966) the primary role of psychological stress in illness behavior is not yet clear. It may cause an increase in the importance of health matters, increase the person's perceived susceptibility to disease, make the consequences of the disease look more threatening, or raise the probability that action will lead to desired results.

A study conducted by Mechanic (1962) revealed that persons who reported high stress as measured by frequency of loneliness and nervousness visited the doctor more frequently for symptoms than those who did not report such stress. Interpersonal stress was a significant determinant for seeking medical care. Tolerance for deviation can be said to be reduced when the individual is experiencing psychological stress.

5. *The information the individual has about the aberrance, his cultural background, understandings, and system of values.* According to certain reports, increased knowledge or additional

information about the aberration elicits no consistent or predictable response. For some individuals the added information was more fear-producing than reassuring. The kind of information transmitted is probably as important as the amount in determining behavior. Blackwell (1967) states in her retrospective study that individuals would tend to seek medical care more quickly when they knew the dysfunction was abnormal than when this fact remained unknown. Generally, in cancer studies there seemed to be no relationship between the amount of information the individual had about the disease and his illness behavior. Better knowledge about cancer symptoms was associated with greater promptness in one study but made little difference in another (Kasl and Cobb, 1966). It appears that the number of interpretations that can be assigned to the symptoms determines when and what kind of action is taken.

Several reports suggest that the ethnic origin of an individual determines when help is sought for a perceived dysfunction. Kasl and Cobb in their comprehensive review of the literature report a study by Zola in which he compares the Italians, Irish, and Anglo-Saxon Americans and their decisions as to when to seek medical care. He noted that when the differences in objective symptoms were held constant, interference with social and personal relations prompted Italian-Americans to seek help for their symptoms, whereas Irish-Americans would seek help for their symptoms only after receiving the approval of others, and Americans of Anglo-Saxon origin would seek help from a physician only when their symptoms interfered with some specific vocational or physical activity. The latter description agrees with the upper-middle-class adult culture, which Blackwell describes as a reflection of the Protestant ethic. Responsibility is placed on the individual for all aspects of his destiny. His personal ambition, self-reliance, and enterprise are all measures of his ability to live up to his responsibility. The basic assumption is that what is best for mankind can be secured by the application of knowledge and action. The individual is responsible for supplying evidence that he is sick. He is expected to know what is accepted as dysfunctional, the extent of his own ability to cope with the dysfunction, and the appropriate professional person to go to when he needs help. He also should be able to pay for the treatment prescribed. Assuming responsibility for his own destiny motivates him to behave accordingly.

Ideological beliefs also determine whether or not medical

or surgical help is sought for an illness. For example, many Christian Science believers refuse to seek help from medical personnel for their illnesses. They seek relief from their symptoms through the teachings of their church.

The dictates of the group and its culture thus serve as determinants of illness behavior. For instance, a symptom might be disregarded if this is what the group decides. An individual might have a severe backache, but so would other people in his group. To do something about the backache would be to deny the expectations of the group and to go counter to one's social heritage. If the group agrees that something should be done about the symptom, then there is a good chance that the symptom will be treated.

Prior training is also considered to have some effect on how and when a person presents himself and his symptoms to his physician. Patterns of behavior are assumed to be transferred from one generation to the next. However, Mechanic (1964) could find no specific relationship between the illness behavior of mothers and their children. The child's attentiveness to symptoms and patterns of illness behavior showed no relationship to the degree of interest in symptoms shown by the mother.

Finally, the place of health in an individual or family's hierarchical value system determines to a large extent whether the symptom is taken care of immediately or whether other needs take priority.

6. *The availability of treatment resources, their physical proximity, and the barriers to taking action in terms of cost, inconvenience, time, effort, and fear.* The problem of availability of treatment facilities is more complex than it appears. The individual may know where to go but not be accepted for treatment; he may know he needs professional help but not know where to get it; or he may not know that he needs professional help.

The doctor's attitude toward the symptoms presented by the patient becomes an important determinant of future behaviors. When a patient has been told more than once that the symptom is nothing, he begins to overlook minor symptoms, feeling that they are insignificant and not serious enough to warrant medical care. He may worry about ridicule or rejection by the physician if he brings these "insignificant" symptoms to his attention. There appears to be a discrepancy between the opinions of the doctor and of patient as to what constitutes serious symptoms and what necessitates treatment and medical attention. In addition, conditioning in popular literature, where emphasis on psychosomatic illness has not received appropriate interpretation, has caused many laymen to delay seeking care for fear of being dubbed a malingerer or hypochondriac.

Barriers to taking action include such factors as time, cost, inconvenience, and fear, and any of these may be strong enough to cause considerable conflict in individuals experiencing the onset of symptoms. Only when the positive forces gain sufficient strength to overcome the negative forces, will the individual take action to regain his previous state of health.

The role of anxiety in illness behavior is not yet clear. It is probable that anxiety is curvilinearly related to illness behavior. Moderately intense fear is most effective in stimulating both health and illness behaviors. As stated earlier, a high degree of fear tends to immobilize the person and prevent appropriate action. Individuals will usually behave in ways that have been most effective in reducing anxiety in past situations. Studies are needed to identify these behaviors and to determine whether they facilitate or interfere with illness behavior. It is possible that at moderate levels of anxiety, prompt action is most effective in reducing anxiety. At more intense levels, only maladaptive responses such as denial or irrational medical practices will effectively reduce anxiety.

7. *Social characteristics of the person: social and economic status, sex, age, and so on.* The exact relationship of age and sex to illness behavior is not clear. Several studies report that men and older subjects are more optimistic about their health than women and younger subjects (Kasl and Cobb, 1966). Older people tend to attribute their symptoms to aging, especially when the symptoms are viewed as nonserious and nonincapacitating. Koos suggests that the older person frequently attributes pain to a change of life and therefore disregards it.

Occupational status plus position in one's social group (including one's relative importance in that group) is an important determinant of illness behavior. The individual who feels he is indispensable to his work or to his family is likely to behave differently toward the dysfunction than a person who does not occupy such an important status.

Sex may also be a determinant of illness behavior. For some males a need to assert one's masculinity makes illness unacceptable. This is especially true for those men who view illness as a sign of weakness and femininity. The role of underreporting by the male sex is not clear because of its relationship to the age of the individual and the nature of the symptoms.

Koos (1960) found a clear social-class gradient in attitudes towards symptoms; the lower the class the less likely was a specified symptom seen as requiring medical attention. McBroom (1970) observed a tendency among upper socioeconomic classes to overreact or to overreport their symptoms, whereas he found no such trend among the lower socioeconomic classes. These findings not only suggest differences in the perceived need for treatment but also reflect the cost of care, access to health services, and fear of treatment. In addition, lower-class people have less information and knowledge about disease and have different cultural interpretations about the cause and course of disease than the upper social classes. As Kasl and Cobb stated, personal income is becoming less acceptable as a satisfactory explanation of illness behavior; other factors such as differences in cultural and social values and orientations between the classes are playing a more important role. According to Mechanic (1969) ethnicity exerts a more powerful effect than social class in illness. Although poverty is not necessarily associated with deviant patterns of illness behavior, neither is affluence necessarily associated with functional patterns of behavior. The fact is, however, that dysfunctional behavior tends to occur more frequently among ethnic groups that are of relatively low-economic class. This was particularly evident among the Puerto Ricans and Blacks in New York City.

Pressure from family members is another important determinant of illness behavior. Without these pressures the patient would tend to delay longer seeking help, believing himself not sick enough to call a doctor.

Once the above variables have been operationalized, they can help define the processes involved in illness. For example, for some disorders the amount and persistence of the aberrance may account for the illness behaviors observed, whereas for another disorder this variable may be much less important. According to Mechanic (1969) the most important determinant of illness behavior is the nature of the symptom, i.e., the intensity, quality, and persistence of the discomfort. What is needed, he suggests, is a theory to explain under what conditions an aberrance is identified and defined. A set of propositions is needed to explain why alternative modes of help are sought or made available to various kinds of people.

Now that an attempt has been made to describe illness behavior and to identify the variables that influence the form of behavior emitted, is there a plausible explanation for the action, delay, or counteraction taken in response to the cues of illness?

SOME THEORETICAL EXPLANATIONS
OF ILLNESS BEHAVIOR

Any experience, according to Blackwell (1964), can be analytically divided into three parts: physical, cognitive, and emotional. In the experience of illness the physical aspect would be the pain, discomfort, change in appearance, or debility actually felt. The cognitive aspect refers to the interpretation and derived meaning for the individual experiencing the symptoms, and the emotional aspect refers to the fear or anxiety that accompanies both the physical and cognitive aspects of the experience.

Causal Theory

According to Heider's Theory of Causality, origin attribution plays an important role in the organization of experiences (1958). There seems to be what some authors call a "causal drive," that is, a tendency toward causal explanation or toward the pursuit of meaning. Following this line of thinking an individual in response to a physical experience such as discomfort, pain, or abnormality will assign an origin to the elements making up the experience. He also responds emotionally not only to the physical experience but also to its name. For example, the name cancer elicits mixed emotions. The judgment of origin or causality is a rational process, according to Heider, whereas the emotional connotation or affective significance is a feeling process, governed primarily by the needs of the personality. The judgment of the origin may be influenced by and/or influence the affective significance of the experience. Thus the symptoms an individual experiences are judged not in medically diagnostic categories but in terms of their interference with normal social functioning.

Rational and affective processes interpenetrate to influence each other. When rational or cognitive elements are inconsistent with affective elements, the individual experiences cognitive dissonance. There is no standard way to interpret a dysfunction. It depends upon the ease of assigning a cause and the emotional significance of the dysfunction. The interpretation of the cause of the symptom or dysfunction must meet the emotional needs of the individual, for example, the need to get rid of the feeling that something is wrong. This probably accounts for the use of rationalization to help explain away some of the symptoms. Having assigned a cause to the experience, the individual is free to direct action toward that cause in such a way that his needs are met.

Heider further states that in the search for causality, the tendency is to assign persons as the origin or cause of events. This was also predicated in Blackwell's study where subjects stated that in response to a symptom of illness they would first determine what they had done or not done that might have caused the dysfunction or aberration. Thus, if the individual assigned himself a role in the cause, he would then attempt to eliminate what he had done in order to get relief from the symptom.

The ease of assigning a cause, according to Blackwell, determines when and whether the individual will seek professional help for the aberration. In her study she found that the shortest delay between awareness of dysfunction and seeking help is when physical conditions are involved, and the longest delay is when psychosocial conditions are concerned. She explains this difference on the basis that physical conditions are overt and the causes limited, being quickly identified as internal or external and either amenable to self-treatment or requiring professional help. Psychosocial conditions, on the other hand, are not clearly identifiable. It is difficult to trace the possible causes because of the transient nature of the manifestations, and thus the individual experiments extensively with coping with the situation prior to seeking professional help.

The assigned cause given by the individual may not be congruent with objective reality. It is important to realize that the assigned cause must be in keeping with the individual's need to defend himself against the perceived threat of illness, and therefore the meaning given may be distorted. The individual selects from the field only what meets his needs. For example, he may attribute his spells of indigestion to overeating, even though he has been eating very little. Attributing the indigestion to overeating is less threatening than attributing it to some feared disease such as cancer. Perceptual distortion is especially possible with dysfunctions that are ambiguous and unclear; contradictory information can easily alter the percept and thus defend the individual against the threat. When objective features are compelling, the individual has no alternative but to agree with reality.

Denial Theory

The use of denial in the presence of a symptom or dysfunction is explained as a form of self-defense. It permits the maintenance of the self-image, even though it may not be realistic. In order for complete denial to occur in adults, relations with reality must be seriously disturbed. If the individual's society, especially his significant others, supports and condones the denial, he could continue to deny the experience of illness. His behavior will thus be modified in terms of the distorted perception; that is, he will ignore it.

A basic theoretical assumption of Freud's is that experiences that elicit a high level of fear tend to arouse outgrown modes of responses learned in childhood (Hall and Lindzey, 1957).* Early in life every individual goes through a learning process of developing fantasies that will function as reassurances to meet recurrent threats. The use of fantasy is a common defense among people who face extreme threat situations. It helps bolster their decision to submit to the perceived threatening ordeal. Denial and the use of fantasy help minimize the probability that the potential danger will actually materialize, and they also minimize the magnitude of the potential danger. As the symptoms continue or increase in intensity the use of denial is no longer effective, and the original fears will return in full strength.

As long as the probability of danger cannot be ascertained, the individual is said to be intellectually denying the potential danger. Denial becomes pathological when the individual disregards clearcut evidence of the dysfunction or symptoms. Denial behavior then becomes a serious deviation in the sense that it is essentially delusional in character and suggestive of a psychotic break with reality.

Conflicting Theory

Berlyne (1960) states that when two or more incompatible responses are aroused simultaneously, the individual is in conflict and exhibits characteristics of hesitancy, tension, vacillation, or complete blocking.

Another conflict theory has been proposed by Barker (1953). He defines the situation of a person who first experiences the discomforts of illness as being in a state of conflict. Using Lewin's Field Theory (Hall and Lindzey, 1957),† Barker describes the region of health that the individual is leaving as highly attractive (+ valence), and the region that the individual is now facing—a subregion of discomfort, pain, or fatigue—as unattractive (− valence). Another region that the individual faces, the one of diagnosis and treatment,

---

*Freud's Psychoanalytic Theory is discussed on pp. 29–75 of Hall and Lindzey's book.

†Lewin's Field Theory is discussed on pp. 205–56 of Hall and Lindzey's book.

is also unattractive (— valence), owing to the pain anticipated, the expense, and the time consumed. The results of diagnosis and treatment lead to two regions: a diagnosis of illness that is unattractive (— valence) because it implies pain, helplessness, expense, dependency, and perhaps death; or a diagnosis of renewed health, an attractive region (+ valence).

Under these circumstances the individual is said to be in multiple conflict as he decides whether or not to submit to diagnosis and treatment. He is experiencing. a double approach–avoidance conflict in which two forces tend to move him to seek help and two forces tend to move him away from seeking help. The desire to avoid the discomfort he is experiencing and the desire to regain his health act as forces to push him into seeking a diagnosis and treatment. However, the desire to avoid the pain and expense of diagnosis and treatment and the discomfort, cost, and danger of illness all will exert pressure to prevent him from seeking help. Only when the approach forces are greater than the avoidance forces will the person persist in securing medical attention. The amount of conflict depends upon the person's conception of the degree of attractiveness or unattractiveness of the alternatives.

The conflict between approach tendencies is said to be more serious and more difficult to resolve than that between avoidance tendencies or that between approach and avoidance. The degree of conflict will increase with the equalization of strength of competing response tendencies and of degree of incompatibilities between response tendencies. In Barker's model both the approach and avoidance tendencies weigh pretty evenly, thus producing considerable oscillating behavior. However, for some people the route to renewed health may not carry the negative valences of cost, discomfort, and inconvenience, thus reducing incompatibility between competing responses. In addition, people differ in their ability to deal with conflict, some having greater tolerance than others.

The means used to reduce conceptual conflict according to Berlyne (1960) include conciliation, i.e., making competing response tendencies or behaviors less incompatible; swamping, i.e., introducing a new response tendency that is stronger than those that are in competition; and strengthening or weakening one or more of the competing response tendencies, thus rendering the conflict unequal. With illness behavior, the persistence of symptoms in spite of self-treatment or the increase in discomfort and perceived severity is usually sufficient to tip the scale in favor of seeking help. Professional personnel might consider reducing the negative valences associated with treatment and illness by improving conditions and removing some of the barriers. Other means to resolve conflict besides acquisition of knowledge include denial, bolstering, obtaining social support for beliefs that are held with some misgiving, seeking out stimulus situations that are likely to reinforce such beliefs, and keeping away from those situations that might implant doubt.

An attempt has been made to provide some theoretical explanations for the illness behaviors described herein. Several theories have been selected as contributing to an understanding of the described behaviors. Whether or not a causal drive really exists is open to question. It does offer a tentative basis from which useful explanations and predictions can be made. There may be better theories, although these are unknown to the author at this writing. Current research on mediational processes and behavioral constructs will add new dimensions to our understanding of behaviors.

SUMMARY. It has been said that illness behavior is elicited in response to cues associated with illness for the purpose of defining one's state of health and discovering a suitable remedy. It was also stated that the kind of person from whom help is sought shall not be the criterion that is used to define the illness behavior but rather the purpose for seeking help. Illness behavior is limited to those help-seeking behaviors that seek to identify and assess changes associated with the experience of illness. In addition, it was stated that illness behavior may be observed at any point throughout the course of illness. It is not limited to the initial or early stages of illness. Whenever an individual is seeking a diagnosis of his state of health or a cure for his illness, he is engaging in illness behavior. Once he has accepted the diagnosis and subscribes to the treatment plan, he becomes a patient and is entitled to play the sick role. Sick role behavior may, however, as mentioned earlier, be displaced at any time by illness behavior. The consequences of such displacement will be discussed in the following chapter.

REFERENCES

BARKER, ROGER G., BEATRICE A. WRIGHT, LEE MEYERSON, AND MOLLIE R. GONICK *Adjustments to Physical Handicap and Illness: A Survey of the Social Psychology of Physique and Disability.* New York: Social Science Research Council, 1953, Chap. 6, "Social Psychology of Acute Illness."

BERLYNE, D. E. *Conflict, Arousal and Curiosity.* New York: McGraw-Hill Book Company, 1960, 350 pp.

BLACKWELL, BARBARA L. "Anticipated Pre-Medical Care Activities of Upper-Middle Class Adults and Their Implications for Health Education Practice," *Health Education Monograph*, No. 17 (1964), pp. 17–36.

———— "Upper-Middle Class Adult Expectations about Entering the Sick Role for Physical and Psychiatric Dysfunctions," *Journal of Health and Social Behavior*, 8, No. 2 (Summer, 1967), 83–95.

BLUM, RICHARD H. *The Management of the Doctor-Patient Relationship.* New York: McGraw-Hill Book Company, 1960, pp. 1–28.

COBB, BEATRIX "Why Do People Detour to Quacks?" in *Patients, Physicians and Illness*, ed. E. G. Jaco. New York: The Free Press, 1958, Chap. 30, pp. 283–87.

HALL, CALVIN S. AND GARDNER LINDZEY *Theories of Personality.* New York: John Wiley & Sons, Inc., 1957, pp. 29–75, 206–56.

HEIDER, FRITZ "Social Perception and Phenomenal Causality," in *Person Perception and Interpersonal Behavior*, eds. Renato Taguire and Luigi Petreillo. California: Stanford University Press, 1958, pp. 1–21.

KASL, STANISLAV V. AND SIDNEY COBB "Health Behavior, Illness Behavior, and Sick Role Behavior," *Archives of Environmental Health*, 12 (February, 1966), 240–66.

KOOS, EARL LOMON "Illness in Regionville," in Dorrian Apple, ed., *Sociological Studies in Health and Sickness.* New York: McGraw-Hill Book Company, 1960, Chap. 1, pp. 9–14.

MACGREGOR, FRANCES COOKE "Some Psychological Hazards of Plastic Surgery of the Face," in Dorrian Apple, ed., *Sociological Studies of Health and Sickness.* New York: McGraw-Hill Book Company, 1960, Chap. 11, pp. 145–53.

MCBROOM, WILLIAM H. "Illness, Illness Behavior and Socioeconomic Status," *Journal of Health and Social Behavior*, 11 No. 4 (December, 1970), 319–26.

MECHANIC, DAVID "The Concept of Illness Behavior," *Journal of Chronic Disease*, 15 (February, 1962), 189–94.

———— "The Influence of Mothers on Their Children's Health Attitudes and Behaviors," *Pediatrics*, 33 (March, 1964) 444–53.

———— "The Sociology of Medicine: Viewpoints and Perspectives," *Journal of Health and Human Behavior*, 7 No. 4 (Winter, 1966), 237–48.

———— "Illness and Cure," in *Poverty and Health.* John Kosa et al., eds. Cambridge, Mass.: Harvard University Press, 1969, pp. 191–214.

SUCHMAN, EDWARD A. "Stages of Illness and Medical Care," *Journal of Health and Human Behavior*, 6, No. 3 (Fall, 1965), 114–28.

TAO-KIM-HAI, ANDRE M. "Orientals Are Stoic," in James K. Skipper, ed., *Social Interaction and Patient Care.* Philadelphia: J. B. Lippincott Co., 1965, pp. 143–55.

ZBOROWSKI, MARK *People in Pain.* San Francisco: Jossey-Bass, Inc., Publishers, 1969, pp. 239–47.

nine | *Sick Role Behavior*

Once an individual defines himself as ill, with or without validation from a doctor, family member, or friend, he will begin to engage in activities congruent with his perception of the sick role. He is said to be occupying a special position accorded by society to those defined as sick and thus is entitled to play the sick role.

For every socially recognizable position in society there is a set of expectations defined by members of the community for persons occupying that position. Rules are learned through intentional instruction, incidental learning, or conjointly. Essentially these rules are copied patterns of behavior, and their adoption depends upon the availability of models. When sick, the individual will behave according to what he has observed and learned from other sick people.

In addition to institutional expectations, behavior is guided by the goals, values, and sentiments of relevant others in the interaction. The patient learns his role as he is interacting. For example, if the relevant other behaves in a manner that encourages dependency, the patient will probably reciprocate in like manner. The relevant other may be a doctor, nurse, friend, parent, relative, or other person. Individuals who care for the sick will, in turn, respond according to their own expectations of their role as well as according to the sick person's expectations of the care-giver's role. If the care-giver perceives his role as comforter and protector, he will be guided by these beliefs, and if these behaviors are acceptable to the patient in terms of his (the patient's) expectations of the care-giver, the care-giver's behaviors will thereby be reinforced by the patient's response. If the behaviors are not acceptable to the patient, the patient will respond in a manner so as to induce a change in behavior more congruent with his expectations of the care-giver's role, and vice versa.

Having accepted the fact of his illness, the patient will engage in activities so as to rid himself of the dysfunction or symptom and regain his previous state of health. However, there is no guarantee that once the patient accepts his illness, he will maintain this position throughout the course of his illness. It is likely that with added experience and knowledge, doubts and skepticisms will arise to cause conflict and resumption of illness behavior. For example, the patient may suddenly deny his illness and resist any form of treatment. Therefore, we shall limit the definition of sick role behavior to those behaviors that a person engages in, once he has determined that he is ill, for the purpose of getting well. This definition includes two necessary conditions: (1) the patient must have accepted that he is ill, and (2) he must want to get well.

Situations in which the individual accepts that he is ill but does not want to get well involve deviant sick role behavior, which will be discussed later in this book. When an individual cannot accept his illness in the presence of dysfunction or symptoms, he is exhibiting illness behavior through the use of defense mechanisms, such as denial, rationalization, and reaction formation. However, we shall concern ourselves for now with nondeviant sick role behavior, as defined by American society today.

Activities for getting well include self-prescriptions as well as medical prescriptions. Self-prescriptions comprise following the advice of family, friend, pharmacist, or one's own past experience. This category means any acts performed on or by the person for the purposes of cure. It may include the intake of medicinal products, and the modification in daily activities of living, such as changes in diet or elimination patterns, decrease in work hours, changing jobs, moving to a more favorable environmental climate, or increase in rest periods. All of these behaviors are directed toward the relief of symptoms and the restoration of health.

Medical prescriptions include following the advice of the doctor and members of the health team. This category means any acts performed on or by the person for the purpose of cure. These acts, when pain inducing, can elicit a whole range of behaviors from the expression of little or no fear to severe fear and sometimes panic behavior. Depending on the amount of discomfort or danger anticipated, past experience, and the amount of trust or distrust vested in the person(s) prescribing or performing the act, there will be a varying display of apprehension in proportion or out of proportion to the threat. In situations of distrust, there is a display of hypervigilant behavior as the individual prepares himself for danger from all sides. He listens to everything that is said and questions every move made in his visual field. This high level of arousal consumes energy and can negatively affect the outcome of the treatment and/or illness itself (Blake, 1961–1962).

Sometimes the individual who has already accepted the fact that he is ill will engage in activities to determine the effectiveness or desirability of a given treatment. Theoretically this is not sick role behavior, since the purpose of the behavior is not to cure but to measure the progress of the illness and the effectiveness of the therapeutic plan. Therefore, the observed behavior is more akin to illness behavior, with the uncertainty associated with the outcome of tests performed, than to sick role behavior.

The behavior elicited by separation from loved ones or from familiar and dependable objects is likewise not sick role behavior. Separation behavior is caused by a disruption in the person's pattern of affiliation and may be experienced in the absence of illness as well as during illness. The separation anxiety associated with hospitalization can influence the course of illness but is by itself a separate category of behavior from sick role behavior. Perhaps to better understand the dynamics of sick role behavior one should observe behavior without the separation variable induced by hospitalization. What then are the typical behaviors displayed once an individual determines that he is ill and wants to get well?

DESCRIPTION OF SICK ROLE BEHAVIOR

In addition to the acts mentioned above, which are prescribed to deal with the signs and symptoms of illness, there are a group of behaviors that do not act directly upon the illness or its symptomatology but instead provide the conditions that are said to facilitate recovery.

1. *Withdrawal in part or in total from one's usual role responsibilities is a characteristic of sick role behavior.* This is in keeping with the nature of illness as defined in this text, in

which it was stated that the presence of signs and symptoms, although necessary, is not a sufficient condition of illness. If the individual does not perceive his dysfunction as incapacitating, he is not experiencing illness as defined herein. If he perceives his symptoms as incapacitating, he is said to be experiencing illness. Due to the felt incapacitation, he will of necessity withdraw from his usual duties and responsibilities. Socially speaking, then, sick role behavior includes some degree of neglect in fulfilling one's usual duties.

2. *The signs and symptoms that are the manifestations of illness, when sufficiently disturbing or intense, tend to draw the individual's attention to his body and its functions.* The things that are of most importance to the patient now are the things that happen to his body and the routines associated with his general welfare. His thoughts, conversations, and preoccupations revolve around his own symptoms. He becomes apprehensive about minor alterations in body functioning, which in health would normally go unnoticed. Weird and unusual sensations act as internal stimuli to continually or intermittently remind the person of his illness. Minor variations in temperature, digestion, pulse, and elimination take on significant importance. The relief of bodily tensions takes precedence over other less important needs. This tendency towards hypochondriasis is frequently observed in persons who experience unpredictability in normal body functions. In wellness the body functions automatically with clocklike regularity, requiring little or no conscious effort. The well individual is thus able to direct his attention to outside, other-directed matters.

3. *Another characteristic of sick role behavior is regression evidenced by an increase in dependent behaviors.* Regressive behaviors include an increase in dependency, egocentricism, a constriction of interests, and a return to earlier patterns of behavior; for example, in a child one might observe bed-wetting, and thumb-sucking.

The amount of regression varies from individual to individual, depending on the kind and severity of illness and on general personality makeup. The physiologic effects of certain illnesses such as fever and biochemical disturbances can cause a narrowing of perceptual range, blurring of vision, and inability to think clearly. As a consequence, behavior is limited to a circumscribed range. There is a greater tendency for regressive behaviors in severe or acute illnesses in which there is considerable instability or fluctuations in the various physiological parameters. Selye (1956) states that man's supply of energy at any given time is limited. Thus, the more energy required by the body to deal with the illness, the less there is for dealing with matters unrelated to the illness.

An increase in dependency is probably one of the most fundamental forms of regression behavior observed in illness. Dependent behaviors can be classified into three general categories ranging in frequency of performance from minimal to maximal: (1) compliance or conformity to opinions and demands of others, (2) the need for physical assistance in the activities of daily living, and (3) the need for emotional support in the form of approval, reassurance, physical closeness, and protection. Some authors describe the second group as instrumental dependency because it is a means to achieve an end, and the third group as emotional dependency in which the means serve as the end or goal of the behavior (Heathers, 1955). As will be observed in the next chapter, the handicapped person may be instrumentally dependent but not emotionally dependent. Sick role behavior is usually accompanied by some degree of emotional dependence.

The more severe and incapacitating the illness, the more the individual will be dependent upon others for help. As the illness progresses favorably, the number of dependent responses decreases accordingly until a balance between dependent and independent responses is regained (the condition of wellness). As recovery proceeds the patient begins to show signs of readiness to resume previously held responsibilities, such as making decisions, choices, dictating to others, and taking the initiative. He demonstrates by his actions and expressed desires that he wants to become an active functioning independent person.

The frequency of dependent responses emitted does not necessarily correspond with the stage of illness. For example, some individuals in the recovery phase are slow about relinquishing their dependent behaviors owing to feelings of inadequacy. They long for health, but they are afraid to resume the responsibilities associated with health. There is usually some conflict during the recovery phase of illness. In the end, however, the healthy world takes precedence over the regressive pleasures of illness.

In contrast to the person who lags behind, emotionally out of step with the progress of his illness, there are those who seem to be in a hurry to get well. They can't wait to resume their former autonomy and independence. These are the people who generally find dependency unacceptable and have difficulty adjusting throughout the course of their illness.

The world of the sick is also described as narrow and constricted. Situations previously of high importance now carry little weight. The acutely ill person displays little interest toward the impersonal events of the day, such as politics, business, and world news. He is cut off from his normal spheres of activity and many of his normal enjoyments. His social relationships are disrupted to a greater or lesser degree. He feels isolated from the outside world (see following passage by VanKaam (1959):

You hear people leaving the house. Out there is the usual beginning of your daily life. The sounds in your house are the same and still they are different. You feel as an outsider who does not participate, who does not have a function in it. There seems a distance between you here in this bed and those familiar sounds. Somebody, before leaving, will come up to your room and ask you how you are feeling. His brief presence makes the distance still greater and deeper. Today the outside receives a new meaning in your life. There is the shouting of boys, the noise of the cars, the sudden screaming of brakes. But again you experience the street as if an outsider, and the polyphony of sounds otherwise so familiar to you seems strange now and at a distance. During the day the telephone rings, the doorbell rings, but you do not participate any longer. Not only does your life become the life of an outsider but another strange thing happens to you. You experience a reduction of the world. The world seems to be reduced to this sick room, to this bed. Not only the spatial world is reduced for you but also the horizon of time in your world of meaning is narrowed down. The plans of yesterday are losing their importance, the future seems to lose its attraction. Past and future are losing their contours.

Many objects around you receive an actual meaning which they did not have as long as you were healthy. You never noticed before the color of the blankets on your bed; now they seem to look like woods of hairy colored threads. The sheets become white plains with clefts, hills and mountain tops. And you catch yourself analyzing the wallpaper into stripes, points and figures. . . .

Along with the narrowing of one's world and the constriction of interests is a preoccupation with matters related to the self. The patient appears to be intolerant and demanding of others and apparently unable to appreciate the needs of others. He becomes the center of a small egocentric world. Egocentricity and self-centeredness are seen in his exaggerated concern with trifling matters, such as expecting people to attend to his wants immediately and to provide services or do errands that would ordinarily be of little concern to him. In most cases he is more subjective than usual in his interpretation of events surrounding him. His world is like that of an infant, singular and egocentric. As his illness becomes less severe and less demanding, there will be more energy available to widen his horizons beyond himself to include the world of people, events, and things.

4. *Compliance is a subclass of dependency behavior and is to some degree a necessary requirement for recovery.* The individual must follow the prescribed medical regime if he is to regain his health. However, there are varying degrees of compliance, from total submission to active participation and cooperation with the therapeutic plan. The individual who refuses to comply with the medical plan is unable to accept his illness or to try and get well. He is ambivalent and in a state of conflict about the illness and displays behaviors falling under the rubric of illness behavior. He either does not believe that he is ill or does not believe that the treatment ordered will help make him well again. Perceived efficacy is an important determinant of compliance. Normally the individual accepts the dependency involved in illness and cooperates with family and physician to hasten recovery.

Accepting the illness means accepting the dependency that goes along with being ill, that is, dependency commensurate with the degree and kind of illness one is experiencing. Inability to accept this level of dependency or overdependency is defined as deviant sick role behavior because it interferes with the goal of recovery.

DEVIANT SICK ROLE BEHAVIOR

We shall make a distinction in this text between acceptable sick role behavior and deviant sick role behavior. It is the author's contention that when illness is used for secondary gains, for gains other than those to get well, this constitutes deviant sick role behavior. The complexity of sick role behavior is magnified when one realizes that the person experiencing illness occupies simultaneously a position of great power and one of extreme weakness. The combination of dominance and dependence places him in a difficult conflict situation. It is easy for him to capitalize on this unusual situation, that is, to gain power he would otherwise not hold. He may attempt to achieve this position of power through overt aggression or displaced aggression. On the one hand the patient tends to be demanding, complaining, and making all kinds of threats, while at the same time he tries to dominate others through the use of pitiable sounding requests and pleas for aid and attention to his sufferings.

Forced dependency as a consequence of illness adds another dimension to the complexity of sick role behavior. The individual may be unable to accept the dependency involved in illness owing to long established fears about being dependent upon others, or he may have strong dependency needs and long to be cared for by others. This second type craves the attention and protection gained through illness and is reluctant about accepting any responsibility. Illness serves as a refuge for these individuals. It protects them from having to meet the demands imposed by the outside world or from dealing with a disagreeable psychological situation. All of us have heard about the child who malingers, not wanting to get well because of the rewards attending his illness. This was recognized by Parsons (1951) when he suggested that the ill be insulated from well persons because of the "contagious" nature of illness. Sickness can serve as an escape from the pressures of ordinary life and thus appear "tantalizingly attractive." Thus, Parsons states that illness, in so far as it is used as a retreat from the outside world, is a form of deviant behavior.

The individual who is afraid or feels threatened when forced to be dependent will find it impossible to accept the fact of his dependency. He is burdened with feelings of shame and guilt when reminded of this intolerable situation. He becomes openly hostile, refusing any offers of help, constantly complaining and tearing people apart. No matter what people do for him, it is never done right!

Another individual may vacillate between accepting and rejecting the enforced dependency. On the one hand he is grateful for the care provided by his benefactors, while at the same time he resents their presence because it reminds him of his weak and inferior relation to them. Hence one observes changes in mood swings, from being cooperative and appreciative at one time to being openly hostile and antagonistic at another time.

A third type of deviant sick role behavior identified to date is that of the individual who no longer appears to care whether or not he will get well. If he at one time did care, the stresses of the illness and therapy have now taken their toll. The individual behaves in a submissive docilelike manner, no longer putting up a resistance to unwanted treatments. He resigns himself to the demands of the regime and communicates through posture and facial expression his feelings of helplessness, hopelessness, and despair, with no power to control the things that are now happening to him. Apathy and withdrawal are described by Strassman (1956) as a defensive adjustment to severe stress. Certain kinds of overt behaviors are inhibited, and most emotional responses are suppressed. Symptoms include a reduced or modulated affect, listlessness, uncommunicativeness, lack of spontaneity, indifference, slowed reaction, lack of enthusiasm, and lack of initiative. Strassman said that these characteristics seem to be a common psychological reaction to the kind of stress experienced by prisoners of war. He labeled this behavior as the "prisoner of war syndrome." He observed that some of the prisoners simply gave up. Deaths occurred among men whose physical conditions seemed to be improving and under control. They "retreated into themselves and refused to eat what was available, eventually lay down and curled up, as if waiting for death." Submission and resignation to one's fate do not contribute towards the goal of recovery and, in fact, may impede or prevent recovery. Thus, this also constitutes deviant sick role behavior. The natural healthy response would be to try to gain control over what is happening and to master it.

SUMMARY.   Sick role behavior includes a class of acceptable and a class of deviant behaviors. Sick role behavior is defined as any activity performed by a person believing himself to be sick for the purpose of getting well. The individual may alternate from sick role to illness behavior as he changes from accepting illness and the dependency involved, to rejecting or becoming doubtful about the presence of illness and/or the benefits of treatment. When the individual engages in activities that do not support the goal of recovery, this constitutes deviant behavior and becomes both a nursing and a social problem. Acceptable sick role behavior involves a whole range of dependent behaviors and leads to some neglect of one's usual duties. It includes receiving treatment prescribed by family, friends, pharmacists, or members of the health team.

VARIABLES THAT INFLUENCE
SICK ROLE BEHAVIOR

The group of variables that influence sick role behavior are similar to those discussed under health and illness behavior, including such factors as the individual's personality, social status, occupation, education, age, and sex. Further elaboration of some of these variables follows.

The Nature of the Illness

Looming larger than ever, now that the illness is a fact and can no longer be denied, is the nature of the illness as perceived by the person experiencing it and the course taken by the illness. As discussed in Chapter 2, illness is experienced as some change in structure and function in the body, a change that is associated with unusual, weird, and sometimes painful sensations. Such changes and sensations are interpreted or are given meaning according to the individual's background and past experiences. His behavior will reflect his perception of his illness as well as his perception of those who care for him.

Where are the aberrations or dysfunctions? Are they overt, readily seen by others, or covert and hidden? Are they serious, that is, life-threatening, or nonserious, with a prognosis of full recovery? What structures are involved? Will the changes interfere with present work or social relationships? Is there stigma attached to the illness, with feelings of shame and guilt? Does the illness involve organs that are personal and private and not usually subject to public inspection? How long will the forced change last? Will it be temporary or permanent? The answers to these and a host of other questions concerning the nature of illness will determine to a large extent whether or not the individual will adopt the sick role. For example, it is conceivable that persons suffering afflictions of the heart or lungs that are perceived as life-threatening would behave quite differently from those experiencing discomforts of the gastrointestinal tract perceived as nonserious. At present there is not enough information to predict that given certain illnesses, certain behaviors will follow. Systematic research conducted now and in the future may provide us with the necessary information to make such predictions.

Furthermore, apprehension, concern, and dissatisfaction with the speed or rate of recovery and remission of symptoms can be sufficiently disruptive to cause doubt and skepticism about the efficacy of the treatment and thereby become important determinants of behavior. Mistrust of the doctor and the therapeutic plan can be responsible for interruptions, delinquency, and abrupt termination of treatments.

Societal Expectations of
Persons Experiencing Illness

According to Parsons (1951), being sick constitutes a social role. The role is partially and conditionally legitimized by a set of institutionalized expectations and corresponding sentiments and sanctions. The patient is helpless and therefore in need of help. He experiences suffering or disablement or both, and possibly is also facing risks of getting worse. His incapacity is legitimated in that he is exempted from "normal social role responsibilities." The failure to perform his normal responsibilities is not his fault. He is not to blame for his illness or held responsible for his condition; he cannot will himself back to health. Actually he may have caused his illness through negligence, but he still is not expected to cure himself.

The exemption accorded the sick may extend beyond the actual disability. For example, a relatively slight impairment may call for staying home from work or school. The limits of exemption are usually specified by the physician as appropriate to the existing incapacitation, and therefore the individual has a moral obligation to accept the prescribed exemption.

Along with the above two rights, exemption from responsibilities and absolvement of blame for illness, are two obligations or duties expected of persons experiencing illness. The sick person should view his illness as undesirable and therefore should desire to get well. His commitment to normal capacities must be maintained. To enforce this duty Parsons recommends that the ill person be insulated from those who are not sick so as to prevent the "spread of disease" and to prevent the sick person from getting too much support for his incapacitation.

Finally, the sick individual is obligated to seek technically competent help and to cooperate with those responsible for his care, in order that his obligation to get well is achieved as expeditiously as possible.

Note that these are four aspects of a system of institutionalized expectations. The degree to which these expectations are met is highly problematic. This is particularly true in our society in which high value is placed on self-sufficiency and mastery over the environment through individual effort. Refusal to play the sick role is essentially a refusal to define oneself as in need of help. Learning the sick role requires in essence the relinquishment of the rights and duties of normal adult responsibilities and entails a desocialization process.

The normally motivated adult finds it difficult to admit that he is unable to fulfill his role obligations. Often the idea of being helpless and in need of help is unacceptable to the person's self-concept. He may recognize his own incapacitation and still insist that he is not sick, or particularly in the case of mental illness he may not recognize his inadequacies in performance. He must often be convinced of the legitimacy of his incapacitation. This involves both the assurance that the illness is not his fault and emphasis on his responsibility to seek help as a symbolic demonstration of his desire to get well. Simply pointing out a clear responsibility is often not enough. A sense of urgency about completing immediate tasks, even though the sick person is relatively inefficient in doing so, mitigates against playing the sick role. Commitment to work roles is accompanied by the natural reluctance to adopt the sick role.

The Role of Relevant Others

The function of lay persons, according to Twaddle (1969), is to guide the individual toward or away from a physician. Once a contact with a physician has been made, the individual and his lay consultants accept the physician's definition of the situation. Twaddle reports a difference among ethnic groups in the use of medical and lay referral systems. Jews consulted physicians most readily, whereas Protestants were most resistant, relying more heavily on nonmedical personnel for advice.

The role of relevant others as determinants of sick role behavior has been recognized as sufficiently important by the sociologists to advocate that care be moved to institutions outside the family home. This is because illness not only causes changes in behavior in those experiencing it, but it also causes changes in the behavior of relevant others, especially members of the family interacting with the patient. Furthermore, handling sickness outside the family serves to discourage falling ill in the first place.

Parsons and Fox (1960) state that the sick person in the home enjoys special privileges not accorded the well person, which could serve to "drive the sick actor deeper and deeper into his illness." In responding to the passive-dependent nature of illness, members of the family may become either overindulgent or hypercritical, both of which attitudes are unfavorable to full and rapid recovery. On the one hand family members may tend to be more sympathetic and supportive of the sick person than warranted, or on the other hand they may display an excessive intolerance with respect to the debilitating features of the illness, imposing overly harsh disciplinary measures on the sick member. Parsons and Fox conclude that therapy is more easily effected in a professional milieu where there is not the same order of intensive emotional involvement so characteristic of family relationships. Too much family involvement can actually impede the recovery of the sick person. The family member can overactivate the sick person's dependency need, bringing about a regression to childhood levels, whereas nonfamily members have better developed safeguards against such eventualities. Sometimes family members neither expect nor genuinely want the patient to get well. This is because the maintenance of the sick role by one member of the family may, according to Kasl and Cobb (1966), contribute to the stability of the whole family. On the other hand, family members may play a constructive role in getting a sick member to accept that he is sick enough to go to bed and call a doctor when he himself would tend to delay action somewhat longer.

The attitude of members of the family and visitors toward the sick as perceived by persons experiencing illness is described by Van-Kaam (1958) as follows:

A hidden conflict (exists) between the sick person and his visitors due to a deep chasm between the way in which the visitor sees the sick and the way in which the sickness is lived by the patient himself. . . . The healthy person shoves him [the patient] out of the world of everyday life. He has classified him as a man of that other world, the universe of the sick. The sickness retains some of its surprising unusual and temporal quality in the experience of the patient himself, but he does not detect any longer a similar surprise on the face of the friend who visits him during the second or third week of his sickness. He is asked how he feels, but when he answers he senses that . . . [his visitor's mind] is occupied with other things which are going on in a world in which he does not seem to belong any longer. His visitor displays tactfulness. This very display emphasizes for the patient that he is different, that he has become someone with whom one has to deal in a very delicate and tactful vein. The sick person cannot communicate with the visitor about his new life, which is a lonely facing of sickness and death. Modern man has repressed the thought of these unpleasant realities, and society cooperates by removing their signs from the public scene, which is dominated by the cult of radiant health. Modern man is an awkward visitor of the sick. He is unable to participate in an easy and natural way in the world of the patient because he would not know how to converse about sickness and death. He feels relieved when he is back in his car among the familiar sounds and sights of the street.

The Culture of the Hospital and of the Medical Care System

Hospitalization that accompanies the sick role, according to Kasl and Cobb, serves as an additional obstacle to the "already difficult process of socialization into and out of the sick role."

Most authors agree with Esther Lucille Brown (1961) and her overall description of the hospital as authoritarian, subordinating the individual and his needs to the larger group in behalf of the bureaucracy and efficient operation of the system. The hospital environment has been characterized as strange, lacking privacy, containing unvarying routines, and deemphasizing external power and prestige. Pain and suffering are expected; compliant and dependent behavior is demanded (King, 1962).

> Perfect strangers appear. They poke things down you, into you, and up you. Many people ask you questions—all manner of questions—and expect accurate and prompt answers. Somehow the questions you have as a patient bring forth evasive answers or receive no answers at all. In fact, often you are given the impression that you have no business asking questions at all. [Larsen, 1961, p. 44.]

The hospital culture does indeed make many demands of the patient that forces him to change from normal living to institutional living.

Every attempt is made, it seems, to remove his personal identity as quickly as possible. Taylor (1962) suggests that the purpose of the admission procedure is to reduce individuals to "appropriate and interchangeable units," to the least common denominator, a process she calls "people stripping" or "sociological sheep-shearing." Each procedure, she states, is designed simultaneously to remove the old frame of reference and to create a meaningful context for new attitudes and new behaviors.

Although Taylor admits to dependency as an outgrowth of the patient's need for help, she claims that the hospital system is set up to treat patients as if they were incompetent in all areas. Exemption from usual responsibilities is interpreted by hospital personnel as meaning that the individual must let others in his new environment make all the decisions for him. A childlike setting evokes childlike behaviors. The patient is expected by hospital personnel to comply unquestioningly with hospital rules and regulations and to follow the decisions made by doctors and nurses. The situation is not at all unlike that of the parent-child situation.

The ambivalence about, and the ambiguity in, the patient role is further enforced by the hospital system. The patient has an obligation to get well—or to die. On the one hand he is expected to submit himself totally to the care-agents, and on the other hand he is expected to retain the desire to get well. At any moment when the doctor decides, the patient must drop the sick role and resume his former well behaviors. The sudden and abrupt change in role expectations adds to the patient's dilemma.

The medical care system serves to offset the psychologically gratifying aspects of illness through the imposition of such penalties as deprivation, subordination, and loneliness; thus it acts to motivate the person to want to get well (Parsons and Fox, 1960). The control of the passive-deviance of illness by the medical care system has brought with it accusations of undersupport, in other words, a failure to recognize the patient as a person. As a result there has been pressure for greater inclusion of the family's supportive role in patient care. What is needed is a proper balance between the supportive and the disciplinary components of the therapeutic process. Research reveals that when the supportive component is heavily weighted, it may be beneficial in facilitating the adoption of the sick role, but it interferes with the person's eventual relinquishment of that role.

People behave according to their expectations of the medical care system. And expectations differ according to whether individuals are members of a cosmopolitan or of a parochial social group. Suchman (1966) suggests that individuals who tend to be open, progressive, instrumental, and individualistic can be characterized as cosmopolitan, whereas persons who tend to be traditional, ethnically exclusive, closed, and highly cohesive are described as parochial in attitude and outlook. The latter tend to subordinate themselves to the primary group values and beliefs. It seems logical to deduce, then, that those who tend to be open and progressive are more receptive to change, scientific advances, and efficiency; whereas those who tend to be traditional and closed, would lack trust in technological innovations and be highly skeptical of the medical care system. Logically the parochial group would place more reliance on traditional concepts of healing carried down from generation to generation, such as folk medicine, which is highly personal and highly subjective and thus nonscientific. Being less open, this group would have a lower level of knowledge about disease and its treatment.

If one described the medical care system in terms of its organization, bureaucracy, and vast complex of specializations that emphasize the application of the latest medical scientific innovations and skills, one could predict with some degree of certainty that members of the cosmopolitan group would have less difficulty adjusting than members of the parochial group. Suchman, Coser, and Taylor support this notion. Those persons classified as cosmopolitan by Suchman tended to adopt a scientific approach towards the medical care system and thus adjusted better to the formal impersonal system than the parochial group who wanted a more personal and less scientific care system.

An examination of the group of persons described by Coser (1960) as having an instrumental orientation reveals a similarity to Suchman's cosmopolitan scientific group. This group of Coser's can be expected to encounter little difficulty adjusting to the medical care system as described by Suchman. As Coser states, they are more scientifically oriented and expect professional competence. They seek information and insight into the interrelations of events, such as the relationship between the competence of medical care and the desired results. In addition they express a need to make suggestions for the improvement of patient care and are in favor of giving more autonomy to patients. They also tend to miss people or activity while in the hospital. Although the latter observations may apply to Suchman's cosmopolitan group, there is no evidence to support that this is necessarily so.

In contrast to the instrumentally oriented group, Coser identifies a class of people who have a predominantly primary orientation. Their orientation is similar to Suchman's parochial group in that they do not try to invoke change but rather accept the status quo, subordinating themselves to the norms of the organization. There is no indication by Coser that the primary group is skeptical of medical care.

Coser apparently views the medical care system from a different vantage point from Suchman. For Coser the medical care system is authoritarian, rigid, and paternal. When viewed from this perspective it is possible to predict that Suchman's parochial group and Coser's primary group should adjust more readily to hospital demands than those who are scientifically and instrumentally oriented. For Coser, the primary group not only submits to societal norms more quickly without question, but they also are oriented to the gratification of primary needs and expect care and attention. They would have a very difficult time adjusting to the scientific and informal medical care system described by Suchman. Likewise Suchman's cosmopolitan group would encounter more difficulty adjusting to Coser's concept of the medical care system than the parochial group.

Taylor (1962) describes a group of patients who appear similar to Suchman's parochial and Coser's primary group. Her "care-oriented" group view doctors as omniscient and protective and call themselves good patients when submitting totally to the system. Her "cure-oriented" group, like Suchman's cosmopolitan-scientific and Coser's instrumental groups, view doctors as applying expert skill and knowledge. They label themselves as good patients when taking an active part in their own therapeutic plan.

Ossenberg (1962) describes the general hospital social environment as formal in contrast to the lower social-class subculture, which he describes as consisting generally of informal modes of interaction. Based on this assumption he hypothesized that the experience of deviance in patient role is inversely related to social class position. The lower the class position, the greater the experience of deviance. Because of the greater primary group cohesion of lower-class patients, there is greater adherence to group sanctioned norms. These norms often contradict the more formal and impersonalized prescriptions of the official medical care system (Suchman, 1966). Individuals who belong to relatively more homogeneous and cohesive groups are more likely to react to illness and the medical care system in terms of social group definition and interpretation of appropriate patient behavior. If the group's interpretation of appropriate patient behavior is in conflict with what is expected by the medical care system, members of the group will experience difficulty in adjusting to hospitalization.

Thus, from the reports of three authors, it is possible to classify patients into two large categories: the cosmopolitan, scientific, instrumental, cure-oriented group and the parochial, popular, primary, care-oriented group. If the medical care system is viewed as a large, impersonal, formal organization with application of the latest scientific advances, the former group will encounter less difficulty adjusting than will the latter. If the medical care system is viewed as a warm, personal, but autocratic, rigid, and highly structured organization, demanding adherence to the hospital norms, the latter group will adjust more readily than the former group. Most persons would agree that the groups are not clear-cut and that there will be many individuals who share characteristics of both groups. For example, although scientific skill and knowledge are important attributes of a medical care system, these factors should be balanced with supportive measures such as the gratification of primary needs. Some persons might argue whether a medical care system can be both warm and autocratic. In other words can one attribute exist in the presence of the other.

Although functional for hospital adaptation and for responding to hospital authority as defined by Coser, primary, care-oriented behavior is dysfunctional for preparing persons to leave the sick role. Therefore this kind of individual is less ready to leave the sick role and to resume his normal social role obligations. Institutions whose members are expected to relinquish autonomous judgment and decision-making ultimately rob the individual of his sense of self-direction and capacity for same. The intensity and length of time the individual is subjected to such regimentation determine the relative willingness or readiness to relinquish the sick role.

Kasl and Cobb (1966) attribute some of the dissatisfaction and ambivalence of patients to the doctor-patient relationship. The relationship has been characterized as mutual role definition in which behavior is shaped by mutual expectations. However, they state that the relationship is actually asymmetrical:

> It is the doctor, who while permissive and supportive, manipulates most of the rewards, denies any reciprocity, and maintains a relatively affective neutrality, whereas the patient is the amateur who has to be socialized into the sick role and eventually out of it again. [P. 537.]

The patient does not know what he is supposed to do, nor does he know what he wants or expects of his doctor. The kind of relationship established by the patient with his doctor will determine, in part, how long he continues treatment. Lower-class patients are known to discontinue treatments and to change family doctors frequently because of dissatisfaction with care and a feeling of rejection, of not being wanted as a patient by the doctor.

SUMMARY. The variables assumed to influence sick role behavior include the nature of the illness, social role norms, interaction with relevant others, the hospital culture, and the medical care system. Variables discussed under health and illness behaviors are also assumed to influence sick role behavior.

SOME THEORETICAL EXPLANATIONS OF SICK ROLE BEHAVIOR

How does one explain or account for the compliance or noncompliance of behavior, the internalization or rejection of social norms, and the regression behavior observed in illness? Is there a theory of human behavior that explains these characteristics? In addition to the theories offered to help explain health and illness behaviors, the following explanations have been put forward: (1) Schutz's Theory of Interpersonal Behavior, (2) the Theory of Disengagement, and (3) Dependency and the Frustration-Aggression Hypothesis.

The Theory of Interpersonal Behavior

In his Three-Dimensional Theory of Interpersonal Behavior Schutz (1960) states that every individual has a need for control. This need can be satisfied only through the attainment of a satisfactory relation with other people. It is defined behaviorally as the need to "establish and maintain a satisfactory relation with people with respect to control and power." Control behavior, according to Schutz, refers to the decision-making process between people. At one end of the continuum, this behavior manifests itself as a desire for power, authority, and control over others and, therefore, over one's future. At the other end of the continuum is the need to be controlled, to have responsibility taken away. The need for control is also manifested in behaviors elicited when the individual is the object of control by others. Independent and rebellious behaviors represent an unwillingness to be controlled, whereas compliance and submission behaviors indicate various degrees of accepting control by others. These behaviors are the ways that the individual tells others how he wants them to behave toward himself.

Schutz hypothesizes that when an adult perceives his position in an interpersonal situation to be similar to his own position in his parent-child relationship, his behavior will covary with his childhood behavior toward his parent or parent substitute. If he was submissive as a child in his relationship with his parent, the present situation that reminds him of the previous relationship will elicit submissive behavior. It will change as it did in childhood under similar conditions. Many authors have described the illness situation as similar to the child-parent situation. Cues in the illness situation recall for the patient certain earlier behaviors relative to control. Thus individuals whose patterns of control in the child-parent relationship were docile and submissive are likely to respond in a similar manner in the illness situation. These individuals comply with a medical regime without question. Conversely, those individuals whose patterns of control in the child-parent relationship were an assertion of independence and rebellion are likely to display the same patterns of behavior in the illness situation because of its similarity to their childhood situation. These individuals are less likely to comply unquestioningly with a medical plan.

Johnson (1967) suggests that willingness or nonwillingness to comply can also be explained by an analysis of the psychosocial construct of powerlessness. She states that persons learn powerlessness through repeated experiences of having future events controlled by forces external to themselves, for example, by fate or chance. Such individuals learn to stop expecting that their behavior will have any influence on the outcome they desire. Powerlessness not only is learned through negative reinforcement but also negatively influences learning. In other words, why should the individual learn something if it's not going to help provide him with a certain amount of power to control what happens to him?

Johnson, who agrees with Schutz on the constancy of learned behaviors in interpersonal relations, suggests that powerlessness in the adult can be said to represent a more or less enduring personality trait. She suggests, however, that when intervention has been identified as a determinant in patient behavior, it should be planned to decrease if possible the feeling of powerlessness. As long as the individual believes that knowledge will add to his power to control future events happening to him, learning will accrue, and a change in behavior will result. She suggests that perhaps the individual experiences feelings of powerlessness in certain settings, whereas the same individual may experience adequate control in other settings. Perhaps the very nature of illness and of the hospital setting makes individuals particularly vulnerable to generalized feelings of powerlessness. Nevertheless, the notion of powerlessness needs to be explored further both in terms of patient willingness to comply and cooperate with treatment and in terms of developing nursing acts to increase feelings of control by the patient about future events.

Unwillingness to comply can also be explained on the basis of cognitive dissonance, especially if what the patient feels and what he is told are dissonant. Take for example the individual who states he feels well but is told that he is sick. If he is to comply, he must convince himself that he feels sick in order to achieve consonance with what he knows. If he cannot achieve consonance this way, he will change what he knows so that it is consonant with what he feels. He will deny the illness and refuse to follow the prescribed medical regime.

Internalization of Social Norms

It was stated earlier that being sick constitutes a social role, since this condition contains a set of norms or rules of behavior that have been institutionalized or accepted by society. Institutionalization of a set of norms in any given society does not necessarily guarantee that the social role that evolves is learned to the same degree by all members of that society. Roles are learned through intentional instruction, incidental learning, or both. Through a process of socialization, by a system of rewards and punishments, the individual learns that certain behaviors are acceptable and others are not. Societal norms that have become a part of the individual's repertory of behaviors are said to be internalized. The individual behaves according to the learned expectations of the role he is playing. If he has learned that sick persons are expected to want to get well and to view illness as undesirable, his behavior should reflect this norm.

However, role behavior is not so simply explained. In addition to a learned set of expectations associated with a given social role, the individual behaves according to the perceived value, goals, and sentiments of the person with whom he interacts at any given time. If the individual accepts his obligation to want to get well and gears his behavior accordingly, only to be met by the relevant other in the interaction with expressions encouraging dependency and regression, he is likely to respond according to what he perceives the relevant other expects of him, regardless of the social norm that previously guided his behavior. Thus, incongruency with sick role norms may be due to the expectancy system established in the interaction.

It is not difficult to realize that the expectations of the behavior of two members in an interaction may differ considerably, each changing according to the perceived expectations of the other—a process that Turner (1962) calls role-taking or role-in-process. In the interaction, each member learns the role of the other while learning their own roles, thus eliminating or minimizing the surprises and unpredictability and consequent disturbances associated with the initial interaction. Role-taking provides stability to an interaction. Obviously if a member in the interaction reciprocated in unexpected ways, there would be a disturbance in the system of interaction. Thus, the interactionists state that social norms are built and reinforced in interaction.

Theory of Disengagement

The response to illness can be compared to the process of aging as described by Cummings and Henry (1961) in their theory of aging. They postulate that certain internal changes in the body due to biological aging result in a change in amount and variety of interaction, quality of interaction, and perception of self-concept. With the changes in the lining of the blood vessels and retina and with the decrease in vitality associated with aging, it seems logical that concomitantly there would be a change in behavior. Cummings and Henry suggest the possibility that there might be some intrinsic changes with age that are analogous to the process of maturation in children. Instead of expanding and enlarging one's world of people and things, the world becomes smaller and more constricted, requiring less involvement and resulting in disengagement from the environment. Admittedly the process is hastened by environmental forces, but until explored further we should not rule out the possibility of an inner change also.

It has been suggested by several authors that there is a narrowing or constriction of the perceptual field in illness. Many times this field is not only narrowed but blurred, owing to fever and biochemical changes that alter the pH and thus result in a clouding of the sensorium. The patient's behavior, as described earlier, reflects this constricted "life space" in ways similar to those of the aged. The individual, in aging, and we postulate in illness, is in a process of mutual withdrawal. He initiates the change, and relevant others may or may not reciprocate. In so far as relevant others do reciprocate, disengagement is achieved.

When the organs of sensation are incapacitated or defective, owing to illness or aging, perception that gives meaning to sensations experienced is also altered. There appears to be first a shift in self-perception, with the need for social interaction becoming less important and therefore less frequent. There is a decrease not only in the variety of interactions but also in the amount of time spent each day in the company of others. Finally, there appears to be a shift in the quality of interaction: both the aged and the ill are accused of behaving in socially unacceptable ways, to the shock and dismay of those around them. With a change in their value systems of rewards, their behavior has become more carefree and less constrained. In the study by Cummings and Henry there was a significant drop in approval-seeking and love-seeking rewards. No longer valuing or needing these rewards, behavior takes on different meaning for the ill or aged. Their behavior no longer requires the sanction or approval of others. In illness, idiosyncratic or irascible behavior is excused on grounds that the individual is not feeling well and cannot be accountable for his behavior.

Another explanation of the regression observed in illness is attributed to adaptation and the struggle for survival. Lederer (1965) suggests that social and emotional regressions allow the sick person to redistribute his energies so as to facilitate the healing process. In other words, Lederer postulates that the regression is in itself an essential factor in the healing process. The biological task of the sick, he continues, is to get well. Achievement of this goal is facilitated by focusing energy on the self and withdrawing energies from other uses and purposes.

The principle of redintegration states that "the greater the frequency with which stimulus events *A* and *B* are associated in the input to an organism, the greater will be the tendency for the central correlates (conscious ideas) of one, *a*, to activate the central correlate of the other, *b*" (Berlyne, 1960). In other words, the helplessness and dependency experienced as stimulus events in illness are associated with the same events experienced in infancy and childhood. Therefore, illness can be expected to redintegrate the only reactions to helplessness and discomfort that a patient has learned. A reinstatement of an earlier reaction under new circumstances is a useful hypothesis to explain the tendency of patients to regress to a more infantile level during their illness.

Psychoanalytic theory explains emotional regression as partly an ego defense against anxiety. The experience of illness is presumed to be anxiety-inducing. The overadaptation seen in overdependency is a reaction formation against deep-seated dependency needs.

Dependency and the
Frustration-Aggression Hypothesis

An analysis of the nature of dependency (Beller and Haeberle, 1959) makes it quite evident that certain aspects can produce much frustration. Dependence on others for gratification of one's needs can be very frustrating, especially when the other person cannot attend to one's needs immediately or "correctly." The dependent person constantly worries that he may do something that will cause him to lose the much needed protection and intervention provided by the care-giver. Frustration leads to feelings of hostility and aggression. Anxiety, which is at the core of dependency, may augment rather than inhibit hostility, rage, and aggression. In turn, aggression may lead to dependency gratification in the form of receiving the much-wanted attention and physical contact. Thus, frustration of dependency needs often leads to aggression. In response to his aggression the individual receives attention and physical closeness, both of which act to reinforce his aggressive behavior. In other words, anger and hostility at not having his dependency needs met will often bring the very help denied to him earlier. The individual therefore learns that aggression is a way of getting his dependency needs met. Some individuals instead of displaying overt aggression will show displaced aggression by playing the role of the weak, helpless person. This behavior is reinforced by the response of others to the weak pitiable cries for help.

SUMMARY. An attempt has been made to describe the characteristics of sick role behavior and the variables influencing the form of the behavior, and to provide some theoretical explanations for the occurrence or nonoccurrence of these features.

It will be recalled that an individual engages in sick role behavior only when he accepts that he is ill and in need of help, and demonstrates a desire to want to get well. The individual who doubts that he is ill, being skeptical and suspicious of the treatment plan, is not engaging in sick role behavior. If he begins to search for another diagnosis or a better remedy, he is engaging in illness behavior. Individuals who display no desire to get well, using illness as a refuge, are playing the deviant sick role.

What about the individual with a chronic illness or physical handicap? Is he experiencing illness, or is he experiencing wellness? Does society expect him to play the sick role or the well role? Gordon (1966) suggests that there are two distinct and unrelated sets of behavioral expectations relevant to the ill person: sick role expectations and impaired role expectations. The next chapter is a discussion of the impaired role.

REFERENCES

BELLER, EMANUEL K. AND A. W. HAEBERLE "Dependency and the Frustration-Aggression Hypothesis," paper presented April 3, 1959, Eastern Psychological Association, Atlantic City, New Jersey.

BERLYNE, D. E. *Conflict, Arousal and Curiosity.* New York: McGraw-Hill Book Company, 1960, 350 pp.

BLAKE, FLORENCE "In Quest of Hope and Autonomy," *Nursing Forum*, 1 (Winter, 1961–1962), 9–32.

BROWN, ESTHER LUCILLE *Newer Dimensions of Patient Care,* Part I. New York: Russell Sage Foundation, 1961, 159 pp.

COSER, ROSE LAMB "A Home Away from Home," in *Sociological Studies of Health and Sickness,* ed. Dorrian Apple. New York: McGraw-Hill Book Company, 1960, pp. 154–72.

CUMMINGS, ELAINE AND WILLIAM E. HENRY *Growing Old.* New York: Basic Books, Inc., 1961, 293 p.

GORDON, GERALD *Role Theory: Illness.* New Haven, Conn.: College and University Press, 1966, 158 pp.

HADLEY, BETTY JO "The Dynamic Interactionist: Concept of Role," *Journal of Nursing Education*, 6, No. 2 (April, 1967), 5–10, 24–25.

HEATHERS, GLEN "Acquiring Dependency and Independence: A Theoretical Orientation," *The Journal of Genetic Psychology*, 87 (1965), 277–91.

JOHNSON, DOROTHY E. "Powerlessness: A Significant Determinant in Patient Behavior?" *Journal of Nursing Education*, 6, No. 2 (April, 1967), 39–44.

KASL, STANISLAV V. AND SIDNEY COBB "Health Behavior, Illness Behavior and Sick Role Behavior," *Archives of Environmental Health*, 12 (April, 1966), 531–41.

KING, STANLEY H. *Perceptions of Illness and Medical Practice.* New York: Russell Sage Foundation, 1962, 405 pp.

LARSEN, VIRGINIA L. "What Hospitalization Means to Patients," *American Journal of Nursing*, 61, No. 5 (May, 1961), 44–47.

LEDERER, HENRY D. "How the Sick View Their World," in *Social Interaction and Patient Care.* Philadelphia: J. B. Lippincott Co., 1965, pp. 155–66.

OSSENBERG, RICHARD J. "The Experience of Deviance in the Patient Role—A Study of Class Differences," *Journal of Health and Human Behavior*, 3 (1962), 277–82.

PARSONS, TALCOTT *The Social System*. New York: The Free Press, 1951, Chap. 10, pp. 431–45.

———— AND RENE FOX "Illness Therapy and the Modern Urban Family," in *The Family*, eds. Norman W. Bell and Ezra F. Vogel. New York: The Free Press, 1960, Chap. 28, pp. 347–60.

SCHUTZ, WILLIAM C. *FIRO: A Three Dimensional Theory of Interpersonal Behavior*. New York: Holt, Rinehart & Winston, Inc., 1960, 267 pp.

SELYE, HANS *The Stress of Life*. New York: McGraw-Hill Book Company, 1956, 324 pp.

STRASSMAN, HARVEY AND THALER E. SCHEIN "A Prisoner of War Syndrome: Apathy as a Reaction to Severe Stress," *American Journal of Psychiatry*, 112, No. 2 (June, 1956), 998–1003.

SUCHMAN, EDWARD "Health Orientation and Medical Care," *American Journal of Public Health*, 56, No. 1 (January, 1966), 97–105.

TAYLOR, CAROL D. "Sociological Sheep Shearing," *Nursing Forum*, 1 (Spring, 1962), 79–89.

TURNER, RALPH H. "Role-Taking, Role Standpoint and Reference Group Behavior," *American Journal of Sociology*, 61 (January, 1956), 316–28.

———— "Role Taking: Process versus Conformity," in *Human Behavior and Social Processes*, ed. Arnold Rose. Boston: Houghton Mifflin Co., 1962, pp. 20–38.

TWADDLE, ANDREW C. "Health Decisions and Sick Role Variations," *Journal of Health and Social Behavior*, 10 (1969), 105–15.

VANKAAM, ADRIAN L. "Nursing the Person," Lecture, School for Psychiatric Nursing, St. Francis Hospital, Pittsburgh, Pa., May, 1958.

ten | *Impaired Role Behavior*

The experience of illness in any society is evidenced by certain manifestations in the living organism, i.e., aberrations in structure and/or function of the body. A change in body structure or customary function becomes an aberration or manifestation of illness when the change extends beyond a normal range established by the medical clinician. For certain structures, facilities, and faculties, the normal range is known and comprises the body of knowledge recognized as medical science. For many human faculties, however, the normal range is not known, and the individual is often uncertain as to whether he is or is not experiencing illness. This is especially true in the case of mental derangement.

It is not enough to define illness as an experience manifested by aberrations in living organisms, for there are many individuals with aberrations who would say that they are not ill. For example, the individual without a limb or with some other body part congenitally absent or surgically removed may not define himself as ill, and yet he manifests an aberration. Are the blind, the deaf, and the dumb experiencing illness? What about the individual who is dependent on drugs or machines for the control of his aberrant condition; can he be said to be ill even though the signs and symptoms of his disability are held in abeyance through artificial and mechanical devices?

How then shall we differentiate between a disabled well person and a disabled ill person? The author suggests that the incorporation of the social dimensions of illness can be used to distinguish between those individuals who are experiencing illness and those who are not. In the presence of an aberration or dysfunction outside the normal range, the criteria for illness shall be the feeling state of the person and his performance capacity. If the defective person states that he does not feel well and suffers an impairment of capacity to perform social roles and valued tasks, he is experiencing illness. On the other hand, if the defective person states that he is feeling fine and perceives no impairment of capacity to perform social roles and valued tasks, he is not experiencing illness. Is he then experiencing wellness? By virtue of a handicap, disability, or chronic condition, the individual may experience wellness congruent or compatible with his handicapped status in society. Because of his defect or aberration his status will differ from that of the normal nondefective member. Whether or not a status for the disabled exists, with a set of institutionalized norms, is not yet clearly known. However, Gordon (1966) suggests that for persons experiencing illness, social pressures serve to discourage normal behavior; whereas for the disabled person not experiencing illness, social pressures serve to aid and maintain normal behavior within limits of a given condition. He calls this the impaired role vis-à-vis the sick role.

In a study conducted by Gordon, persons assessed as ill were those whose conditions appeared to be getting worse or critical. As the prognosis becomes more serious and uncertain, the tendency increases to treat the individual as ill. As the condition becomes better, is controlled, or reaches a state of chronicity, neither better nor worse, the individual is no longer viewed as experiencing illness. He is encouraged to maintain normal behavior within the limits of his condition. Thus an individual may move from sick role behavior to impaired role behavior, and to the extent that there is residual disability limiting his activity, he will continue in this impaired role. He may also engage in illness and health behaviors whenever he experiences new and unusual sensations alerting him to an impending illness, or when he desires to take special action to protect his health.

Supporting Gordon's plea for an impaired role, Cogswell (1964) advocates a disabled or chronic disease role, and Baumen and Kassenbaum (1965) suggest that certain diagnoses are incongruent with sick role expectations, and therefore a different set of expectations are needed whereby the degree of impairment is considered. Hadley at the end of her study, on "Becoming Well: A Study in Role

Change," suggests that children born with a cardiac defect may be enacting a handicapped role rather than a sick role (as implied earlier in the same study). It appears that the role the individual plays depends on his perception of his disability as well as on the perception of relevant others. Some will play the sick role, whereas others with the same congenital defect will play the impaired role. Most authors seems to agree that there is a need to identify a set of norms for the chronically ill, the handicapped, and the disabled.

It has already been suggested by Gordon that the distinguishing feature between illness and any of the above conditions is that in the former case (illness condition) the individual is encouraged to relinquish normal behaviors, whereas in the latter case (impaired condition) the individual is encouraged to resume normal behaviors within the limits of his abilities. The next step, then, is to ask what distinguishes chronic illness from disability, and disability from a handicapped condition.

Wright (1960) differentiates between a handicap and a disability. She suggests that a handicap is usually a result of a disability. When the disability, defined as a condition of impairment (either physical or mental), hinders the individual from achieving at his maximum functional level, it is also a handicap. The differentiation between the two is apparently made to emphasize that not all medically diagnosed disabilities are viewed as "obstacles," and that there will be some who have no known disability but still experience a "handicap." For the purposes of this text a person is viewed as disabled when he is observed to have an aberration in structure and/or function that causes an actual restriction on activity and/or arouses a psychosocial prejudice. The disabled person who does not perceive himself as handicapped shall be classified as healthy. In other words, a disabled person, as long as he does not perceive his disability as handicapping (incapacitating), will be defined as experiencing wellness. A distinction should be made between actual objective impairment and perceived impairment. The individual who perceives himself as handicapped in the absence of any known physical impairment, with or without medical sanction, is an enigma. His status is not known at this time, and therefore he is neither disabled nor well.

Cogswell has defined chronic illness as any impairment or deviation from normality with one or more of the following characteristics:

1.   The impairment is permanent.
2.   There is residual disability.

3. The impairment is caused by nonreversible pathological alterations.

4. The impairment requires special training of the patient for rehabilitation.

5. The patient is expected to require a long period of supervision, observation, or care, all of which can usually be administered by the patient himself.

Since the goal of treatment for chronic diseases cannot be cure, it must be control. Any condition that meets one or more of the above criteria and causes a restriction on activity and/or arouses psychosocial prejudice is classified as a disability. Thus, a disability may be long term or short term, permanent or temporary, and with potential for cure or control. A disability may or may not require special rehabilitative procedures. An individual may be disabled at birth or suffer disability sometime during his life span. Once the signs and symptoms of illness are removed, controlled, or reach a state of chronicity, the individual is no longer considered ill; he is classified as either disabled or well. The rights granted to persons experiencing illness are gradually withdrawn as the individual is pressured to resume normal role obligations achievable within the limits of his condition.

A disability may be obvious or hidden. Examples of obvious defects include amputations, deformities, facial disfigurement, a limp, mental retardation, stuttering, or any impaired function that provokes attention. Examples of hidden defects include disabilities that are disguised or camouflaged by a substitute or prosthesis (in amputation cases), or disabilities that are hidden by the nature of the defect, such as epilepsy, chronic hypertension, and controlled diabetes. A disability may also be classified according to whether it is a static or a dynamic condition. *Static* refers to conditions that are permanent and fixed. No further change is expected at least in physical makeup, and perhaps none in mental performance, e.g., a condition such as that caused by the loss of a finger or a leg. *Dynamic* refers to a condition that is subject to change if props are removed and includes such illnesses as diabetes, heart disease, and phobias. However, the individual with a dynamic impairment is not considered ill as long as his illness is under control. But because this kind of condition is subject to change, the individual must remain under the direction or aegis of medical personnel so that control measures can be modified to keep up with the changes going on in the body (such as growth, maturation, or decline).

A disability therefore is any impairment, physical or mental, obvious or hidden, static or dynamic, in which signs and symptoms of illness are receding or controlled, but which continue to impose restrictions on activity or to provoke psychosocial prejudice. Included in this category is the individual who is described as convalescing, or whose condition is considered incurable but controlled. As long as this individual does not experience the disability as incapacitating (handicapping), he is not experiencing illness per se. Therefore he will be expected to relinquish the sick role and to adopt the impaired role. In summary, impaired role behavior may be observed in the transition from illness to wellness, or it may become a way of life for the permanently disabled.

What are some of the assumed characteristics of the impaired role? Thomas (1966) suggests that the impaired role is an extension of the sick role (as defined by Parsons*) only it is made more "enduring." Thus the first assumption of the impaired role is that the chronically ill (disabled) person experiences an impairment that is permanent rather than temporary, and the right to be exempted from ordinary social responsibility is expected to be permanent; whereas in the case of the ill person, this exemption from responsibility is a temporary privilege granted by society.

In contrast to Thomas' position, this book takes the position that the disabled person is not exempted from ordinary social responsibility as defined for the sick person. The disabled person is expected to maintain normal behavior within limits of his condition. He is expected to assume the responsibilities of his role(s) in so far as it is possible, and to help modify his life situation (e.g., job and home) in the light of his disability. Thus automatic exemption is not granted to the disabled; rather exemption is permitted relative to the degree of disability. Generally speaking, there is a modification of the role(s) of the disabled rather than an exemption.

The second assumption is that many disabled persons as defined herein cannot fulfill the obligation to "want to get well" in terms of a cure as implied in the sick role norms. For example, the chronically ill person is encouraged to make the most of his remaining capabilities, and in this respect he must want to overcome the disability so as to realize his potentialities. In order to achieve proper realization of his capabilities he must accept the fact of his impairment. Acceptance implies that the disabled person recognizes his limitations realistically and that rules for performance are made commensurate with his true degree of disability, his capabilities, and environmental opportunities.

---

*See discussion on page 167.

The third assumption is that the disabled person should not be insulated from the well population. Insulation of the ill has been suggested by Parsons (1951) as a device to protect the well from the temptations of becoming ill. But it is contended here that the rewards attending the disabled are of a different order than those of the ill and therefore not as contagious to others.

The primary reason for proposing that an impaired role be identified as such is that many disabled persons do not perceive themselves as incapacitated (handicapped) and therefore ill. Thus it is wrong to impose upon them a set of sick role norms. But it is equally wrong to classify these individuals as healthy persons in terms of the nondisabled group. The sick role in our society carries with it the assumption that medical personnel or family will care for the patient as long as he is ill. This is not an appropriate norm for the disabled. Many disabled persons are able to carry out their own medical program but refuse to do so or are prevented from doing so by the mistaken assumption of sick role norms. The disabled person needs a set of norms to provide consistency to his behaviors and to the behaviors of those who interact with him. Until a set of norms is established, the disabled person will behave according to his perception of what relevant others expect of him.

Impaired role behavior shall be defined as any activity undertaken by a disabled person who no longer views himself as ill, but is restricted physically and/or psychosocially, for the purposes of maintaining control of his impaired condition, prevention of complications attending such conditions, and resuming role responsibilities commensurate with his controlled or convalescent state. It includes activities directed towards resumption of normal behaviors and the full realization of one's potentialities. It incorporates the concepts of rehabilitation and peak wellness for the disabled.

In contrast, the individual who is unable to accept the disability and attending limitations will behave in a manner that interferes with the goals of maintenance and prevention and therefore is defined as deviant. His behavior will be detrimental to his well-being. He will either try to camouflage the defect or to deny it. In either case the consequences will be disruption to the controlled condition, with a recurrence of illness or psychological disturbances due to repeated failures to perform at the unrealistic level aspired to by him. On the other end of the continuum are those persons who continue to view themselves as ill in spite of medical consensus that their condition is controlled. This behavior is deviant. It perpetuates a socio-psychological condition inconsistent with the medical condition. This inability to relinquish the sick role may be due to a distorted perception of one's condition or to enforcement of sick role norms by relevant others. Both situations become problems for members of the health team.

DESCRIPTION OF IMPAIRED ROLE BEHAVIOR

The form the impaired role takes depends upon the specific nature of the disability. All of the patterns described below are not necessarily applicable to every disabled person (Thomas, 1966). One or more of the patterns, however, should apply to every disabled or convalescent person, for each of these individuals is confronted with either congenital absence or the partial or complete loss of certain responses and thus the need to relearn old responses (e.g., to be independent again), to substitute one response for another (e.g., hearing with lip reading), or to learn a new and different response (e.g., walking with a prosthesis or reading Braille).

If the individual has an impairment from birth or acquires one early in life, he must learn the behavioral patterns of the impaired role in the process of growing up. If the disablement occurs later in life, he must learn new behaviors, and in addition he must unlearn other behaviors no longer possible or appropriate. A large proportion of disabilities occur rather suddenly, and this requires rather rapid socialization into the new disabled role. The process of role change from a well role to an impaired role or from a sick role to an impaired role carries with it certain problems for the disabled.

Handicapped Performer

By definition the impaired role differs from the well role in that the performance of the disabled person is restricted. His impairment may range from complete loss of certain functions at one extreme, to a very minimal loss at the other extreme. His behavioral repertoire will be limited and less complete than that of his nondisabled counterpart. Some behaviors added to his behavioral repertoire will be unique and different, unfamiliar to the nondisabled group. He must innovate ways to achieve goals no longer achievable by previously learned ways. For example, the deaf individual substitutes hearing with lip reading and hand gestures, and the blind person substitutes visual reading with finger reading (Braille).

Activities commensurate with the individual's role as male or female, father or mother, son or daughter, or bread-winner or house-wife may have to be modified because of the disability. For example, the disabled person may have to change his image of the father role so as to be consistent with his capabilities rather than to give up or exempt himself from the role altogether. However, the individual whose disability makes it impossible for him to assume any aspect of his sex, family, or occupational role is said to be experiencing illness and therefore plays a sick role. Impaired role implies the ability and an obligation to assume certain role responsibilities within limits of one's condition. According to this definition the father who is incapable of assuming some activities, even partially, relative to his role as father-husband is ill rather than disabled. He is therefore exempted from his obligations. Thus, a characteristic of impaired role behavior is that behavior or performance is limited relative to the well role.

Instrumental Dependence

The impaired role includes a dependence upon others for aid. The individual with a disability naturally receives more aid than does his nonimpaired counterpart. The degree of dependence will vary with the disability. Also the kind of dependence is an instrumental, means-to-an-end dependence rather than an end in and of itself. The instrumental dependence characteristic of the impaired role differs markedly from the emotional dependence of the sick role. In the former case the individual requires help to complete a task or meet a physical need, whereas in the latter case the individual is dependent upon others, like a child, for protection, approval, and reassurance. Examples of instrumental dependence include the blind person who is dependent upon a seeing-eye dog to locomote safely; or the hard-of-hearing person who is dependent upon a hearing aid to communicate with others; or the person with diabetes who is dependent upon medications and special diets to maintain proper metabolism of carbohydrates.

As part of the impaired role the disabled person is expected to learn to adjust, accommodate, and respond to being an object of aid. This dependence upon others departs from the dominant cultural emphasis upon self-reliance and independence. This is especially felt by the individual who has been trained to be self-reliant, autonomous, and independent in the course of his social learning prior to the advent of the disablement. Americans esteem active mastery more than passive acceptance. Therefore, the disabled person feels hurt at times because of his inability to repay others for the assistance or help he is receiving. He displays ambivalence and negativism with regard to the help he receives, especially when it is accompanied with a drop in his self-esteem. It is not easy to surrender mastery and control to passive acceptance.

Co-manager of His Condition

The disabled person is expected to share in the management of his impaired condition. He is actively involved in his medical care program. In contrast, persons experiencing illness are passive recipients of care as long as the medical and surgical treatments are administered by trained personnel. The disabled person is expected and encouraged to help make decisions relative to his care and rehabilitation. For example, he may participate in the selection of an artificial limb, assume responsibility for giving himself injections and taking medications, or follow a prescribed diet and balanced schedule of rest and exercise. He remains under the care of a physician or other health person, but he assumes considerable responsibility for the control, maintenance, and/or improvement of his condition.

Public-Relations Man

The disabled person is called upon to explain his impairment to others. He learns to be not only an object of aid but also an object of curiosity. The relative uniqueness of the impaired condition places a burden of explanation and interpretation on the disabled over and beyond what is expected of the nondisabled. Thus the disabled person is expected to be his own "public-relations" man. Sometimes he is asked to satisfy the curious, sometimes to resolve inconsistencies in behavior between himself and those interacting with him, and sometimes to clarify his disabilities in order to gain employment or admission to a college, or to enlighten a prospective marital partner as to his capabilities and limitations. As a public-relations man he strives to reduce social prejudice through education of his public. As long as shame, inferiority, and pity are linked with disability, opportunities for realizing one's potentialities are precluded.

DETERMINANTS OF IMPAIRED ROLE BEHAVIOR

Perhaps the most important factor responsible for the variability and somewhat unpredictability of impaired role behavior is the lack of a set of institutionalized norms for the individual who is disabled. There are no uniform, clear rules for disabled persons in the same way that there are rules for the performance of ill and nondisabled persons. The rules and conceptions held for the disabled are generally diverse and lacking in agreement. Furthermore, ignorance about the various types of disabilities and stereotypes concerning the disabled only add to the confusion and inconsistency of behaviors observed.

Without rules of behavior to serve as bases for the development of more complete roles for the disabled, the choice of behavioral alternatives increases, allowing for wide variations. Even the purpose or sentiment that guides the interaction tends to lack unity and consistency. It is difficult to be consistent when the assigned objective in the interaction remains circumspect. Should the disabled person be treated as ill or well? How can he be expected to learn his role when he is confronted with a different set of expectations by the different persons with whom he interacts?

In the absence of a set of norms to guide him, the individual can choose to behave so as to imply a greater or lesser handicap than he has, or he may behave consistently with the true degree of his disability. Persons who interact with the disabled person also have a choice of behaving toward that person in a manner that is commensurate with the actual degree of disability or of behaving in a way that implies a greater or lesser degree of handicap than actually exists. What factors, then, influence the choice of options for the disabled person and for those interacting with him?

The Degree of Disablement

Various diagnoses or disabilities have different consequences for different kinds of people; for example, a restriction on strenuous activity has different consequences for people with dissimilar occupations. The minimum requisite degree of exemption from certain obligations is determined by the attributes of the disability. For the severely disabled and those interacting with him the rules of behavior are fairly well defined. The confusion is greatest with the moderately disabled person. What are the capabilities of this individual, and what expectations can be set that are realistic, that is, neither too high nor too low? In Hadley's study (1966) of children born with congenital heart defects, she found that some parents were highly restrictive and protective of their children, whereas others tended to push their children into behaving like their nondisabled siblings. The inconsistency of behaviors toward the disabled was attributed to sociopsychological factors inherent in the parent-child relationship rather than to the severity of the disability. A relationship between degree of disablement and set of expectations was not made apparent in this study.

Visibility of the Disablement

The visibility of the disablement influences how the disabled person will behave as well as how others will behave toward him. Generally speaking, people behave toward such individuals as if they were more disabled than they actually are. The situation is different for the disabled person with an essentially nonvisible impairment, for there are no cues to alert others to the disablement, and therefore the tendency is to behave toward him as if he were normal.

It is interesting to note that when a group of children, ages 10–11, were asked to rank pictures of children shown with various types of visible handicaps or with no handicaps according to which were most likable or least likable, they ranked the nonhandicapped child as first in preference (Richardson et al., 1961). The rank order of preference was as hypothesized: (1) a child with no physical handicap, (2) a child with crutches and brace on the left leg, (3) a child sitting in a wheelchair, (4) a child with the left hand missing, (5) a child with a facial disfigurement on the left side of his mouth, and (6) an obese child. Although the subjects tested included handicapped as well as nonhandicapped children with varying socioeconomic and cultural backgrounds, there was no significant difference in their rankings. The authors noted that the social (cosmetic) impairments (obesity and facial disfigurement) were more disliked than the functional impairments. In a later study Richardson (1970) observed that the only age level at which the nonhandicapped child was not rated as the most liked of the six choices was between 5–6 years. He postulated that this could be due to less exposure to the handicapped and to a failure to understand the concept of liking.

He also postulated that the reason the nonhandicapped is generally preferred to the handicapped, in the absence of known explicit training towards such a bias, can be attributed in part to dominant cultural deprecatory attitudes toward persons with physical disabilities. Thus, according to the findings of the above reported studies, the kind of disability and its visibility are important determinants of friendship patterns.

Acceptance of the Disability

If the disabled person is able to accept the impairment, he is more likely to behave in a way that is consistent with the degree of disability. Although proper acceptance of the disability by the disabled person does not guarantee that others will reciprocate in like manner, it does increase the possibility of consistency with assigned purposes or sentiments between the two actors.

On the other hand, if the disabled person is unable to accept his impairment, he will behave unrealistically and act as if he were not handicapped; whereas others who recognize the true degree of the handicap will behave toward him on a more realistic basis. The inconsistency between these two sentiments is obvious.

Inconsistent behavior is also elicited when the handicapped person accepts his disability with resignation and denigration, and consequently behaves in a way that exaggerates the disability. This individual displays more handicapped behavior than the disability warrants. Others realizing the true nature of the handicap will behave toward this person commensurably with the true degree of disability. Thus, both members in such an interaction will behave inconsistently toward one another, creating role conflict.

Role conflict exists whenever there are two opposing expectations held for the behavior of an individual such that he cannot perform consistently with both at the same time. Role conflict takes many forms. As described above, the disabled person may hold different expectations for himself than those held by relevant others. A child with a heart defect may hold expectations for himself to behave normally, whereas the child's parents expect him to behave as if he were disabled and sometimes ill, with a need of enforced rest and restricted activity. Another source of role conflict derives from inconsistent expectations among those who interact with the disabled person. The parent may define certain rules of behavior that are contrary to the expectations set down by the physician. A more subtle source of conflict is found in the disabled person's own set of expectations. The father with a recent heart attack realizes he must care for himself if he is to recover, but be also realizes at the same time that as a member of the middle class he is expected to achieve and succeed in his world of work.

Confronted with such a situation of conflict, the disabled person and his relevant others either must choose one set of expectations to be more desirable than the other set, or as Turner (1962) suggests, they must make "creative compromises by which viable relationships can be maintained." Thus conflict is resolved between self and other(s) through a process of role-taking and role-making. Each member reciprocates according to his perception of the changing purpose or sentiment of the other in the interaction.

Society and Culture

Society, generally speaking, is built and organized to benefit the normal individual. Conditions perpetuated by society, because of ignorance, constrain the disabled to behave in ways that exaggerate the true degree of disablement. Society has assigned the disabled to a dependent minority group rather than to a potential productive force. The traditional attitude toward the crippled and disabled has been one of charity. These individuals have been regarded with sympathy, and their plight is seen as one of inevitable helplessness and dependency. These attitudes have encouraged the disabled to feel self-pity, to seek secondary gains from the disability, and to solicit the help of others in general.

This attitude is exemplified in the general labor market wherein the disabled are discriminated against and employment opportunities restricted. Kessler (1953) suggests that discrimination against the physically handicapped or disabled is based on the following economic grounds:

1. The employer maintains that a physical disability means a loss in productivity and thus an economic liability.
2. The disabled person is said to be more prone to accidents because of his physical limitations.
3. If the disabled person sustains an injury, the employer feels that he will be obligated to pay for any aggravation of a preexisting disability.

Some employers also believe that the crippled and disabled are psychologically instable and therefore too risky to employ. Kessler suggests that these assumptions are without foundation!

In addition, the disabled person is surrounded by nonhandicapped adults who serve as models for his behavior. He wants to be "just like anyone else." He strives to emulate the model, to be self-reliant and independent, but often due to his disability he experiences only repeated failures. Thus, idolizing normal standards may only serve to increase feelings of inferiority.

Adoption of the impaired role is facilitated by the following conditions:

1. If there is congruence between the old behaviors and the new ones the disabled person is expected to learn.
2. If the individual is capable of learning the new behaviors.
3. If he is motivated to adopt the new role.
4. If he has had some preparation through rehearsal, imaginative or actual, of the new behavior.
5. If the transition from a well or sick role to an impaired role is gradual rather than sudden.

Unfortunately the characteristics of most disabilities acquired late in life are accompanied by a sudden, rapid onset, basic incongruence between the old and expected new behaviors, a lack of motivation to change (especially true for older persons), and inability or incapacity to perform the new and different behaviors.

Based on Interruption Theory (Spielberger, 1966), such discontinuity between two roles that follow one another sequentially produces a state of arousal that is followed by emotional behavior. The interrupted organism (disabled individual) tries to maintain the old behavior in an effort to complete the response sequence learned prior to the disability, or failing this the individual will try to substitute some other learned organized response. When no alternative response is available, the individual will not be able to complete the sequence or planned course of action, and consequently he experiences anxiety, distress, or fear. The important point is to provide continuity between role transitions by making alternative responses available so that the disabled person can once again behave in an organized, unitary fashion, smoothly and without pause.

AMBIGUITY OF IMPAIRED ROLE

Does being disabled constitute a social role? According to Parsons (1951), the test of whether a role has been accepted by society is the existence of a set of institutionalized expectations and corresponding sentiments and sanctions. In the case of the person experiencing illness the situation is clearly defined. This individual is viewed as helpless and clearly in need of external assistance. He is recognized as being in a state of suffering or disablement or both. In addition he cannot be blamed for his illness, nor can he extricate himself by his own efforts. He is said to be technically incompetent, requiring professional attention, and he faces complex problems of adjustment. Based on these sentiments, certain rights and obligations are granted, which were discussed in Chapter 9.

In contrast to the person experiencing illness the disabled person lacks group sanction and the personal valuation necessary to endorse behavior reflecting his disability. In his case, due to a lack of group sanction, realistic acceptance of his position and himself is precluded. The sentiments surrounding the disabled person are varied, inconsistent, and contradictory. These feelings range from viewing the disabled individual as unfortunate, dependent, helpless, and tragic to a more positive approach in which he is viewed as a member of a potentially productive group.

In the absence of a set of institutionalized expectations, who or what defines appropriate behavior for the disabled group? As stated repeatedly throughout this book, people respond according to the perceived values, goals, and sentiments of persons in interaction. Patterns emerge as a consequence of repeated interactions between the disabled person and his relevant others.

SOME THEORETICAL EXPLANATIONS OF IMPAIRED ROLE BEHAVIOR

An understanding of the behavior of the disabled is perhaps best understood from the perspective of role theory.

Role Theory

Roles, according to Turner (1962), are defined, created, and stabilized or modified as a consequence of interaction between self and others. A role is a set or collection of possible actions that belong together and are consistent for a given actor.

A set of obligations and privileges, such as has been defined for persons experiencing illness, best fits those roles that are attached to formally acknowledged statuses. These so-called formalized roles are merely devices to set the full role in motion. In fact, sometimes the norms associated with formalized roles cramp the role-taking process, which is characteristically tentative, changing, and innovating.

The performance of the disabled person is based on his identification of the role of the other person toward whom he is orienting himself. His own role of dependency can exist only to the extent that others in the interaction are playing the role of care-giver. Thus in order for a disabled person to play a role, he must have some idea of the expected behavior of the person or persons toward whom he is relating. He behaves in such a way as to forestall or provoke some anticipated behavior. This individual identifies the role of the other either from knowledge of his own status, by generalizations drawn from observing the other's behavior, or from imaginatively placing himself in the other person's shoes in order to predict what might be that person's course of action. The disabled person thus prepares himself to interpret and to respond to a range of behaviors. When he changes his behavior toward another, it is assumed that he first perceived a change in the role of the relevant other. Individuals continually test the conception they have of the role of others. Expectations refer not to the specific action the relevant other will take but to the perceived guiding sentiment and goal of the role played by that relevant other. The expectation is that the sentiments or goal will be shared or reciprocated, or else met by some countersentiment.

The disabled person plays a variety of roles, depending on the sentiments or goal of relevant others in the interaction. Thus, he may play comanager, public-relations man, handicapped performer, and so on, as discussed earlier in this chapter. He may also play the sick role if this seems expected of him by relevant others. In some situations he is expected to behave as if he did not have a disability, a source of much frustration when the reality of the situation prevents the achievement of the unrealistic goals set by himself or others.

Individuals born with a disability or with one acquired early in life learn the behavioral patterns associated with the impaired role in the course of growing up. It is the individual who acquires a disability late in life who not only must learn new behaviors but also must "unlearn" other behaviors no longer possible or appropriate. He may be suddenly confronted with a set of behaviors incongruent with those learned in earlier role-training. His pathway from dislocation to reintegration is fraught with emotional and interpersonal crises. He must first come to terms with the fact of the disability and his feelings of inadequacy, and then face the need to accept help or to be the recipient of aid. Some persons have to go through a period of mourning, grief, and depression for the lost part or function before they can move on to reintegration. Ultimately the individual either accepts help and thus temporarily affiliates with the world of the disabled, or he rejects this alternative through denial or some other compensatory mechanism. With assistance from others, the newly disabled person is able to rechannel and mobilize energy away from his loss and move toward vigorous development of his remaining assets and finally achievement of optimal self-autonomy along with social reintegration.

The Self-Concept

Disability often forces an individual to modify his conception of himself. New and confusing bodily sensations, reduced abilities, and a less than perfect body now challenge the individual's previously established self-identity. Shame, inferiority, and worthlessness are often experienced to a degree that is not justified by the disability. What is the cause of this discrepancy?

A person learns to accept the image that the group holds up to him. Self-conception or the cognitive awareness of one's self is derived from interaction with others. Self-conceptions are learned, and the evaluative reactions of others play a significant part in this learning process. Self-concept derives from a self-estimate of one's performance coupled with the evaluation delivered by others. The disabled person's conception of himself as worthy or unworthy is certainly influenced by the evaluation of his performance by relevant others. Constant deprecatory sentiments toward disabled persons serve only to create self-concepts of low esteem. Most persons accept in good faith the position that the group provides for them and thus become more or less committed to the behavior expected by the group. Apprehension about future worth and concern about losing the regard of family and friends are partially reflections of anticipated group behaviors toward the disabled person. Achieving a coherent self-picture and value for one's self will succeed or fail depending on the kind of relationship the disabled person is allowed to establish in his community.

The Need for Inclusion

Another dimension to Schutz's Three-Dimensional Theory of Interpersonal Behavior (1960) is the interpersonal need for inclusion —the need to feel that the self is "significant and worthwhile." Of particular relevance to the disabled is the need to feel that one is a competent, responsible person, plus the need to feel that the self is lovable. The disabled person needs to be accepted by others for what he is, in spite of his handicap. In a study by Richardson et al. (1961), the fact that 10–11-year-old children did not choose a disabled person for their *best* friend (even though some of the children were disabled themselves) lends some support to the notion that the disabled are often excluded from establishing certain valued relationships with the nondisabled group. Inability to satisfy this need may help explain the ambivalence and resentment often expressed by the disabled toward the nondisabled.

All persons need to experience the feeling of mutual interest with other people. The disabled person wants to be able to take an interest in other people to a satisfactory degree and to have other people interested in him—his personal self and not just his disability. Being stared at or quizzed about the disability with consequent intrusion into the privacy of one's life is not the kind of interest solicited. The disabled individual will regard such an intruder as a fatuous boor and will want to retaliate in kind. The disabled person would like to exclude his disability from the situation, to minimize the disability in an effort to establish a viable relationship. His greatest fear is the fear of rejection. His efforts to be just like everyone else are guided by this need for inclusion. All people want to establish satisfactory relations with others, but it is the disabled group that is most often denied this satisfaction.

SUMMARY.   The reasons for including a discussion of the impaired role in this text are based more on the recognition of a need for such a role rather than on any evidence that such a role exists. Many observers would agree with Gordon that most individuals have a different set of expectations for persons whose illness is deteriorating than for persons whose illness is improving or stabilizing. However, the distinction is not always made clear, and thus the confusion and inconsistency in the behavior of disabled persons: sometimes the disabled individual is expected to behave as a well nondisabled person, and other times he is expected to play the sick role.

Gordon suggests that behavior is guided by the prognosis of the illness. If *A* perceives that *B*'s illness is deteriorating, *A* can be expected to behave quite differently toward *B* than if *A* perceives *B*'s illness is improving or stabilized. On the other hand, if *B* perceives his illness to be deteriorating, he will behave in a way that communicates this·feeling and *A* will reciprocate accordingly.

In other words, the element of prognosis can serve to determine the response of both parties in interactions. In the course of repeated interactions, rules and standards of conduct will be defined.

Ultimately, perhaps, the disabled group will be accorded a formal status with certain rights and obligations appropriate to their newly recognized status.

REFERENCES

BAUMAN, BARBARA O. AND GENE G. KASSENBAUM "Dimensions of the Sick Role in Chronic Illness," *Journal of Health and Human Behavior*, 6, No. 1 (Spring, 1965), 16–27.

COGSWELL, BETTY E. AND DONALD D. WEIR "A Role in Process: The Development of Medical Professional's Role in Long Term Care of Chronically Diseased Patients," *Journal of Health and Human Behavior*, 5 (Spring and Fall, 1964), 95–109.

GORDON, GERALD *Role Theory and Illness*. New Haven: College and University Press, 1966, 158 pp.

HADLEY, BETTY JO *Becoming Well: A Study of Role Change*. Doctoral dissertation, University of Calif., Los Angeles, 1966.

KESSLER, HENRY H. *Rehabilitation of the Physically Handicapped*. New York: Columbia University Press, 1953, pp. 6–24.

PARSONS, TALCOTT *The Social System*. New York: The Free Press, 1951, pp. 250–57, 431–47.

RICHARDSON, STEPHEN A., NORMAN GOODMAN, ALBERT H. HASTORF, AND SANFORD M. DORNBUSCH "Cultural Uniformity in Reaction to Physical Disabilities," *American Sociological Review*, 26, No. 2 (April, 1961), 241–47.

———— "Age, Sex Difference in Values Toward Physical Handicaps," *Journal of Health and Social Behavior*, 11, No. 3 (September, 1970), 207–14.

SCHUTZ, WILLIAM C. *FIRO: A Three-Dimensional Theory of Interpersonal Behavior*. New York: Holt, Rinehart & Winston, Inc., 1960, 267 pp.

SPIELBERGER, CHARLES D. *Anxiety and Behavior*. New York: Academic Press, 1966, p. 265.

THOMAS, EDWIN J. "Problems of Disability from the Perspective of Role Theory," *Journal of Health and Human Behavior*, 7, No. 1 (Spring, 1966), 2–14.

TURNER, RALPH H. "Role Taking: Process Versus Conformity," in Arnold Rose, ed., *Human Behavior and Social Process*. Boston: Houghton Mifflin Co., 1962, pp. 20–38.

WRIGHT, BEATRICE A. *Physical Disability, A Psychological Approach*. New York: Harper & Row, Publishers, 1960, 408 pp.

eleven | *Reflections*

Behavior and Illness represents only one small content area that the author has delineated as essential to the practice of professional nursing. Perhaps this study can be viewed as a bridge, connecting a previous unit on the bio-psycho-socio-cultural features of man to a succeeding unit on problems that arise because of man's failure to adjust and to adapt to the threat or actual experience of illness. Thus the reader has been parachuted so to speak into the middle of a course of study. The text began with an analysis of the nature and perception of illness and concluded with a description of man responding to the different phases or stages of illness. It was assumed that a course on the bio-psycho-socio features of man had already been completed.

The author began with the suggestion that a definition of illness, to be useful for nursing, must provide for the explanation and prediction of behaviors associated with the event. Many persons may not agree with this definition of illness. They may find that it is too general and ambiguous. After all, a phenomenon can encompass many things. Perhaps it is foolhardy to suggest that the merit of the definition lies in its broad application as opposed to the more narrow version of a distinct entity or status orientation adopted by other disciplines. Such a definition, however, does provide content for observation and study. It suggests that if illness is viewed as a form of punishment vis-à-vis an adaptive response of the organism to injury, one can predict that the behavioral responses to illness will differ. An individual's own interpretation of phenomena experienced is an important determinant of his behavior.

Treatment and hospitalization are viewed as stressors superimposed upon the experience of illness. It is quite simple to distinguish conceptually between these three events: illness, treatment, and hospitalization. Some would question whether it is useful to make such a distinction, especially in view of the fact that patients themselves do not distinguish between them. Patients, however, are not aware of the fact that their behavior may reflect response to one event as opposed to the other two events at any given point in time. In addition, each of these events has parts that are capable of eliciting separate responses. Intervention is based on a correct analysis of the entire situation. It would seem that disturbances due to separation from loved ones would elicit a different class of responses from those due to anticipated pain from an impending treatment. Thus this author maintains that the distinction is necessary for accurate diagnosis and prescription.

The theoretical framework chosen for the analysis of the perceptions of illness, treatment, and hospitalization has been criticized by some individuals as too abstruse and of little heuristic value. Perhaps there is some truth to this criticism. Used properly, however, this technique offers the only route known to this author for the nonparticipant to literally "get under the patient's skin" and co-experience the event with him. If nurses want to be able to explain and predict behavior in illness, assuming that behavior is a function of perception, then some framework must be used for evaluating how things *appear* vis-à-vis how things *are*.

A study of man and the nature of illness seems on the surface to be quite logical and reasonable for nursing. After all, nurses care for and about patients experiencing illness. Substantive content for any discipline should center on the subjects and events of primary concern to that discipline. We have assumed that nursing-care measures are carried out for the purpose of achieving comfort. Furthermore, we have assumed that comfort can be measured in terms of some calibrated tension level. These assumptions have yet to be subjected to empirical design for tests of reliability and validity. For example, many would question the proposition that behavioral stability is possible in illness. The idea appears sound, but can it be measured? A theory is useless if it cannot be subjected to scientific procedure. In other words, this theory must not only be capable of generating predictions or propositions concerning relevant events, but these propositions must also be able to be verified. Can one measure equilibrium-disequilibrium? Can one measure stability-instability in the human organism? During a period of homeostatic disequilibrium is it possible to experience simultaneously behavioral stability? Does stability really facilitate the recovery process? These and other questions have no answers today. The assumptions are reasonable only in so far as the theory of systems upon which they are based is sound and the analogies drawn, proper and reasonable.

The four categories of behavior—health, illness, sick role, and impaired role—were presented as descriptive material to demonstrate typical behaviors associated with each stage of illness. Much of the data included in this book is from reports and studies culled from the literature. Many more studies are needed to lend validity to those currently reported.

Knowledge about behavior in illness provides us with a partial base from which to make a preliminary diagnosis of stability, precarious stability, and instability. Certain signs and symptoms of precarious stability and instability are seen to occur and recur together. Like the problems of medicine, nursing problems are identified through careful assessment of the patient's behavior, past and present, and the events or situation currently affecting him. Additional theoretical knowledge is needed to diagnose specific clinical nursing problems and to prescribe an appropriate plan of care. This knowledge when developed will comprise the practice theory of nursing.

The foregoing is based on the assumption that nursing is an applied science with its own theoretical problems and methodology. Like medicine, dentistry, pedagogy, and engineering, nursing is an applied science because it is concerned with practical ends that have social consequences. Basic sciences do not have this orientation. The aim of basic science research is the discovery of general laws and the advancement of knowledge. Basic science research is not intended to solve problems in the applied sciences. The relationship, if any, is apt to be indirect and unsystematic with no immediate applicability. This is not to deny the very defensible proposition that nursing along with all other applied sciences is ultimately related to knowledge in the underlying sciences. Just as progress in medicine can be attributed to progress in biochemistry and bacteriology, progress in nursing is similarly dependent upon advances in the natural and social sciences.

Research in the applied sciences must be conducted under the conditions in which it is practiced. For example, medical research is conducted in the clinical setting, pedagogical research in the classroom, and nursing research in the patient setting. The typology and resolution of applied and clinical problems in nursing require meticulous and empirical research. A theory of nursing practice will evolve following rigorous and systematic observations of hundreds of case studies and the recording of behaviors and responses to prescribed manipulations. When behaviors occur consistently and predictively following carefully controlled manipulations, nursing will have achieved "control" of the situation.

The ultimate goal of nursing's practice theory is to be able to diagnose nursing problems manifested by instable or precariously stable behaviors and to prescribe treatment for the restoration and maintenance of stability. In addition, realizing that certain events or elements of events tend to evoke instable behaviors, nurses will intervene by means of anticipatory guidance to avert an imbalance. Nursing's practice theory should also provide guidelines for initiating change when stability is being maintained with the use of unhealthy coping devices. Timing is not the only important factor; the size and frequency of steps to be taken as the patient is moved from the use of unhealthy devices to the use of healthy devices are of equal significance. The maintenance of stability with the use of unhealthy devices is, at best, tenuous and precarious. Unless isolated from society the individual is constantly pressured to conform and to adjust. Thus efforts are directed towards modifying behavior as expeditiously as possible with minimum disturbance to system stability.

The author hopes that the ideas presented in the chapters of this book will be challenged through dialogue and systematic research. Certainly nursing will not come of age until nurses dare to disagree. Constructive criticisms are needed and solicited. Piaget has stated that the child should be encouraged to interact with his peers, especially at the beginning of reflective thought, so that he is confronted with arguments, conflicts, and contradictions concerning his ideas. This is necessary to rid him of egocentric thought. Thus, nursing, too, in its present developmental stage requires similar practice and exercise to rid itself of narrowness, invalid assumptions, and traditional thought.

REFERENCES

PIAGET, JEAN *Judgment and Reasoning in the Child.* Paterson, N.J.: Littlefield, Adams and Co., 1959, 260 pp.

Author Index

Subject Index